Oxford Essays in Jurisprudence

(Second Series)

Oxford Essays in Jurisprudence

(Second Series)

EDITED BY

A. W. B. SIMPSON

Fellow of Lincoln College, Oxford

CLARENDON PRESS · OXFORD

Oxford University Press, Walton Street, Oxford OX2 6DP

OXFORD LONDON GLASGOW
NEW YORK TORONTO MELBOURNE WELLINGTON
IBADAN NAIROBI DAR ES SALAAM CAPE TOWN
KUALA LUMPUR SINGAPORE JAKARTA HONG KONG TOKYO
DELHI BOMBAY CALCUTTA MADRAS KARACHI

ISBN 0 19 825313 3

© OXFORD UNIVERSITY PRESS 1973
First published 1973
Reprinted 1978

PRINTED IN GREAT BRITAIN BY
LOWE AND BRYDONE PRINTERS LIMITED
THETFORD, NORFOLK

Preface

In this second collection of essays in jurisprudence the emphasis has been placed upon central issues in the theory of law. This is a subject which crosses traditional pedagogic boundaries; consequently we hope that what we have written will be of interest not only to lawyers, but also to those working in other disciplines concerned with the study of human social organization through law, whether they are categorized as philosophers, political scientists, social anthropologists or whatever. The individual contributions have been written independently, and are not the production of the group; nevertheless there exists some degree of family relationship between the work of the eleven contributors, and I suppose in some unpleasingly mysterious sense the team might be said to be the same as before, though only four original members have written for this volume. My own contribution as editor has been confined in the main to arranging the mechanics of production, and here I am grateful for assistance from Mr. David M. Parker in compiling the tables and to Mrs. Jennifer Hebb for secretarial assistance; thanks are also due to the anonymous copy editor of the O.U.P. Professor H. L. A. Hart has also as ever been helpful to many of the contributors both in criticizing drafts of their work and by founding the discussion group (continued under his successor) which has, for nearly twenty years now, provided a local forum for the discussion of topics in jurisprudence.

A. W. B. S.

Oxford, July 1972

Contents

Table of Cases

I

Groups, Laws, and Obedience

A. M. HONORÉ

LEGAL theory may be looked at from two different points of view. On the one hand it may be thought of as the enterprise of describing the conditions which must exist in order that there may be laws and of giving an account of the characteristics of laws. On the other hand it can be conceived as the advocacy of political and moral ideals within the framework of a convention which requires them to be put forward as versions of the meaning, definition, or function of law. Legal theorists are engaged in a form either of cartography or of ideological warfare.

In the last resort it is the second of these points of view which more closely represents the truth. Even when they lay an elaborate smokescreen to disguise their emplacements the legal theorists are committed. This is and must be so so long as the notion of law is intimately linked with that of obedience. When we say that something is a law we are, among other things, striking a special posture towards the question whether it should be obeyed, and, if it is disobeyed, how that disobedience is to be justified. A theory of law is, *inter alia*, a theory about the appropriate attitudes to obedience and disobedience to certain prescriptions, and it would be less than candid to pretend that such a theory can be morally or politically neutral. Legal theory is a form of practical reason, not a science. In contrast with law-making and law reform, which can in theory be scientific to the same extent as other goal-determined techniques like medicine, legal theory is in the end an elaborate form of exhortation or an elaborate display of commitment.

For this reason the grand contests of legal theory are never conclusive. Decade after decade Positivists and Natural Lawyers face one another in the final of the World Cup (the Sociologists have never learned the rules). Victory goes now to one side, now to the other, but the enthusiasm of players and spectators alike ensures that the losing side will take its revenge.

At the Cup Final the legal theorist can only cheer or jeer, label the other side moral lepers, or disingenuous romantics. In the intervals of the competition, however, the first descriptive view of legal theory comes into its own. For it too has a certain viability if not pressed too far.

Under the heading 'theories of law' a vast profusion of descriptions has been offered, and it seems certain that, after so much has been said, there is nothing radically new to say. Yet the descriptions remain in varying degrees unsatisfying. Either they seem remote from the facts of human society, or they describe the scene from too narrow and specialized a point of view. Being impressed by the admittedly important differences between laws and other forms of social control or social service, some theorists seem unable to place laws in a more general context. In their writings laws dangle mysteriously in the air, perched over a void.

In the belief that others may share my dissatisfaction I offer this elementary sketch of a description which may be more promising than some of those currently in vogue. Most of these share two characteristics which I find dissatisfying. First, they begin, as it were, from too far in—from the notion of a rule, command, norm, or the like. These notions presuppose, it seems to me, too much. It would be better to start from the outer framework of the problem, which is set by the axiom that all laws are laws of a society or group. The first question must be 'What is a group?' not 'What is a rule?' Secondly, they overlook or misrepresent the specific connection of the institution of laws with the problem of securing obedience from members of a group. The hope of pointing a better way persuades me that even the schematic and over-simple account which follows is worth giving.

GROUP UNDERSTANDINGS

All law is the law of a group of individuals (I do not necessarily exclude animals). No one can make a law purely for himself. He may form a resolution, frame an ambition, or adopt a rule, but these are private prescriptions, not laws. Even if we assume, for the sake of argument, that the content of a law may refer to a unique individual (X is to sound the alarm), still the prescription would have to be adopted by a group before it could plausibly qualify as a law. Thus, if the inhabitants of the village all agree that X is to sound the alarm, we have arguably the makings of a law, but not if X privately decides to do so, or even publicly announces his intention of doing so.

The groups to which laws relate vary in size and importance. It is linguistically correct to speak of laws of the international community, of territorial states, of religious groups, of professions, of the participants in certain sports, of revolutionary movements, of tribes. Even when the word 'law' is not used, almost every association tends to have something similar (rules, regulations, statutes, orders). The existence of a group, therefore, is a necessary and almost a sufficient condition of the existence of laws or something comparable. It seems sensible, then, to begin to study the conditions for the existence of laws by asking the question 'What is a group?'

Clearly a group is not a mere collection of individuals. A crowd is not a group, even if it exhibits the patterns of behaviour called 'crowd behaviour'. On the other hand, a band of conspirators, a mountaineering expedition, those engaged on a scientific experiment form groups. What unites them? A common purpose may be necessary, but hardly seems sufficient. All those who want H for president share a purpose, objective, or desire, but they do not form a group. To make a group the members must at least know that the others share their purpose. Even this is not enough. Suppose that scientists in several countries know that their colleagues elsewhere are trying to solve a certain problem in chemistry. This does not make them a group. Some understanding as to the means to be pursued is also necessary. Let it be agreed that A is to try a certain method of solving the problem, B (in another country) another, etc. We now have the makings of a group consisting of the chemists who are devoting their efforts to its solution. Far more clearly, the scientists in a particular laboratory, who are carrying out a detailed programme of research form a group.

It is a matter of degree whether the shared understandings of individuals are firm, numerous, important, and lasting enough for them to count as a group. Subject to this qualification, a group may be described as a collection of individuals who share a fairly definite understanding of what is to be done by one or more of themselves in given circumstances, or how the question what is to be done in those circumstances is to be decided. 'What is to be done' here includes 'What is not to be done' and 'What may be done'. The latter (permissions) can be construed, roughly but with sufficient accuracy for present purposes, as a form of prohibition, viz. 'what is not to be prevented from being done'.[1]

For example: certain persons share an understanding that the main building is to be occupied by a concerted attack at 5 p.m. today, that corpses are to be buried within five days of death, that X is to give orders during the expedition, that Y is to decide the dispute between Alpha and Beta. In each case they qualify as a group rather than a mere collection, though the first group is rather evanescent.

On the other hand, if certain persons oppose the Vietnam war, or find themselves on a railway platform, or are lawyers practising in the town of X, they have something in common, but are not *ipso facto* a group. Either they lack a common purpose, or they have no shared understanding of what is to be done in given circumstances, or the understanding is too vague to constitute them a group.

Such a shared or common understanding, or a number of such understandings, is a defining characteristic of a group. People form a group rather than a collection only because they have (besides a common purpose, known to the other members) at least this much in common. Those who do not share these understandings are not members of the group. If C does not agree that X is to give orders during the hunt he is on a private hunt of his own, albeit in the company of the rest of us.

What, however, do I mean by a shared understanding? In the first place, each member must understand what the others profess to regard as the proper thing to be done in given conditions. The prescription (a better word here than norm or rule, because it may so far refer to quite special and particular circumstances) must be communicated by word, example, or attitude to others, or to one's own conduct. A purely

---

[1] The subject is complex. Permissions not coupled with prohibitions of interference are of little normative significance; they simply endorse a competitive situation. The permissions here referred to are those protected by a prohibition of interference, or at least to a limited extent, or coupled with duties, at least in some circumstances.

private prescription cannot be the basis of group existence. Principles which a person adopts for himself but does not display or communicate to or advocate for others (ranging from private morality to private eccentricity) are clearly not part of what cements the group. This fact serves partly to explain the often repeated but misleading statement that morality is an internal, and law an external, matter. There can be private morality, but no private law.

In order that there may be a shared understanding, and so a group, the prescription must therefore be communicated, and it must be adopted by the members of the group. It is often said that the members must 'accept' the prescription, but this, though in a sense correct, is apt to mislead. They may have no choice in the matter, since fear or necessity may dictate that they must remain with the group. If, therefore, 'acceptance' implies voluntary adhesion, it expresses the wrong idea. Again, the member need not accept the prescription for himself in the sense of thinking it right or adopting it as part of his personal morality or attitudes. He may adopt it by professing to do so or simply by conforming to what is prescribed or by adopting the appropriate attitudes of approval or condemnation to those who conform or violate. He must refrain, it is true, from a professed rejection of the assumptions on which the cohesion of the group is based, for to do so is to abandon the group. But this is all. And in a society which lacks verbal communication there is no way of not 'accepting' the shared understandings except that of the lone wolf who leaves the pack.

What is needed, then, is understanding minus professed rejection rather than understanding plus acceptance. Another way of putting this point is to say that the shared understanding need not come about or be maintained in any particular way. It may originate in an agreement, meeting, referendum, or the like. It may have come from an assertion of authority by one person or collection of persons, acquiesced in by others. It may be that the members of the group were led to it by a rational consideration of their respective interests, by idealistic enthusiasm, or by fraud and coercion. The existence of the group depends not on the origin of the group understanding but on its present existence. Hence, just as the history of the shared understandings or conventions on which the existence of a group depends does not alter the fact of the understandings. (though it may affect their moral force) so the means by which they are now maintained may be anything ranging from free acceptance to tradition, custom, naked force, propaganda, and trickery. The existence of group understanding as to how certain things are to be done is one thing; how they came to exist and how they now continue in existence quite another.

It is therefore important to grasp the distinction between the present shared understanding which is a condition of the existence of laws and other group prescriptions (and so, in the fuzzy terminology of some theorists, the 'basis' or 'foundation' of law), and the manner in which that understanding first came about or is now maintained. Military dictators turn into democrats, popular governments become squalid oligarchies. Good laws may be maintained by tyranny, bad laws freely accepted. In the welter of moral considerations on which the problem of obedience to laws depends the questions how the present understandings came into being and how they are now maintained have their place, but unlike the present existence of the understandings, they are not defining characteristics of the group.

Can the prescriptions to which the understandings relate have any content whatever or are some prescriptions ruled out? It seems to me that at least one convention, viz. 'Everyone is to do as he likes' would be ruled out as the defining element of a group, because it would make it impossible for any member to rely on any other doing anything in particular. 'Those who want to, fish; those who do not, don't' cannot be used to define the group consisting of both those who go fishing and those who do not. It must be defined somehow else. Another way of putting this point, perhaps, would be to say that the understanding must relate to a prescription. No prescription is necessary to tell people to do as they please. Natural liberty is the state of affairs existing in the absence of prescriptions. The understanding must relate to something which involves a curtailment of liberty. Membership of a group means a sacrifice of freedom, in the sense that no collection of persons constitutes a group unless they share an understanding which involves a sacrifice of freedom, actual or potential. It may be that not everyone need sacrifice his freedom. When the uniting understanding is 'Do what X says', X does not sacrifice his. Nor need the sacrifice be immediate. 'All go fishing this morning', all now being willing, does not involve a sacrifice of freedom at the moment. It does so potentially, if someone should change his mind, or get bored.

So far I have mentioned certain necessary conditions for the existence of a group, and so of laws, positive morality, canons of good manners, etiquette, social obligations, religious duties (where the religion is conceived as a group function), and the like. There must be a known common purpose, and one or more shared understandings as to what is to be done in given circumstances by one or more members of the group, or of how this action is to be determined. The prescription to which the understandings refer must restrict the freedom of at least some members of the group. The understanding must be communicated, not kept private.

But this is not yet a full statement of the conditions for the existence of a group. We have still to deal with the need for the prescriptions to which the understandings relate (group prescriptions) to be effective.

EFFECTIVE PRESCRIPTIONS

If the common understandings of which I have spoken cease to exist the group ceases to be a group and becomes at most a collection of individuals, unless the understandings which have ceased to exist are replaced by others. Thus 'Do what X says' may be replaced by 'Do what Y says' without disintegration, but if the group comes to reject 'Do what X says' without replacing it by something else, the group will dissolve.

If, however, the continued existence of shared understandings is a necessary condition of group survival it is not a sufficient condition. In order that the group may exist it is also necessary that the understandings on which it rests should, within limits which are not easy to define, be honoured. In other words, the prescriptions to which the understandings relate must be broadly effective.

They may be effective for various reasons. It may be that, because of tradition, habit, lethargy, or the like, no one thinks of violating them. On the other hand, it may be that some or many would like to do this but are constrained by the opinion of others. Thirdly, it may be that some do violate the prescriptions. In that case, if the violations are known, the other members of the group may either display disapproval and hostility or not. If they do, the violators may either show repentance, be prepared to conform in future, offer amends and so forth, or resort to open defiance. If they agree to conform, the prescription remains effective, though violated. If they defy the other members, we must ask whether this defiance is met with hostility or acquiescence. If it is met with hostility, the effectiveness of the prescription depends on whether this hostility in turn induces repentance. If acquiescence ensues, then, given sufficiently grave and repeated violations, the prescription ceases to be effective. The same result follows, subject to the same qualifications, if the other members of the group do not initially display hostility towards the violation. In that case the prescription, though apparently based on a firm social understanding, is like a worm-eaten beam, ready to fall at the first blow.

If the members of the group are sufficiently hostile towards violations of the prescription in question they will probably resort to violence, as a last resort, in order to maintain it. They may threaten, beat, kill, or forcibly expel the violator, or they may let him starve, deprive him of amenities, fail to protect him against his enemies. Let us call these methods (infliction of violence, deprivation of essentials) 'extreme measures'. The group may, then, react to violations with extreme, moderate, or slight measures, or may acquiesce.

The use of such measures is to enforce prescriptions. 'Enforce' is here used not in the sense of 'inducing conformity by force', since the pressure does not always amount to the use or threat of force, and it need not always be successful in inducing conformity. On the other hand, the enforcement of prescriptions is something more than the inculcation of ideals. A prescription is not effective merely because lip-service is paid to the desirability of certain conduct in a given situation. There must also be a substantial measure of compliance with the prescription. 'Enforcement' means inducing, by whatever form of pressure, that degree of compliance.

Prescriptions may be effective without being enforced, if,

owing to the docility of the members of the group, pressure is not needed to enforce them, or if the members have some other motive sufficient to induce them to comply with the prescription (altruism, desire for emulation, idealistic fervour, rational conviction, shrewd appreciation of the advantage to be gained by compliance). But, since group understandings involve a restriction of liberty, enforcement will often be necessary. One method of enforcement is by the spontaneous directing of pressure against the violator. This, though often effective, especially in a small and coherent group, is less efficient and less secure in a large or diverse group. The group may be too loosely knit to run the risks connected with spontaneous enforcement. There are two ways in which it can minimize this risk. These correspond to two important social inventions, which help to make possible the existence of laws.

They both involve the same idea, namely the interlocking of different types of prescription. The first simply consists in superimposing on the group understanding as to what is to be done in given circumstances a further understanding as to what is to be done in case the first prescription is violated. Instead of 'Everyone is to hunt', we have 'Everyone is to hunt; if not, he is to be given no food', or 'Everyone is to hunt; if not, he is to contribute from his stocks', or 'Everyone is to hunt; if not, he is to be summoned to do so the next day.' This device, of backing up an initial prescription with a subsequent, remedial prescription has the disadvantage that it openly recognizes the possibility of violation. On the other hand, it has the advantage that reinforced concrete has over plain concrete. Inviting stress, it provides a mechanism for resisting it. Moreover, the process of welding prescriptions together may be continued for several stages. 'Everyone is to hunt; if he does not hunt, he is to contribute from his stocks, if he does not contribute, the others may raid his stocks; if he resists, he may be told to leave; if he does not leave, he may be expelled by force.' This chain of prescriptions (remembering that apparently permissive principles are to be construed as prohibitions of interference) is designed to ensure that the effort at enforcement does not break down merely because the members of the group, faced with defiance, do not know or cannot agree what the next step should be. It is not, obviously, a substitute for the will to enforce prescriptions; it merely ensures an accepted method for the expression of that will, if it exists. In effect, it serves to channel the supply of hostility, to prevent indignation running to waste.

The first example of the interlocking of different types of prescription is therefore the concatenation of initial prescriptions with remedial prescriptions. It should be noted that these remedial prescriptions need not amount to sanctions. They need not consist in the infliction of unpleasant measures on the violator by force or against his will. The remedial measures may consist in the offer of rewards, in persuasion, conciliation, negotiation of a compromise, or the like. For example, 'Everyone is to hunt; if he does not, he is to be given an opportunity of hunting the next day; if he still does not, three of the eldest men are to visit him and persuade him to change his mind; if he still persists, then . . . ' These persuasive steps represent rational ways of reinforcing the initial prescription. It may be that these steps are in practice effective and that there is no need for a further step prescribing that something unpleasant be done to the violator. Or it may be that the chain of enforcement prescriptions peters out in a diffused unspecific hostility. On the other hand, it is characteristic of a chain of remedial prescriptions that very often it will at least ultimately provide for a specific sanction to be applied to the violator, which may or may not consist in the infliction of 'extreme measures'. Much depends on whether sanctions are necessary in the context and whether it is practicable to organize them. Sanctions, therefore (prescriptions which provide for something unpleasant to be done to the violator), are a general but not a necessary feature of a chain of enforcement prescriptions.

The second type of interlocking prescription we have already met. This is the arrangement by which an initial prescription (genetic prescription) merely determines the way in which the content of a derivative prescription is to be settled. Thus, given a genetic prescription 'Do what X says', X may instruct 'All sharpen their knives.' Here the genetic prescription is sustained by a group understanding; the derivative prescription may not be supported in this way. It may not be generally accepted, apart from X's instruction, that the correct thing to do is for all to sharpen their knives, yet the instruction 'All sharpen their knives' may be accepted because of the group understanding 'Do what X says.' Conversely, it is of course true that independent acceptance of 'All sharpen their knives' will reinforce 'Do what X says' where X issues such an instruction. Hence two prescriptions supported by group understandings, the one genetic and the other not, may support each other, or one supported by a group understanding may support one which is derivative. These arrangements have the advantage that violations of the supported prescription need not involve a direct challenge to the supporting provision and so need not endanger the existence or stability of the group. One may defy a particular derivative prescription while not in general rejecting the source prescription and the related group understanding. As in the first type of interlocking of types of prescription, the group is simultaneously opened to stress and provided with the means of meeting it. It is opened to stress because the derivative prescription does not carry with it all the force of the source prescription, in that it is possible, at least sometimes, to reject the former while adhering to the latter. On the other hand, this arrangement promotes the resilience of the group by making it possible for it to be so structured that isolated violations can occur without disruption.

Now it seems reasonable to attribute a special status to those group prescriptions which have the function of supporting other prescriptions (whether group prescriptions or simply the orders of individuals). These, whether of the form 'Do what X says' or 'If he does not hunt, he is to contribute from his stocks' are dual-function prescriptions. They function as group prescriptions in their own right, and possess whatever psychological weight the members of the group are prepared to put behind them. But in addition they have a reinforcing function in regard to other derivative or preceding prescriptions. They furnish an additional reason for compliance with the derivative or preceding prescriptions. Thus 'Do what X says' furnishes an additional reason for complying with 'All sharpen their knives' (an instruction given by X) and 'If he does not hunt, he is to contribute from his stocks' furnishes an additional reason for compliance with 'He is to hunt'.

Genetic and remedial prescriptions may together be classed as *reinforcing prescriptions*. They, together with the prescriptions which they reinforce, count as *interlocking prescriptions*. Now we can make a further approach to the statement of the conditions necessary in order that laws shall exist, by saying that nothing is to count as a law which is not an interlocking prescription or derived from an interlocking prescription. Clearly this formula has a functional basis. It invites us to think of laws as belonging to a structure which has the function of reinforcing (providing additional reasons for compliance with) prescriptions which may or may not be independently supported by group opinion.

Let us see whether this step is justified. It could be attacked either from a linguistic or from a logical point of view. It may be said that as a matter of usage the word 'law' is applied to customs, usages, conventions, agreed rules, etc., which are not interlocked with either remedial or genetic provisions. Some arrangements of primitive and international society and of informal groups which fall within this class could perhaps be called laws. In reply to this one might argue that, if we survey the force of the word 'law' over the whole range of its use, it generally serves to draw attention to the existence of a *special* reason for conformity. In other words, to say of a certain prescription or provision that it is law is to say that, over and above the inherent rationality of doing what is prescribed, or the fact that one has agreed to do just that, or the charisma of the person issuing the instruction, there is an additional (not necessary conclusive) reason for obeying, namely the enforcing or genetic provision which is interlocked with the provision to be obeyed. Most laws are doubly prescribed.

A logical objection to my suggestion is that *all* prescriptions arguably interlock with other prescriptions and that, in any case, until the principle on which prescriptions are to be individuated is made clear, the meaning of the suggestion is obscure. A brief answer to the first part of this objection is that no prescription which is logically derivable from another in the sense that it would be inconsistent to advocate the latter without advocating the former is to be treated as interlocking with it. Thus 'X is not to steal A's car' does not interlock in the required sense with 'All are to respect the property of others.' Clearly if 'All are to respect the property of others' is accepted, it follows that 'X is not to steal A's car' in the sense that no additional reason is needed for commending the latter proposition to one who accepts the former. On the other hand, 'If X does not pay, Y may seize his goods' gives an additional reason for X's conforming to the provision 'X is to pay.' Likewise, 'Do what A says' gives an additional reason for B's conforming to the instruction 'B is to guard the camp', where A has so instructed B.

The second part of the objection, that a principle is required for individuating prescriptions, is perhaps more serious. It can, however, for present purposes, be met in the following way. A prescription will count as a different prescription from another prescription (and so be capable of being regarded as an interlocking prescription) when its content is an action to be done or not to be done before or after the action prescribed by the first prescription. Thus the relation between 'X is to pay' and 'If X does not pay Y may seize his goods' is that of successive prescriptions. The seizure is (not to be prevented from) taking place after the non-payment. So is the relation between 'X is to decide' and X's instruction 'Y is to guard the camp.' The decision is to precede the guard duty. Of course, whether prescriptions are linked in this temporal way depends on the intention of the prescribers and the persons who share the understandings on which the prescriptions rest. The difference between 'X is to pay and if he does not pay Y may seize his goods' and the Kelsenian form 'If X does not pay Y "ought" to seize his goods' is social and psychological. Is the first step, X's paying, separate in the sense that it is treated by the persons concerned as something to be done not merely, even if partly, in order to avoid the second step?

It seems possible, therefore, to defend the thesis that every law must interlock with a distinct prescription. This will serve to exclude many types of social provision (canons of positive morality, good behaviour, social obligations, and the like) which lack this characteristic. Most of these are neither thought of as representing rules or decisions set by persons having authority to rule or decide, nor as leading, in case of violation, to prescribed further steps. 'Lies are not to be told; if someone tells a lie, he is to . . .' 'Invitations are to be returned within a reasonable time. If an invitation is not returned . . .' (the person concerned need not be invited again—but then he need not be invited even if the invitation is returned). In some cases of breach of social obligation some simple step, such as an apology, is prescribed, so that a remedial element is present. 'No one is to step on another's foot. If he does so accidentally, he is to apologize.' If he does so intentionally, social obligation does not prescribe any particular move, at least at the present day, though in former times it would have been possible to define the steps leading from insult to challenge and duel. In any particular social context it will usually be possible to identify a particular prescription either as standing on its own feet (apart from the support given by a diffused group hostility to contravention) or as supported by genetic and remedial provisions.

RULES, FUNCTIONS, INSTITUTIONS

The distinction between interlocking and independent prescriptions is important, but not adequate to explain the special status of those prescriptions which count as laws. For this purpose several further notions need to be introduced, the first of which (and the starting point of many contemporary inquiries into legal theory) is that of a rule. Not all prescriptions are rules. 'X is to have his hair cut today' does not express a rule. Nor are all laws rules. 'Anne is to be Queen' is not a rule, nor is 'A minor is a person under eighteen years', yet both can be laws. What, then, is a rule, and what is the significance of rules in relation to laws?

A rule may be defined as a prescription having the form 'whenever . . . then . . .'. Thus, 'X is to have his hair cut today' does not express a rule, but 'X is to have his hair cut every month' (whenever a month has elapsed), 'X is to have his hair cut when told to by Y' (whenever Y so instructs him) express rules for X. For ordinary prescriptions (non-genetic and non-remedial) the significance of rules is economic. They serve to save time and effort by providing for an unspecified number of situations without the need to think out the appropriate action on each occasion. Most provisions of positive morality, etiquette, good manners, political and religious duty, and the like take the form of rules, but some social obligations do not: for example, 'We meet at Z's house at 8 p.m.'

Now clearly the fact that a prescription takes the form of an effective rule gives it some additional force. The additional force derives from the fact that similar action is taken in similar cases (of course if the rule is not effective this additional force is not present). Rules therefore exploit the force of imitation, precedent, and the principle of like behaviour in like cases.

This feature can be exploited by the group if it adopts rules as genetic and remedial prescriptions. Suppose there to be a group understanding that 'Whenever X has a dispute with Y, A is to decide.' X has a dispute and A decides that X is to apologize. Now the decision 'X is to apologize' has a threefold force. First, there is the force arising from whatever diffused group opinion sustains the requirement of an apology, from A's charisma etc. Secondly, there is the derivative force of the understanding 'A is to decide.' Thirdly, there is the force of example: 'A decided the last dispute between X and Y and his decision was then accepted.' A similar analysis will do for a remedial prescription in the form of a rule, for example 'A is to offer a sheep to the chief each month; if ever A does not offer a sheep, B may seize one', where an additional force may be drawn both from A's having offered a sheep in the previous month and from B's having seized sheep on some previous occasion when A did not offer it.

We have now a further concept, that of interlocking prescriptions reinforced by group rules, that is to say doubly reinforced. Still, whatever name we adopt for these, they are too informal and *ad hoc* to count linguistically or functionally as laws. A further step is needed, namely that of institutionalizing the genetic and remedial rules. This step involves two stages. In the first (the jurisdictional stage) the genetic or remedial rule is to be applied, in appropriate circumstances, to all the members of the group, or rather to any who may fit the given circumstances. Thus in 'Do what X says in war' (X may give instructions in matters of war to all other members of the group, or to all fighting men), the genetic prescription is given a group scope. The rule adopted gives X a group function (to lead in war), and makes him an official of the group (war leader). Similarly, a remedial prescription may be given a group scope. 'If any member of the group fails to offer the chief what he should offer, Y may seize his goods to an appropriate extent.' This creates the office of bailiff and gives Y a group function, viz. the seizure of goods in certain circumstances.

The group function and group officer represent stages on the path towards laws, but it might be rash to say that interlocking prescriptions supported by genetic and remedial rules which create group officers and group functions are necessarily laws. No doubt the existence of such officers and functions tends to reinforce the relevant prescriptions, because these prescriptions are now supported not just by rules, which carry with them the force of imitation and precedent, but by the fact that the prescriptions emanate from them or that the breach of them will be remedied by group officers performing group functions, so that a challenge to them involves indirectly a confrontation with the group as represented by its officers. Not only is there, as in the case of an ordinary rule, the force of precedent or example, but the person giving the instruction or (potentially) taking the remedial step represents the group, i.e. his authority extends over the whole group ('authority' here simply meaning that a prescription entitles him to take certain steps). Hence to the reasons for conforming to the instruction 'All sharpen their knives' (given by X) we can add that fact that the instruction comes from a group officer, issues from a group institution. Not only must the potential violator take account of the independent backing for the prescriptions 'All sharpen their knives' and 'Do what X says', not only must he consider that in previous instances X's instructions have been followed, but he must also recognize that X is a group official. In other words, we have here yet another technique for bringing into play the individual's desire for the group to cohere and for himself to remain a member of it.

One can think of situations in which this whole apparatus of interlocking prescriptions, rules, and official functions is present, yet its transient or informal character tends against the use of the formal terminology of laws, regulations, statutes, etc. For example, an impromptu game, expedition, or other enterprise may be organized by a group which agrees on certain rules and officials (leader, umpire, recorder, treasurer), without our being tempted to say that the enterprise is being conducted according to laws. Hence a further stage is needed, viz. the institutional stage. In this stage there is a group understanding as to a rule determining how the group officers are to be selected (and often how their functions are to be determined). Thus 'Let the oldest fighting man be war leader' (whenever there is a vacancy let the oldest man be chosen), 'Let the war leader be chosen by the majority', 'Let the most learned man decide disputes' would constitute appointive rules, and these together with the jurisdictional rules, will generate group institutions. Thus, given such rules, we can speak not merely of the function and office of leading in war, but of the institution of the War Leadership, of the Bailiffdom, of the Dispute Tribunal, etc. Clearly the appointive rule yet further adds to the group coherence by making it unnecessary to reach a fresh understanding on the mode of appointment of group officials on each occasion and thereby reinforces the authority of the officials.

In a full analysis a great deal would need to be said about institutions. Very often an institution is a group within a group or, if one prefers, a group within a society. In that case its internal structure, with rules, officers, and functions, will mirror what has already been described. But though this 'corporate' type of institution is the most familiar one, the idea can be sufficiently illustrated from the example of an institution comprising at a given moment a single officer performing a given function. If we take the elements distilled by Hauriou in his classic account of institutions,[2] the *idea*, the *organized power*, and the *manifestation* of common activity, it will be seen that these are all paralleled in the account given, though adjustment must be made for the fact that Hauriou is speaking of a 'corporate' institution. To the 'idea' corresponds our 'function': the institutional officer has some given function to perform, some social objective to pursue. To the 'organized power' corresponds our notion that the organization and allocation of the function, including provision for successive appointments to the office, rests on group understanding. In this way the 'organized power is put at the service of the idea for realization.' Finally, the notion of 'manifestation' merely means the actual execution by the officer of his given function. If, then, we add to what has been said the possibility that the institution

---

[2] For an accessible account see *The French Institutionalists* (ed. Broderick), 20th Century Legal Philosophy Series VIII (1970), pp. 93, 100.

may itself constitute a group, we link our analysis to the classic characterization of corporate institutions.

But for the purpose of giving an account of laws it is not essential to introduce the complication of corporate institutions. Given even an institution or institutions of a very simple character, embodied at a given moment in a single officer, we can reasonably claim that the reinforcement of social group understandings has now reached the stage at which it is linguistically and functionally justifiable to speak of laws. When we find prescriptions which are reinforced by genetic or remedial rules of an institutional character (i.e. supported by group understandings as to the jurisdiction and appointment of the relevant officials) we can speak of the prescriptions and rules that support them as laws, while acknowledging that, in proceeding from structures of less to those of greater complexity, the precise stage at which to mark a linguistic boundary is to some extent a matter of choice.

Following this institutional basis, very many groups (associations of all types, religious, political, professional, and cultural groups, besides the territorial state and its subdivisions and the international community) will have their laws, sometimes called rules, regulations, statutes, orders, decrees, instructions, and the like. On the other hand, the modern western family is probably not sufficiently institutionalized to have laws, though it certainly works by interlocking rules and recognizes a degree of authority.

THE TERRITORIAL GROUP

Within the class of groups which, in this broad sense, have laws, it is widely felt that the laws of the territorial states (and their sub-divisions such as England) and possibly the laws of the international community have a special status, and are, indeed, the only laws in the full sense of the word. What justification is there for this selectivity? It does not rest on the fact that there are specialized institutions concerned with the identification and application of the group laws, such as courts. Any group or association can have a tribunal with these (and generally also with some remedial) functions, and the existence of such an institution will generate a special sense of 'law' in relation to the group in question, namely the sense in which group laws are the rules and specific prescriptions recognized, rightly or wrongly, by the institution in question. Nor does it rest on the systematization of the laws of these particular territorial and international groups. Apart from the sense in which the expression 'legal system' means all the laws of a given group, or (by derivation) all the laws of the group recognized as such by a group institution specializing in the identification of laws (a court or tribunal), the set of laws belonging to a group can be made into a system, made systematic, by writers who put them in some order and explain their interrelations. This, though useful and educative, does not change the force of the laws except in so far as to diffuse knowledge of them and make them more intelligible is to make them easier to obey. The special attention paid by writers to municipal and international laws, and the elaborate structure of the tribunals concerned with these laws, is to only a small extent the cause, to a much larger one the consequence, of the special status of these laws.

The explanation of the special status of these laws must be sought elsewhere than in their systematic character or the existence of special institutions to identify them. We must once more take note of the intimate connection between law and obedience. If law is an elaborate group structure designed to secure obedience to certain group prescriptions, then in a conflict between groups and the laws of groups a special preeminence will naturally attach to the laws of that group which is in a position to compel other groups to conform to its prescriptions. In the modern world the territorial state and its subdivisions are by and large in this position *vis-à-vis* private associations, religious and political movements, and professional bodies. This is, of course, not universally true even today. In some countries the State is subordinate to a political party or (rarely) a church. Still, the general predominance of these groups over rival groups is sufficiently striking to justify the usage by which the laws of these territorial groups are treated as pre-eminently laws in the full sense of the word. The laws of the international community are also so classed by derivation from municipal laws, not because they fully share, in relation to the laws of other groups, this substantial predominance, but because they are the laws of the community formed by the territorial state groups, which themselves possess this predominance.

The reason for the predominance of the territorial groups is simply that they have managed to institutionalize, to a greater extent than other groups, the use of force in remedial situations, to mobilize greater force for employment in those situations, and to minimize the use of force on an institutional basis by other groups. To this extent, but only to this extent, the description of the necessary conditions for the existence of laws, must take account of the importance of sanctions and of the use of force. In an intergroup conflict the predominance of institutionalized force on the side of a particular group will be decisive in earning for the laws of that group the title of laws in the full sense of the word. This should not be converted into the proposition that all laws must be backed by sanctions, or even that a group could not operate a system of laws without sanctions, as opposed to remedial procedures. There may be groups whose procedures of conciliation are in practice sufficient to secure a broad compliance with group prescriptions. Conversely, the application of social pressures, including force, in a haphazard or non-institutional way does not amount to the operation of a legal system. Law is a system for the reinforcement of group pressure by the adoption of rules and institutions of certain types. But the intimate connection of laws with obedience does not carry with it the implication that all methods of securing obedience amount to the application of laws. A group may rely on unorganized pressures to secure conformity to what its members require; it may allow them freely to resort to force to that end. In that case it may secure obedience by force and without laws, just as it might do so in some cases without either. It would, however, be less than candid to recognize that the special predominance of the laws of the state in modern conditions rests on the fact that the state usually commands greater force than its rival groups, and this potential predominance entitles the laws of the state (and by derivation, of the international community) to special status even when, as is normally true, no conflict actually arises between the laws of the state and those of another group.

It remains to enter the caveat that the foregoing descriptive analysis, though intended to reflect the realities of social life, is not meant to be taken historically. For the sake of clarity I have expounded the various notions—the group, shared understandings, interlocking genetic and remedial prescriptions, rules, functions, and institutions, the special status of municipal and international laws—in a particular order. This is to be taken as a device necessary to an expository sketch of this sort, and no more.

II

Principles of Revolutionary Legality[1]

J. M. EEKELAAR

Actio personalis moritur cum persona. This axiom expressed the rule of the common law that actions for personal injury did not survive the death of the victim. As a consequence, a wrongdoer was in a better position in civil law if he killed his victim than if he left him injured. A series of statutes[2] has rectified this anomaly of the civil law. But in recent years an analogous doctrine seems to have appeared in constitutional law. It is generally accepted that courts are under a duty to declare *ultra vires* governmental acts which conflict with statute or a specific constitutional provision and to allow the aggrieved citizen the appropriate remedies against the authorities. But if those in power go further and totally disregard the constitution, promulgating a new constitution of their own making, or if power is usurped by revolutionaries, four Commonwealth tribunals have held that the very fact that the old constitution has been inflicted a mortal wound not only frees its successful slayers from its restraints but entitles them to judicial recognition as being legitimate and therefore, it seems, to legal immunity with respect to their revolutionary acts.

The tribunals were the Supreme Court of Pakistan,[3] the High Court of Uganda,[4] the Appellate Division in Rhodesia,[5] and the Judicial Committee of the Privy Council.[6] The Privy Council did not uphold the legitimacy of the revolutionary regime in Rhodesia, but this was only because it thought that

---

[1] This essay is based on a lecture delivered at the University College of Rhodesia, Salisbury, on 14 August 1969.

[2] Fatal Accidents Acts 1846–1959; Law Reform (Miscellaneous Provisions) Act 1935.

[3] *The State* v. *Dosso* (1959) 1 Pakistan L.R. 849.

[4] *Uganda* v. *Commissioner of Prisons, ex p. Matovu* [1966] E.A. 514.

[5] *Madzimbamuto* v. *Lardner-Burke N. O. and others* 1968 (2) S.A. 284 and *Archion Ndhlovu* v. *The Queen* 1968 (4) S.A. 515.

[6] On appeal from the first Rhodesian decision: [1968] 3 All E.R. 561.

the violated constitutional order might yet respond to the artificial respiration then being applied to it by the British Government. If the facts had allowed the legitimate constitution to have been pronounced dead with certainty, the Privy Council appeared to approve the doctrine which would allow legitimacy thereby to be conferred upon the usurpers. The facts of these cases will be found in the voluminous literature which now surrounds the Rhodesian decision[7] and will not be recited here. But the fact that a conclusion of this nature was reached by each of these tribunals after a consideration of constitutional and jurisprudential theory to a degree probably unprecedented in the Commonwealth warrants reflection on its wider implications. There is a view, professing a pessimistic realism, which would attribute the results of these cases to personal or political motivation on the part of the judges.[8] Sympathy with the revolutionaries, unwillingness to relinquish office, even an altruistic desire to prevent their replacement by lesser men may indeed all have played a part. But the decisions should not be so simply dismissed, since the judges sought to justify their conclusions by a reasoned appeal to principles of constitutional law and jurisprudence. These principles deserve the closest attention, not only because of the interest inherent in their selection, but because on one juristic view they attract the unique criticism that they cannot form the basis of a truly 'legal' decision.

It is the main purpose of this essay to argue that that view[9] is not only mistaken, but that it also arbitrarily and dangerously limits the scope of juristic thought. It derives from that form of legal positivism which asserts that 'legal' rules can exist only within the framework of an operative legal system. Once that system collapses, decisions about it and any possible successor to it cannot be 'legal' decisions. They must *necessarily* be of a

---

[7] See (1967) 30 M.L.R. 156 and (1969) 32 M.L.R. 19 (J. M. Eekelaar); (1967) 83 L.Q.R. 64 and (1970) 87 S.A.L.J. 168 (R. S. Welsh); (1968) 26 C.L.J. 233 (R. W. M. Dias); (1968) 8 R.L.J. 138 (A. J. E. Jaffey); [1968] C.I.L.S.A. 390 (R. H. Christie); (1969) 19 U.T.L.J. 326 (F. M. Brookfield); [1969] P.L. 293 (Claire Palley); [1969] P.L. 325 (L. J. Macfarlane); [1969] *Annual Survey of Commonwealth Law*, 71 ff.

[8] See Claire Palley, '*The Judicial Process: U.D.I. and the Southern Rhodesia Judiciary*', (1967) 30 M.L.R. 263.

[9] To which I formerly adhered: see (1969) 32 M.L.R. at p. 34. It also seems to be accepted by F. M. Brookfield, loc. cit.

'personal' or 'political' nature. The reasoning leading to this conclusion can be seen from the analyses of the structure of a legal system advanced respectively by Professor Hans Kelsen and by Professor H. L. A. Hart. For the former, norms obtain the character of law by reason of their creation in accordance with the requirements stipulated by the highest norm (e.g. the constitution) of a coercive system which is generally effective. For the latter, rules are legal rules if properly derived from an ultimate rule of recognition. It follows from this that the question whether or not to accept the highest norm of the system (or the ultimate rule of recognition) cannot be decided in accordance with legal norms (or rules) because their existence as *legal* phenomena depends on their derivation from the accepted norm (or ultimate rule). Kelsen's theory makes the additional demand that, in order to represent the legal norms as 'objectively valid', it is necessary to 'presuppose' a norm above the highest norm of positive law. This presupposed norm he calls the basic norm. Hart, however, denies the necessity of making this 'presupposition' in order to assert the validity of the system's laws. Either the ultimate rule and its derivatives exist or they do not exist, and this is simply a question of fact.[10] It will be necessary to consider the implications of Kelsen's additional requirements further, but it may be remarked that Hart's dismissal of the existence of the ultimate rule as no more than a factual matter seems to preclude study about its acceptability as a serious subject for jurisprudence. To refute the positivist position it is necessary to show, first, that the question whether an ultimate rule is acceptable is one *capable* of judicial determination and, second, that such determination need not *necessarily* be subjective and unprincipled and may indeed be no different from many other judicial decisions. In attempting to establish those propositions, it will be further submitted that not only is judicial determination about the ultimate rule possible, but that it is crucial in distinguishing between one type of social organization and others.

JUDICIAL DETERMINATION

The degree of significance, if any, to be attached to judicial decision about the ultimate rule does not emerge clearly from

[10] *The Concept of Law* (1961), pp. 105, 245.

the positivist theorists. In the extreme view of John Austin, the presence of commands reinforced by a threat of the imposition of a sanction if broken suffices to identify rules of law. The question of judicial acceptance or non-acceptance of the authority of the ruler does not therefore arise. In the highly sophisticated model expounded by Hart, an ultimate rule will exist (and therefore form the foundation of a legal system) if 'judges, officials and others' in fact act in accordance with its precepts.[11] Hart considers it essential that the judiciary adopts a *uniform* attitude to the ultimate rule, for if the judges were to diverge amongst themselves in its application, we could not logically speak of the existence of a distinct legal system.[12] However, it is not clear whether a division between the judiciary and *other* officials on the acceptance of the ultimate rule is to be considered as of any greater significance to jurisprudence than a division of loyalty between, say, the police and the army. It seems that the jurist can do no more than wait along the sidelines until the uncertainty resolves itself.[13] It may be, however, that Kelsen's exposition is consistent with, and indeed suggestive of, placing a crucial emphasis on the presence or absence of judicial acceptance of the ultimate rule. Unfortunately, his reasoning is so obscure on this point that there is some danger that attempts to determine his 'true' view will lead to unprofitable wrangles amongst commentators similar to those which have long bedevilled Marxists and Hegelians.[14] It is hoped therefore that the question whether the insights extracted from his writings are an accurate representation of Kelsen's own position will be considered of secondary importance to their intrinsic value.

When Kelsen insists that a basic norm must be presupposed in order to establish the objective validity of a constitution and of acts performed under it, it is important to realize that the basic norm is here performing a logical function. When a jurist expounds the norms of a system as objectively valid laws he must, according to Kelsen, be presupposing the existence of a basic norm which confers validity on the highest norm (e.g. the

---

[11] Op. cit., pp. 106, 113–14.   [12] Op. cit., pp. 112–13.
[13] Op. cit., p. 115.
[14] See J. Raz, *The Concept of a Legal System* (1970), pp. 136 ff. Kelsen's discussion of the subject is said to be 'beset with confusion'.

constitution) and all its derivatives.[15] A textbook writer writing a book on Rhodesian criminal law in 1971 would seem implicitly to accept the validity of the constitution at that time operative in the country. But has Kelsen conceived the basic norm merely to make this somewhat banal point? It would seem that he has not, because he expressly states that the basic norm is relevant to a much more interesting problem.

The problem that leads to the theory of the basic norm . . . is how to distinguish a legal command which is considered to be objectively valid, such as the command of a revenue officer to pay a certain sum of money, from a command which has the same subjective meaning but is not considered to be objectively valid, such as the command of a gangster.[16]

Kelsen, then, is concerned with differentiating between social phenomena. Rules validly enacted by a legitimate government are a different type of phenomenon from directives foisted upon a community by a group of bandits, even though a professor of law might be able to produce a systematic account of the latter. Kelsen uses his concept of 'objective validity' and accordingly of the basic norm to make this distinction. However, the passage immediately following the extract quoted above fails to clarify how he means the concept to be utilized.

The difference consists in that we do not consider the subjective meaning of the command of the gangster—as we consider the subjective meaning of the legal command of a revenue officer—as its objective meaning because we do not presuppose in the former case a basic norm. A Communist may, indeed, not admit that there is an essential difference between an organization of gangsters and a capitalist legal order which he considers as the means of ruthless · exploitation. For he does not presuppose—as do those who interpret the coercive order in question as an objectively valid normative order—the basic norm. He does not deny that the capitalist coercive order is the law of the State. What he denies is that this coercive order, the law of the State, is objectively valid. The function of the basic norm is not to make it possible to consider a coercive order which is by and large effective as law, for—according to the defini-

---

[15] Both Brookfield, loc. cit., and J. W. Harris, *'When and Why does the Grundnorm Change?'*, (1971) 29 C.L.J. 103, very properly emphasize this function of the *Grundnorm* in the descriptive task of the legal scientist.

[16] Kelsen, *'A Reply to Professor Stone'* (1965) 17 Stanford L.R. (vol. 2) at p. 1144.

tion presented by the Pure Theory of Law—a legal order is a coercive order by and large effective; the function of the basic norm is to make it possible to consider this coercive order as an objectively valid order.

Kelsen does not state whether it is as citizens or as 'legal scientists' that 'we' do not presuppose a basic norm in the case of the gangster nor whether he is referring to the Communist as a citizen or as a 'legal scientist'. If he is saying that a Communist citizen may regard a capitalist legal system in the same manner as any citizen would regard the commands of bandits in his society the passage, while adverting to a possibly interesting aspect of the Communist's outlook, provides us with no tool with which we may seek to discover whether there is any important manner in which the two types of coercive organizations differ. However, elsewhere in his writings Kelsen suggests that one can explain a system of law as a valid system of law, and thereby presuppose its basic norm, without approving of it.[17] So a Communist professor might presuppose a capitalist basic norm in explaining a capitalist legal system. Yet it seems that Kelsen would probably deny that the same professor would presuppose a gangster's 'basic norm' if he were to give an account of the coercive stipulations of bandits. The professor would not interpret them as being 'objectively valid'. The reason for this is that, even though a Communist might consider a capitalist system as analogous to banditry, the organization of a capitalist state and of gangsters present distinct social phenomena. This thesis, which, it is submitted, Kelsen is attempting to restate in the extracts quoted, was presented by him with clarity in his *General Theory of Law and State*.

This legal order, considered as a system of valid norms, is essential also to the sociological concept of domination as applied to the State; for, even from a sociological point of view, only a domination considered to be 'legitimate' can be conceived of as 'State'. The bare fact that an individual (or a group of individuals) is in a position to enforce a certain pattern of behavior is not a sufficient ground for speaking of a relation of domination such as constitutes a State.

---

[17] 'Even an anarchist, if he were a professor of law, could describe positive law as a system of valid norms without having to approve of this law': *The Pure Theory of Law* (1967), p. 218 n.

Even the sociologist recognizes the difference between a State and a robber gang.

The sociological description of the State as a phenomenon of domination is not complete if only the fact is established that men force other men to a certain behavior. The domination that characterizes the State claims to be legitimate and must actually be regarded as such by rulers and ruled. The domination is legitimate only if it takes place in accordance with a legal order whose validity is presupposed by the acting individuals . . . Sociology has to record the existence of this legal order as a fact in the minds of the individuals involved, and if society interprets the domination as a State organization, then sociology itself must assume the validity of this order. Even as an object of sociology, 'State domination' is not a bare fact but a fact together with an interpretation. This interpretation is made both by the rulers and the ruled and by the sociologist himself who is studying their behavior.[18]

It is therefore clear that the notion of 'objective validity' and the presupposition of a basic norm are not confined to an explanation of what a legal textbook writer does when he explains laws. They are concerned not with the nature of the activity of the observer of society but with the phenomena he observes. The legal scientist writing a legal textbook and the sociologist describing the State are not simply explaining systems of coercive acts. They are explaining systems of coercive acts which are accepted as valid by the communities concerned, and, in making their descriptions, they too presuppose the validity of the systems.

The practical significance of Kelsen's position (as here interpreted) can be illustrated by a simple analogy. Suppose two groups of people live confined in separate establishments. Upon investigation it might be found that in each a small minority lives apart from the rest and from time to time draws up rules governing meal hours, recreation times, and other matters. These rules are habitually obeyed. The minority is assisted in rule-enforcement by a small number of people drawn from the majority who make administrative arrangements, detect offenders, and punish some of them. In fulfilling their tasks they invariably act on the directions of the minority. This information would probably be sufficient to allow some positivists

[18] *General Theory of Law and State* (1961), pp. 187–8.

the conclusion that we have a model of a legal system. But for Kelsen, before the rules can be represented in their objective significance, the additional question must be asked whether the acting individuals, *rulers and ruled*, regarded the basis of the authority as valid. An answer to this question might reveal that one institution was a boarding-school run by popular masters assisted by dutiful prefects and that the other was a concentration camp in which obedience was compelled by threats of torture and execution. It would then be open to deny that the second institution was an 'objectively valid' system. It may be objected that little is to be gained by distinguishing between the two institutions, and still less by stigmatizing the authority of the second as 'invalid', for in each case effective social control is being exercised by a process of rule enforcement. Yet the one institution is different from the other in important and characteristic ways. Surely the distinction is one which should arouse jurisprudential as well as sociological interest because it appears to relate to the very distinction made by Hart himself between acting because one is *obliged* and acting because one is *obligated.*

If it is accepted that this distinction is relevant to jurisprudence, the significance of judicial acceptance or non-acceptance of the validity of the rule-making authorities becomes apparent. For to make a distinction between nation states parallel to that made in the boarding-school/concentration camp analogy would involve an investigation into the psychological attitudes of populations which, even if it were possible, would certainly take jurisprudence beyond practical bounds. Undoubtedly Kelsen himself would exclude such an investigation from his conception of the task of legal science. But in a developed community there exists an institutionalized substitute into which community judgments are channelled. This is the court structure. Conflicts between the community and its rulers find their solution there just as do those between individual citizens. Even if some societies may be reluctant to ascribe this role to their courts, there is no *necessary* reason why courts should not assume it. Indeed, in most societies the courts are the means, recognized by rulers and ruled alike, through which questions of validity and legitimacy are resolved. In practical terms, then, whether the 'ruled' can be taken to have accepted the validity of the rule-making authorities and, indeed, whether there exists a 'juristic postulate' about this validity depends upon whether this validity has been accepted *by the courts*. Jurisprudence can in this way recognize that a society whose judicial agencies accept its rulers as legitimate is radically different from one in which this acceptance is lacking.

RULES AND PRINCIPLES

If it can be accepted that an executive supported by a national judiciary must be viewed in a very different light from one which is not, the central problem now arises. The positivist might accept the point and yet maintain that the decision whether or not to support the executive is inherently a non-legal one. On this thesis, where a constitutional order is overthrown, the courts are placed in an insoluble dilemma. The only rules properly considered 'law' were those deriving from the vanquished basic norm. The courts are faced with the stark alternatives of either insisting that the previous order is the only legal one or, apparently, of acting in a non-legal vacuum. If the courts choose to follow their duty and apply the 'law' so defined, an absurd result could be reached. If an absolute monarch died without making provision for a successor, the 'law' would compel them to insist on regarding him as the lawful ruler. To avoid such futility, it would be reasonable to limit the legitimacy of a ruler to the period in which he remains in effective power. This proposition was called by Kelsen the 'principle of effectiveness' and it has an analogy in the principle of domestic law that the courts will not make orders that would obviously be in vain.

While it may be safe to assume general assent to the application of this principle in appropriate circumstances on the ground of common sense, the positivist may yet insist that the principle is not a legal one. Such an assertion has the appearance of Austinian dogma about it. Why should it be less of a legal principle than, for example, the statement that the courts will not permit themselves to be used as instruments of fraud, simply because no reference was made to it in the constitution? Like most dogma, it is founded on an oversimplified view of law and the nature of a legal decision. Professor R. M. Dworkin has drawn attention to the narrowness of the positivist position.[19] He takes the situation where a judge is faced by a problem not covered by any identifiable rule. The positivists seem to suggest that, in those circumstances, since there are no applicable rules, the matter must be decided according to the judge's personal discretion. This, Dworkin contends, puts the matter in too extreme a form. The judge may indeed have a discretion, but it must be exercised in accordance with legal principles and if this is not done the decision is open to criticism and may be reversed. Dworkin sharply distinguishes legal *principles* from legal *rules*. He suggests that there is a difference in *kind* between them. Rules apply in an all or nothing fashion. Where a rule covers the case, it must be applied unless an exception to it can be found. Theoretically, all the exceptions to it are capable of being listed, thus making more complete the original statement of the rule. Principles, on the other hand, have a dimension which rules lack. This is one of *weight*. Courts are not *bound* to apply a principle in the same way as a rule; they weigh them against other principles. Countervailing principles do not 'eat away' at a principle as exceptions do to a rule. They exist alongside it.

Before proceeding to a second and, for the present purposes, more interesting distinction which Dworkin finds between the characteristics of principles and rules, a caution should be entered as to whether the contention that they are different in kind can be accepted. Dworkin cites an American case[20] in which a court considered all the following principles: (*i*) that no man shall profit from his own wrongdoing; (*ii*) that courts will not permit themselves to be used as instruments of injustice; (*iii*) that freely negotiated contracts are to be enforced; (*iv*) that, in the absence of fraud, one who chooses not to read a contract before he signs it cannot later relieve himself of its burdens; and (*v*) that an automobile manufacturer is under a special duty with regard to the construction, promotion, and sale of his products. In order to avoid pre-empting discussion by definition, these statements will be called neither principles nor rules, but *normative propositions*. Two things about them are noteworthy. They are of differing degrees of *generality* and of

[19] '*Is Law a System of Rules?*' (1967) 35 U.Chi.L.R. 14, reprinted in Summers (ed.), *Essays in Legal Philosophy* (1968), p. 25.
[20] *Henningsen* v. *Bloomfield Motors, Inc.* (1960) 32 N.J. 358, 161 A.2d. 69.

weight. Normative propositions have to them two limbs. The first refers to a set of hypothetical facts; the second directs what should or should not follow on their happening (or failure to happen).[21] The reference to facts can follow an infinite gradation in degree of generality from the very precise (an automobile manufacturer manufacturing an automobile) to the extemely general (a court faced with the possibility of administering injustice). The direction as to consequences will similarly vary in weight of compulsion. The direction that an automobile manufacturer is under a special duty seems a strong directive. But the stipulation that a freely negotiated contract is to be enforced seems a much weaker one because there may be many cases where it would be unjust or contrary to public policy to do so.

Some examples will illustrate how this works. While most propositions formulated with generality will have a weak direction as to consequences, in many cases the direction may be so compelling that few or no exceptions are admitted. One may cite the principles that no one should be put in double jeopardy for the same offence, or that where an administrative decision affects the basic rights of an individual he has a right to be heard. A general proposition to which an exception seemed almost inconceivable appears in Lord Pearson's statement in *Verrier* v. *D.P.P.*[22] that he could not imagine circumstances in which it would be 'right' to sentence a person convicted of an attempt to a term greater than the maximum for the completed crime. This was contrasted with the propositions that '*normally* it is not right to pass a higher sentence for conspiracy than could be passed for the substantive offence' and that 'it should undoubtedly remain the *general rule* that where a substantive offence is charged, the addition of a charge for conspiracy is undesirable.' Although all the propositions are in general terms, the degree of weight attached to the directives varies from the almost absolute in the first case to the somewhat mild in the last.

The degree of weight properly to be placed on the directive is a matter of great subtlety. It may vary over the course of

[21] This follows Kelsen's description of the nature of a legal norm, but must not be taken as implying general acceptance of his description of the normative structure of a legal system.

[22] [1966] 3 All E.R. 568; see now Criminal Law Act 1967, s. 7 (2).

time and (a point of significance, returned to later) according to the source of its enunciation. The principle underlying the maxim of English law, *caveat emptor*, was once very strong. It is now almost eclipsed. There has also been a decline in the strength of the principle that *volenti non fit iniuria*. An early principle of the English divorce law that the courts would be slow to assist an adulterer was gradually replaced, over the course of a hundred years, by the principle that a marriage that has completely broken down should not be kept in legal existence.[23] On the other hand, it is not uncommon for comparatively weak normative propositions to gain in strength so that 'practices' are said to 'harden into rules of law'. But vulnerability to atrophy is not confined to generalized propositions. The precise 'rule' in *Rylands* v. *Fletcher*[24] has been steadily eroded by exceptions since its formulation in 1866. By the time the House of Lords, in *Conway* v. *Rimmer*,[25] effectively laid to rest an earlier rule, initially understood to be of absolute character, that a certificate from a Minister that production of a document would be contrary to the public interest was sufficient to withhold it from a court, the authority of that rule had been greatly shaken by both judicial and extrajudicial criticism.

These examples could be multiplied but should be sufficient to support the point that the gradations in the generality and weight of normative propositions are so fine that no real demarcation line can be drawn between those which should properly be called 'rules' and those which should be called 'principles'. Lawyers tend to describe as principles those propositions which are couched in terms of comparatively wide generality with a correspondingly weak directive, though these are also sometimes referred to as 'general rules'. But general propositions, too, might precede a strong directive. These could be described either as principles or as rules.[26] Where the factual part of the proposition is more precisely formulated, the normative statement is likely to be more compelling and the exceptions to it

---

[23] Compare *Morgan* v. *Morgan* (1869) L.R. 1 P. & D. 644 with *Blunt* v. *Blunt* [1943] A.C. 517.
[24] (1866) L.R. Ex. 265.
[25] [1968] 1 All E.R. 874.
[26] An example is the first proposition of Lord Pearson referred to earlier.

more readily identifiable. On this analysis the nomenclature allotted to different classes of normative proposition is unimportant. The differences between them are of degree and not of kind.

But this criticism of Dworkin's position leaves untouched a dimension of law to which he draws attention and which was lacking in the positivist thesis. He claims that the *origin* of principles is to be found 'not in a particular decision of some legislature or court, but in a sense of appropriateness developed in the profession and the public over a time'. Principles cannot be identified by reference to a rule of recognition as may be the case with most rules. Their authority lies outside the four corners of the positivist legal system. The proper gradations of weight to be attached to them cannot be ascertained by applying a mechanical test of identification provided by a basic norm. Every lawyer knows that statements of principle by some judges possess greater authority than those of others. This was true to an even greater extent of the writings of the jurists in the Roman legal system. The intangible quality of *authority*, the presence or absence of which may be decisive as to whether a principle is accepted, arises from the fact that the writer or judge is respected for his learning and expresses propositions in a clear, orderly, and accurate fashion which have become accepted in the professional tradition as possessing sound sense. This enables lawyers to accept as authoritative normative propositions emanating from sources outside their own jurisdiction. This fact is not weakened by the observation that English courts consider such authority as being 'persuasive' rather than binding. On the view taken here that the difference between principles and rules is one of degree only, these considerations apply equally to the more precisely worded propositions, though such statements are unlikely to be given as much weight outside their own jurisdiction as more general statements are because they will usually have been framed with a specific local context in view. Nevertheless, when Roman law was received into Europe, many of its detailed rules were imported alongside its more general principles. Even in England, where the judiciary has traditionally been very insular in its use of authority, the Court of Appeal has recently strongly relied on a decision of the High Court of Australia when reversing an earlier decision of its own on the law relating to bigamy.[27] Diplock L.J. referred to the outstanding reputation of the Australian judges in the case in question and remarked: 'The decisions of the High Court of Australia, even when so constituted, may be persuasive only, but how persuasive they are.'

Further examples will show that the assessment of relevant principles may involve inquiries into sources so remote from those indicated by formal constitutional rules that any attempt to comprise them within a 'basic norm' would so inflate the concept that it would lose all coherence. The traditional exclusion of textbooks as authoritative sources in the English system should not blind English jurists to the fact that in many systems certain respected textbook-writers hold an authority of their own. But even the English courts on occasion appeal to textbooks as supporting propositions they wish to apply.[28] Furthermore, when faced with new problems, or when devising new solutions to old ones, English judges have taken into account principles which cannot be said to be derived even from the authority of legal textbooks. Lord Denning has proclaimed the emergence of a 'right to work' which may have an important impact on legal doctrine.[29] Lest this be dismissed as an instance of inadmissible radicalism, Viscount Simonds, a follower of a more conservative tradition, has on one occasion appealed to 'abstract principles of justice' in deciding a novel point of private international law[30] and, on another, to 'contemporary ideas of justice or morality' when refusing to follow the rule laid down in the Court of Appeal that a tortfeasor is liable for all the direct consequence of his negligent act.[31] In jurisdictions less shy to sully the purity of judicial pronouncement by reference to non-judicial sources one might have

[27] *R. v. Gould* [1968] 1 All E.R. 849.

[28] See, for example, *Beswick* v. *Beswick* [1967] 2 All E.R. at p. 1219 where Lord Upjohn refers to Seton on Judgments and Orders as 'that great book of authority' and *The Mihalis Angelos* [1970] 3 All E.R. 125, where heavy reliance is placed on Scrutton on Charterparties.

[29] See *Nagle* v. *Fielden* [1966] 1 All E.R. 689 and *Edwards* v. *Society of Graphical and Allied Trades* [1970] 3 All E.R. 689.

[30] *Metliss* v. *National Bank of Greece and Athens* [1958] A.C. 509; see also *Jones* v. *Maynard* [1951] Ch. 572 where Vaisey J. appealed to Plato's definition of justice as a 'kind of equality' as support for his decision.

[31] *Overseas Tankship (U.K.) Ltd.* v. *Morts Dock and Engineering Co.* [1961] A.C. 388, not following *re Polemis* [1921] 3 K.B. 560.

expected citation of support for Lord Denning's proclamation of the 'right to work' and for Viscount Simonds's interpretation of contemporary ideas of justice or morality. Support for the former might have been found in the Universal Declaration of Human Rights, 1948[32] and for the latter, perhaps, by reference to the writings of Professor A. L. Goodhart.

Despite the reticence of British judges to refer to them directly, there can be little doubt that the expression of contemporary views about policy and social ends has a strong influence on the formulation and re-formulation of legal principles. A striking case where a judge disclosed his source is found in *Chaplin* v. *Boys*[33] where Lord Wilberforce expressly based his re-formulation of an important rule of English private international law on a proposition enunciated in the proposed official draft of the Restatement on the Conflict of Laws of the American Law Institute. It is not surprising that judges resort to authoritative sources outside their own immediate system in an area of law like private international law where local judicial authority is scant. The same is true of constitutional law. The norms of proper constitutional behaviour may appear only fleetingly in the case law and even more rarely in statutes. Yet principles upon which judicial decision may be founded are not wanting even though their statement may appear only, or mainly, in non-judicial sources. To cite but two recent English cases, in *Nissan* v. *Attorney-General*[34] reference was made to the opinions of the Law Officers of the Crown and in *Burmah Oil Co.* v. *Lord Advocate*,[35] which concerned the question whether a citizen has a right to compensation against a government which seizes his property in an emergency, careful attention was paid to the views of Scottish and European institutional writers, to decisions in the United States and to the work of the political theorist, John Locke.

If it can be accepted that English courts can and do turn to sources whose origin falls outside the narrow limits of 'law'

---

[32] Article 23 (1); see C. Wilfred Jenks, *The Common Law of Mankind* (1958), ch. 6.
[33] [1969] 2 All E.R. 1085.   [34] [1969] 1 All E.R. 629.
[35] [1964] 2 All E.R. 348. In *Liyanage* v. *R.* [1967] 1 A.C. 259 the Privy Council implied the principle of the separation of the powers into the constitution of Ceylon (which made no express reference to it) in such a manner as to invalidate legislation. The application of the principle was supported by reference to U.S. judicial dictum and to Blackstone's *Commentaries*.

laid down in positivist jurisprudence, the further point should be made that the freedom with which courts do this may vary between jurisdictions. The argument at this point is not that these sources are to be regarded as 'law' within a jurisdiction in the same sense as, for example, a local authority by-law. They do, however, distil normative propositions. Whether those propositions are considered 'legal', 'moral', or 'social' is unimportant. Their significance lies in the fact that they provide guidelines which are seen by courts as being relevant to the solution of the problem in hand. The degree of respect accorded to the source will depend upon the judge's individual assessment of the inherent worth of the proposition and the degree of its acceptance within the professional and cultural tradition of his society. In systems where judicial precedent is given greater weight than non-judicial sources, the latter may be preferred to be called 'sources of law' rather than 'law'. But in systems where judicial decision is not given pre-eminence, the line between law and its sources is one which cannot be precisely drawn. It would therefore be rash to conclude that the sources which have been considered cannot form the basis of a truly legal decision.

CONSTITUTIONAL PRINCIPLES

We may now revert to the situation confronting a judicial tribunal in the event of a revolution. Common sense, it has been suggested, dictates that the courts should cease to regard the decrees of the vanquished ruler as being authoritative and support for this was found in Kelsen's principle of effectiveness. Professor A. M. Honoré has suggested that there might be some implication within the old constitution that it should be considered frustrated if it becomes impossible to carry out its terms.[36] But he recognizes that this analogy with the contractual doctrine, like most analogies, does not fit the case exactly. It is probably better to regard this principle as one which exists independently of the old order and which accordingly survives its demise. The weight which it carries can, like that of other principles, be derived from sources quite distinct from the formal constitutional rules.

If this principle can survive the collapse of the previous

[36] '*Reflections on Revolutions*' (1967) Ir. Jur. (N.S.) 268.

system there seems to be no *a priori* ground for excluding the possibility that other principles, too, might have survived. The question now arises whether it is possible to conceive of principles according to which prima facie illegal acts may be sought to be justified. It appears that such principles do exist and can be applied even to override the enacted law of an effective legal system. Two examples will be given. One is drawn from the principles of sentencing offenders. In the vast majority of cases in which a court finds a mitigating factor it cannot be said that the presence of that factor *justifies* the offence (in the same way as, for example, self-defence). In some cases, however, it may come near to doing so, as where a penniless person who steals food for his family is given an absolute discharge. In one case[37] a defendant had refused to produce his national registration identity card when a policeman demanded it in connection with a traffic offence. The police power derived from wartime legislation enacted for security purposes. A Divisional Court of seven judges upheld the validity of the legislation, but 'emphatically' approved of the absolute discharge given to the defendant and encouraged magistrates similarly to discharge any other person convicted of this offence. The decision amounts to an assertion that disobedience to this law is justified and it can be supported only by reference to a principle, which must override the enacted law, that legislation passed for security purposes cannot be used for other purposes when the emergency is over. Not only, therefore, may courts take cognizance of criteria according to which unlawful acts may be justified, but where their application involves consideration of the motives of the authorities, investigation into these motives appears to be within their competence.

Perhaps a more immediately analogous principle is that of necessity. This may be used to justify invasions by private citizens against others which would otherwise be unlawful[38] and can also be considered the basis of the English doctrine of martial law.[39] By this doctrine the 'ordinary law' is suspended while the courts refuse to intervene during the course of an

---

[37] *Willcock* v. *Muckle* [1951] 2 K.B. 844.

[38] See Glanville Williams, 'The Defence of Necessity' (1953) 6 *Current Legal Problems* 216, who writes: ' "The law", in a word, *includes* the doctrine of necessity; the defence of necessity is an implied exception to particular rules of law.'

[39] See R. F. V. Heuston, *Essays in Constitutional Law* (1964), p. 159.

emergency. But it would be mistaken to suppose that there was a legal vacuum during this period because acts which would otherwise have been unlawful will be justified only if they survive careful scrutiny as to whether they exceeded the limits reasonably set by the exigencies of the situation. It was this principle which was relied upon by the court at first instance in the first Rhodesian case to justify those acts of the authorities which were 'predominantly motivated' with a view to maintaining the functioning of society. There is also substantial authority for the principle to be found in the writings of the Roman–Dutch jurists, a judgment of Lord Mansfield, American decisions arising out of the Civil War, and in decisions from Pakistan and Cyprus.[40]

The present purpose is not to attempt to make an exhaustive list of the kinds of principles that may be relevant to a decision whether revolutionary activity should be given legal justification, but the more limited one of salvaging this area of investigation from total extinction by the operation of positivist dogmatism. But it may be helpful to set out some of the principles which may be pertinent to revolutionary situations.

1. The principle of effectiveness.

2. The principle of legitimate disobedience to authority exercised for improper purposes.

3. The principle of necessity.

4. The principles that violation of a right demands a remedy and that no one should profit from his own wrongful act. As a revolution will invariably have involved the violation of some of the 'rights' protected by the previous constitution, a combination of those principles suggests that, even if the new order is considered legitimate, some recompense should be offered to those whose rights were infringed.

5. The principle that a court will not permit itself to be used as an instrument of injustice.

6. The principle that it is in the public interest that those in *de facto* impregnable control should be accorded legal recognition. This was the main principle upon which the four Commonwealth tribunals rested their decisions. Put more

---

[40] See (1969) 32 M.L.R. at p. 31 n. The majority of the Privy Council refused to apply the doctrine to the Rhodesian situation. But see the strong dissent of Lord Pearce.

crudely, the principle states that might, once established, *ipso iure* becomes right. It gives effect to the acceptable policy value that it is in the interests of the community that order be preserved. But one might be reluctant to hold that it is the *only* relevant principle and that there *cannot* be others which would militate against automatically accepting revolutionaries as legitimate regardless of any other circumstance.

7. The principle, common to both public and private international law and which Grotius considered a central tenet of natural law, that promises are to be kept: *pacta sunt servanda*. A government elected under a constitution expressly or impliedly pledges with the electorate that it will hold to the constitution. If it abrogates that constitution, it breaks faith with the electorate and therefore contravenes this principle unless and until it submits itself once more to the same electorate to express its acceptance or rejection of the action.

8. The principle that government should be by the consent of the governed, whether voters or not. There is nothing new in this principle. Authority can be found in political writings at least from the Middle Ages to the present day.[41]

9. International law now probably supports the principle of the right to self-determination[42] and of the unacceptability of racial discrimination.[43] As the Rhodesian court, in particular, relied heavily on an appeal to international law for support for the principle it in fact applied (that revolutionary success demands legal recognition) it would have been proper to have weighed against that principle other norms of international law relevant to the situation.

AUTHORITY OF THE COURT

In concluding the defence of the proposition that principles of the kind enumerated above may properly be taken into account by a court in order to determine whether or not to uphold the legitimacy of a revolutionary regime, it is necessary to consider two oblique arguments which would attempt to

[41] See Gierke, *Political Theories of the Middle Ages* (1900), pp. 39 ff. The medieval writers supported the principle by reference to a maxim taken from the Roman law: *quod omnes tangit debet ab omnibus approbari.*

[42] See I. Brownlie, *Principles of Public International Law* (1966), p. 483.

[43] See U.N. Declaration on the Elimination of All Forms of Racial Discrimination (1963).

undermine it. One is to take theoretical objection to the jurisdiction of a court which indulges in the exercise. The claim is that, as the court acquired its authority to determine disputes by virtue of jurisdiction conferred on it by the old constitution, the disappearance of that constitution implies the collapse of the court's own authority. The other argument is the severely practical one that, whatever the legal theorist or the judges may say, any court making a finding adverse to a revolutionary regime is certain to be disbanded so that in reality a judiciary will be allowed to function only if it is subservient to the new regime.

The first argument weighed heavily with the Rhodesian court, which felt bound to conclude that the authority which enabled it to continue to function must have been derived from the new Government. This view, however, rests on two premisses which are not necessarily true. The first is the assumption that, because the source of the court's authority arose from the old constitution, it must necessarily have fallen with the other branches of that order. This implies that there must be one single source of authority for all lawmaking institutions which accordingly stand or fall together. Belief in a Kelsenian basic norm or a Hartian rule of recognition might encourage this view. But is there any good reason why it should not be supposed that the source from which the court's authority arose has survived independently of the demise of the old executive? The second questionable premiss is that by suffering the court to continue to function, the new executive thereby assimilates the court into its own revolutionary order and that this compels the *de iure* recognition of the Government. But against this it might be urged that the very submission by the revolutionaries to litigation before the court concerning their own legitimacy suggests that the court may have an inherent authority arising from the submission of both parties, rulers and ruled, to its jurisdiction. As Honoré puts it: 'Any group can agree on the submission of disputes to adjudication and this agreement is (unless one holds the preconception that all the laws in a given territory must necessarily be systematized) itself a source of law.'[44]

The second objection must be met by an appeal to faith. It

[44] Loc. cit., p. 276.

is certainly true that many revolutionaries are unlikely to be deterred by judicial opposition. On the other hand the extent to which even revolutionary politicians wish to appear to be acting in accordance with acceptable principles should not be underestimated. The dismissal of judges is an extreme step which might have dangerous domestic and international consequences for a revolutionary executive. Nor should it be too readily assumed that a regime which takes this step will easily find a replacement judiciary without leaving itself open to ridicule. The difficulty of such a task will depend upon the degree of strength with which constitutional principles are held in the cultural and professional traditions of the society in question. Insistence upon these principles in the face of threats of dismissal would have the salutary effect of underlining the unprincipled nature of the threatened governmental conduct.

But perhaps the most important advantage to be gained by the recognition of principles of this kind is that revolutionary situations would no longer be seen in absolute terms: that either the usurpers must always and inevitably remain illegitimate or that they must always and inevitably be held legitimate once they have succeeded, irrespective of the reasons why they took power, how they have behaved while in power, and how long they have held power. The answer to the problem of legitimacy may be a qualified one, involving the judicious balancing of a wide variety of factors. Had the Rhodesian court, for example, held that the revolutionary regime could be considered lawful only if confirmed in office by the electorate which had elected them under the old constitution and if some satisfactory evidence was produced that the new constitution was broadly acceptable to the majority of the population[45] (in accordance with principles 7 and 8 listed above) is it *inconceivable* that the regime might have preferred to attempt to comply with that finding rather than to dismiss the judges?[46] The opportunities open to the judiciary to influence the course of events should not be dismissed out of hand. It may be that

[45] In discussions between the British and Rhodesian Governments before the declaration of independence it was suggested that a Royal Commission might seek such evidence, but the proposal then came to nothing.

[46] Had the matter proceeded in this fashion, a powerful precedent would have been created which another court faced with a similar situation would have found difficult to ignore.

this is unaccustomed territory for the judiciary to enter. But this is true for many areas of law in modern times, especially with respect to the interaction between the executive and the citizen. It is hard to believe that our legal and cultural tradition is too weak to develop sound and acceptable principles in this new context. But in order that they may take root, it is necessary to rid ourselves of the conceptual block which would forever bar the entry of juristic thought into this domain.

III

Revolutions and Continuity of Law

J. M. FINNIS

' . . . the State and its legal order remain the same only as long as the constitution is intact or changed according to its own provisions.'[1]

INTRODUCTION

Devolution of authority from the Imperial Crown in Parliament has been followed, rather regularly, by revolution within the new states of the Commonwealth. Judicial and academic accounts of both devolution and revolution have been largely dominated by a theory of legal discontinuity. In its simple form, this theory asserts that every illegal change in the constitution of a state is a revolution, and that a revolution overturns the entire legal order, replacing it with a new system.[2]

[1] Kelsen, *General Theory of Law and State* (1946), p. 368. See also Kelsen, *The Pure Theory of Law* (1967), p. 209. Below, nn. 2, 14.

[2] Hans Kelsen is the principal exponent of this view, and has been relied upon in the judicial decisions mentioned below, notes 22 and 62. There are, however, problems in interpreting his texts. Thus in *General Theory*, p. 117, he appears to be defining 'revolution' as that which 'occurs whenever the legal order of a community is nullified and replaced by a new order in . . . a way not prescribed by the first order itself'. But other passages show that Kelsen's argument is not simply *ex definitione*. For example, on p. 368 of the same work he says: 'To assume that the continuity of national law, or—what amounts to the same—the identity of the State, is not affected by revolution or *coup d'état*, as long as the territory and the population remain by and large the same, is possible only if a norm of international law is presupposed recognizing victorious revolution and successful *coup d'état* as legal methods of changing the constitution. No jurist doubts, for instance, that it is legally the same Russian State that existed under the tsarist constitution and that now exists under the bolshevist constitution and under the new name of U.S.S.R. But this interpretation is not possible if we, ignoring international law, do not go beyond the Russian constitution as it exists at a given moment. Then the continuity of the legal order and the identity of the Russian State become incomprehensible. If the situation is judged from this point of view, the State and its legal order remain the same only as long as the constitution is intact or changed according to its own provisions.' See also ibid., pp. 117–19, 220–1; Kelsen, *Pure Theory of Law*, pp. 209–10. For expositions of similar views, see Cattaneo, *Il concetto di rivoluzione nella scienza del diritto* (1960), pp. 96–8, and the works cited in O'Connell, *State Succession in Municipal Law and International Law* (1967), i, p. 101, n. 2.

Exponents of this theory of discontinuity are well aware that in almost all cases the content of the post-revolutionary legal system is similar, if not identical, to that of the pre-revolutionary system.[3] Both the general rules of law (especially private law) and the particular rights (contractual, real, remedial, etc.) actually acquired under those rules are likely to survive, in the sense that 'the same' rules and rights will be enforced after as before the revolution. Still, the fact that the law of property is 'the same' in one country as in another does not imply that one and the same rule is in force in both countries. Likewise, the fact that the law of property in a certain country is 'the same' at one time as at another does not entail that one and the same rule is in force at both times. If the two times are separated by a revolution, then on the theory of discontinuity the law will not be one and the same, since the basis or reason for the validity of the rules will be different. Every rule has its particular identity as part of a particular system, and the identity of a system changes (it is said) when its constitution, its basic norm, its rule of recognition, is changed in a manner not legally permitted or provided for.

The theory, so stated, has an engaging elegance and simplicity. Closer examination reveals, however, that it is ambiguous and arbitrary, and that these defects are the short-comings of a central tradition of modern legal philosophy. So before raising questions about the truth of the theory, it will be as well to clarify its meaning. Two questions immediately arise, the first concerning the *sufficient* conditions of a change in the identity of a legal system, the second concerning the *necessary* conditions of such change:

(i) Does every illegal or 'unconstitutional' act, of the sort that would usually be called a *coup d'état*, amount to a change in the constitution and thus in the identity of the legal order? Or is there a class of *coups d'état* that, while illegally supplanting legal officials, nevertheless leave the constitution, in Kelsen's sense, intact?

[3] 'Usually, the new men whom a revolution brings to power annul only the constitution and certain laws of paramount political significance . . . A great part of the old legal order "remains" valid also within the frame of the new order . . . The laws which, in the ordinary inaccurate parlance, continue to be valid are, from a juristic standpoint, new laws whose import coincides with that of the old laws': Kelsen, *General Theory*, pp. 117–18; cf. *Pure Theory*, pp. 209–10.

(ii) Can there be a change in the identity of a legal system otherwise than by violation of some rule of the system existing at the time of the supposed change?

I. THE PROBLEM OF THE COUP D'ÉTAT

In his exposition of the theory of discontinuity, Kelsen says that he includes *coups d'état* among the revolutions that effect the destruction and creation of legal systems.[4] But other exponents have been hesitantly willing to recognize a category of unconstitutional acts which involve a modification of the law in force without bringing to birth a new legal system, because these acts do not affect the supreme source or criterion of validity of the system.[5] It will be convenient stipulatively to name this category the 'mere *coup d'état*', without assuming either that this is what Kelsen means when he uses the term *coup d'état*, or that the distinction thus drawn will still be viable at the end of a jurisprudential analysis.

A modern lawyer, contemplating the accession of a usurper to the throne, is likely to say: 'The answer, which Kelsen has taught us to analyse correctly, is that the old legal order [gives] way to a new, which [may] happen to coincide largely in content with the old . . . it [is] the rules of the new, not the old order, which require his subjects to bear him allegiance.'[6] The Year Books thought otherwise. When, for example, the Yorkist Edward IV seized the throne in 1461, the Lancastrian kings from Henry IV to Henry VI were officially regarded as usurpers who had overthrown the true line of succession. So when a question arose about the validity of the acts of the Lancastrians, counsel argued, apparently with success:

It is necessary that the Realm should have a king under whose authority laws will be held and upheld, and though [Henry VI] was in power by usurpation, any judicial act done by him and touching Royal jurisdiction would be valid, and will bind the rightful king when the latter returns to power.[7]

---

[4] *General Theory*, p. 117; *Pure Theory*, p. 209; cf. below, text at p. 50, n. 14.

[5] See, e.g. Cattaneo, op. cit., p. 70.

[6] Honoré, 'Allegiance and the Usurper' [1967] Cam.L.J. 214, 233; but cf. Honoré's later article, 'Reflections on Revolution', (1967) 2 The Irish Jurist 268.

[7] 'Pluis d'assis Bagot, ore fuit le matter reherce et touche, que non obstante cel act les patentes de legitimation sont bones, car le roy H. fuist roy en possession, et il covient que le roialme eit un roy south que les leyes serront tenus et maintenus,

The language of this successful argument of counsel brings out the issue. There is a 'realm' in which 'authority' is exercised by the 'King' by way of 'judicial acts' of 'Royal jurisdiction'. Into this structure of offices or jurisdictions the usurper inserts himself; he disturbs the monarch but not the Monarchy. Of course, usurpations were not without legal consequence; for example, all royal commissions had to be renewed and all suits in the royal courts recommenced. But this in any event occurred, in English law, on the death of the monarch. Significantly, constitutional law in the age of usurpations dealt with usurpation and the death of the King alike as 'demise of the Crown'.[8] There was no question of glossing over or minimizing the illegality of usurpation; the constitutional lawyers did not deal kindly with the attempts sometimes made to justify treason by alleging that allegiance is due to the Crown rather than to the King.[9] But the self-interpretation of English law has been clear and definite in its assertion that the law, even the constitutional law, of the kingdom is affected neither in content nor in identity by *coups* and counter-*coups*.

This interpretation, moreover, seems eminently reasonable. So it is not surprising that some exponents of the theory of

---

donque par ce que il ne fuist eins forsque par usurpation, uncore chescun act judicial fait par luy que touche jurisdiction roial serra bon, et liera le roy de droit quant il fait regresse, etc.' *Bagot's Case* (1469) Y.B. 9 Edw. IV, Pasch., pl. 2. See Chrimes, *English Constitutional Ideas in the Fifteenth Century* (1936), pp. 55–6, 369; Vinogradoff, *Collected Papers* (1928), i, 199. On *Bagot's Case* and subsequent authorities, see *State* v. *Carroll* (1871) 38 Connecticut 449; *In re Aldridge* (1894) 15 N.Z.L.R. 361 at p. 369 ff; *Adams* v. *Adams* [1971] P. 188 at p. 210.

[8] E. Kantorowicz, *The King's Two Bodies* (1957), p. 371 and works there cited. See also the argument of counsel (following the opinion of the judges in the *Case of the Dutchy of Lancaster* (1561) 1 Plowden 212 at 213) in *Willion* v. *Berkley* (1561), Plowden 225 at p. 234 (75 E.R. 339 at p. 355) '... the King has two capacities, for he has two bodies, the one whereof is a body natural, consisting of natural members as every other man has ...; the other is a body politic, and the members thereof are his subjects ...; and this body is not subject to passions as the other is, nor to death, for as to this body the King never dies, and his natural death is not called in our Law (as Harper said) the death of the King, but the demise of the King, not signifying by the word (*demise*) that the body politic of the King is dead, but that there is a separation of the two bodies, and that the body politic is transferred and conveyed over from the body natural now dead, or now removed from the dignity royal to another body natural. So that it signifies a removal of the body politic of the King of this realm from one body natural to another'. See also Blackstone, I *Comm.* 249.

[9] See Kantorowicz, op. cit., pp. 364–6; Blackstone, I *Comm.* 249.

discontinuity are unwilling to include *coups d'état* among law-destroying revolutions. But their hesitations are also understandable, for if an exception is to be made in favour of mere *coups d'état*, where is the line to be drawn? May not the exception in favour of continuity swallow up the rule of discontinuity?

It is tempting to suggest that a line between law-destroying revolutions and mere *coups d'état* can be fixed as follows: in a mere *coup d'état* only the rules governing the succession of persons to legal office are affected; the rules concerning the powers and hierarchy of the offices themselves are unaffected. This suggestion seems to correspond to a suggestion made by Hart, that there is a category of acts which entail only the legally unauthorized substitution of a new set of individuals as officials;[10] the suggested distinction would, moreover, explain the attitude of English lawyers to usurpations of the Crown. But before the suggestion could be adopted, it would be necessary to show that it is consistent with the premises of the theory of discontinuity which it is designed to make more palatable. So it is necessary to examine those premises more closely.

In any constitution distributing authority among officials or estates there will be, *inter alia*, three categories of rules:[11]

    A. *rules of succession to office*, including rules governing both accession to and succession in office or estate;

    B. *rules of competence*; rules governing the distribution of powers as between offices or estates;

    C. *rules of succession of rules*, including all rules (whether or not included also in category *A* or category *B* or both) governing the amendment, suspension, or replacement of rules of each of these three categories.

Even in the simplest absolute monarchy, the *rules of succession to office* governing succession to the Crown may be liable to lawful alteration, and such alteration will be regulated by a *rule of succession of rules* which happens to coincide with the simple

---

[10] Hart, *The Concept of Law* (1961), p. 115.

[11] The analysis which differentiates these three categories is adapted *ad hoc* to the problem of the *coup d'état*, and is not intended to supplement or supplant more fundamental analyses of types of rule or norm.

rule of competence governing legislative authority, viz. 'What Rex enacts, and only what Rex enacts, is law.'[12]

Granted the clear and distinct conception of *rules of succession of rules*, it is open to the jurist to explain the validity of the existing constitution by reference to the rules of the preceding constitution, and in particular by reference to that rule of the preceding constitution which governed the amendment or replacement of that constitution. Thus, with Kelsen, the jurist can proceed back, via a succession of *rules of succession of rules*, to a 'historically first constitution'. This constitution, by definition, emerged without legal authority, and can be regarded as the ultimate and highest posited source of validity of the existing constitution and thence of the whole existing legal system. On Kelsen's recent analysis, the *Grundnorm* is an injunction (not posited but 'fictively' postulated 'as if' it were the content of an act of will) to obey the will of the founders of this 'historically first constitution'.[13]

But although *rules of succession to office* are distinct from *rules of succession of rules*, rules of the former category cannot be violated by an overt usurper without violating some rule of the latter category. For because overt usurpation is not a once-for-all act accomplished at some *punctum temporis* like a murder, but involves a claim to *hold* office, it is more than merely the violation of some rule or rules. To usurp the Crown in an absolute monarchy is to insist that the particular *rule of succession to office* identifying the lawful holder of royal office shall be *changed*, at least so that it becomes a rule identifying the usurper as the present lawful holder (even if the usurper has no dynastic ambitions and is content that, after him, the succession to office shall be determined as if there had been no usurpation). Now *ex hypothesi*, this change or amendment or abrogation in suspension of some *rule of succession to office* is accomplished in violation of some *rule of succession of rules* which governs the change, amendment, abrogation, or suspension of constitutional rules: otherwise an overt usurpation would not be identifiable as such.

Therefore, even if Kelsen were to accept the suggestion that

---

[12] Cf. Hart, review of Fuller's *The Morality of Law*, (1965) 78 Harv. L.R. 1281, 1295.

[13] Kelsen, *Pure Theory*, p. 200; *General Theory*, pp. 115–16; (1966) 1 Israel L.R. 1 at p. 6.

there is a distinguishable category of mere *coups d'état* in which the *rules of succession to office* are affected while leaving the *rules of competence* governing the powers of the offices unaffected, he would have to point out that the effect of a *coup* on rules of the former category entails a violation of some *rule of succession of rules*. Because of this violation, rules generated and legal acts done after the *coup* cannot be traced back to the same sources of validity as rules and acts before the *coup*; the unity of the system is broken; there are two systems, and only the system interpreted as including the post-*coup* constitutional rules (of each category) is effective and, consequently, existent as an object of legal cognition (i.e. valid). Thus Kelsen is bound in consistency to reject the distinction between law-destroying revolutions and mere *coups. d'état*. And this, on the whole, he does (although he accepts, perhaps inconsistently, that a usurpation of supreme *judicial* office effects only a 'revolutionary partial change', not a 'revolutionary total change' of the constitution).[14]

But if the notion that the unity of a legal system is constituted by derivation, via rules of succession of rules, from a historically first constitution demands a clear and unequivocal rejection of the mere *coup d'état* as a jurisprudential category, it is the occasion of doubt and equivocation in answering our second question, to which we now turn.

II. THE PROBLEM OF LAWFUL DEVOLUTION

On the theory of discontinuity, all revolutions effect a change in the identity of a legal system. But can such a change be effected otherwise than by a 'revolution'?

At one level, this question raises no more than a terminological difficulty, visible in Kelsen's expositions,[15] in the use of the term 'revolution'. For on the one hand, the term can be used to indicate simply an effective seizure and exercise of

[14] *Pure Theory*, p. 276. Note that it is possible to imagine circumstances which might be styled a *coup d'état* but which might involve no violation of constitutional law and would thus constitute an exception to our demonstration that all *coups d'état* are revolutions in the Kelsenian sense: for example, if the Vice-President were to assassinate the President of a state whose constitution provided that the Vice-President should succeed the President on his death from whatever cause (provided that the legal system did not contain the rule that no man may profit from his own wrong).

[15] Above p. 43, n. 2.

rule-making power or authority in violation of, at least, some rule of succession of rules. On the other hand, the term can be used to indicate any situation in which the speaker considers that a change in the identity of a legal system has been effected, whether by division of one system into two, or by absorption of several into one, or for some other reason. When, in the theory of discontinuity, it is affirmed that 'all revolutions effect a change in the identity of a legal system', the term 'revolution' is used in the former sense; and this is its sense throughout this essay.

However, at another level, the present question—Can the identity of a legal system be changed without violating some existing rule?—exposes important difficulties in the Kelsenian model of a legal system. According to that model, all the rules of a system are linked to each other by common derivation from the rules of competence in a 'historically first constitution', the derivation being governed and verified by reference to rules of succession of rules. Now, given these rules of succession of rules, it is clear that the *original* rules of competence in the historically first constitution need no longer be 'in force'; they may have been replaced by other rules of competence in accordance with the relevant rule of succession of rules; and this rule may have itself replaced an earlier rule of succession of rules in accordance with the earlier rule's reflexive provisions for its own replacement. As Kelsen puts it:

If we ask for the reason of the validity of the constitution . . . we may, perhaps, discover an older constitution; that means the validity of the existing constitution is justified by the fact that it was created according to the rules of an earlier constitution by way of a constitutional amendment. In this way we eventually arrive at a historically first constitution that cannot have been created in this way and whose validity, therefore, cannot be traced back to a positive norm created by a legal authority; we arrive, instead, at a constitution that became valid in a revolutionary way, that is, either by breach of a former constitution *or for a territory that formerly was not the sphere of validity of a constitution and of a national legal order based on it.*[16]

The passage italicized is ambiguous: it may refer simply to formerly 'uncivilized' regions; or it may refer to territories that

[16] *Pure Theory*, p. 200 (emphasis added).

once were merely *part* of a larger territorial sphere of validity, as (say) Pakistan was once, in law, a part (and not even a sub-unit identifiable as such) of the British Empire and constitutionally subject to the general imperial rule that 'what the Queen in the Imperial Parliament enacts is law'. But in the latter case, the problem becomes evident: save by way of a *breach* of a former constitution, how can the Pakistan legal system have managed to separate from the Imperial (British) legal system? After all, ultimate rule-making authority over Pakistan was transferred to the Constituent Assembly of Pakistan by the Indian Independence Act 1947, an Imperial statute enacted in accordance with British constitutional rules of succession of rules. No breach or violation of law occurred.

Indeed, the Kelsenian analysis is often felt to derogate from the genuine independence of former imperial territories. The demand has been raised for a 'local root' of sovereignty or constitutional authority, for a 'shift in the *Grundnorm*', for 'autochthony'. Great care has, on occasion, been taken to perform some unauthorized act in the course of transfer of authority, so that it may be claimed that, *because* there has been a revolution, *therefore* the validity of the new constitution legal order *cannot* be traced back to the British imperial constitution.[17] The problem has been familiar to continental jurists, too: when an absolute monarch grants a constitution purporting to limit his rule-making authority (an *octroi* constitution), one can dispute endlessly whether the new rule perhaps gets its validity from the old, or whether the old rule has been completely superseded and eliminated.[18]

These disputes get their heat from the practical question whether or not the new rule and constitution could be repealed by an exercise of authority under the old rule and constitution. Could the Imperial Parliament reassert its authority over

---

[17] See Wheare, *The Constitutional Structure of the Commonwealth* (1960), ch. IV. Cf. also Latham, *The Law and the Commonwealth* (1949), esp. pp. 534–40; Roberts-Wray, *Commonwealth and Colonial Law* (1966), pp. 289–301.

[18] Joseph Raz's discussion, in *The Concept of a Legal System* (1970), pp. 102–3, of a case of 'peaceful transfer of powers' (cf. p. 107), while making a valid point against Kelsen (along lines similar to those developed in this essay), rather minimizes the need for a fully developed legal theory of independence by relying on a supposed 'general consensus of both lay and professional opinion', which consensus is in fact often lacking. 'This opinion is completely justified' says Raz; but this he assumes rather than explains (and cf. pp. 34, 188). See also below p. 65, n. 49.

Pakistan? Perhaps one will be inclined to say, with Hart, that according to British law it can, but according to Pakistan law it cannot.[19] This answer, however, evades rather than settles the theoretical problem, which arises from the fact that, on the Kelsenian analysis back to a historically first constitution, the 'Pakistan legal system' seems to be no more than a sub-unit in the British legal system, from which it cannot be freed save by way of some violation of British law. Nor will it suffice to say that the Indian Independence Act was *intended* to transfer rule-making authority over Pakistan irrevocably away from the Imperial Parliament. For, on the one hand, one can reply that the British rule of succession of rules, as it existed in 1947, did not itself authorize the Imperial Parliament to transfer parliamentary authority irrevocably away ('Parliament cannot bind its successors'). And on the other hand, one can reply, more radically, that if, as the Kelsenian analysis entails, an earlier constitution is the source of the validity of later constitutions, there seems no reason why it should not validate a rule purporting to repeal a later constitution, whether or not the later constitution authorizes such repeal. To this radical suggestion, it would be no sufficient rejoinder to say that the old constitution (or rule of succession of rules) and the new 'relate to different periods of time';[20] for the whole problem, on the Kelsenian analysis, is *how* they relate to different periods of time, granted that the earlier constitution is as much the *present* source of the validity of the remotest and latest of its lawful successors as it was (is?) the source of the validity of all the intermediate and lawfully repealed constitutions in the historical succession of constitutions.

Various attempts have been made to escape from the obviously unsatisfactory analytical state of affairs indicated in the preceding paragraph. The most common escape is by arguing that a constitution, or at least an ultimate rule of succession of rules, *cannot* be wholly replaced in accordance with its own stipulations; purported replacements are really 'legal camouflage' for a 'peaceful revolution' in which the replacement is a *break* with the past, accomplished by 'universal consent', or

---

[19] Hart, *Concept of Law*, p. 118.

[20] Cf. Hart, 'Self-Referring Laws', in *Festskrift till ägnad Karl Olivecrona* (1964), at p. 314.

transfer of allegiance,[21] or by a 'factual social-psychological change in the political ideology', accomplished by a 'magical act which alone can loose the bond forged by' the pre-existing rule of succession of rules.[22] In this argument we discern the theoretical pressures underlying the ambiguity, mentioned at the beginning of this section, in the legal use of the term 'revolution'. To minimize the ambiguity Alf Ross named the relevant 'social-psychological change' not 'peaceful revolution' but 'evolution'[23] (to be contrasted, no doubt, with lawful 'devolution').

In favour of this view, Ross offered a number of arguments. One was that it is logically impossible for a proposition to refer to itself; thus a rule of succession of rules cannot provide reflexively for its own supercession.[24] The alleged logical impossibility, however, has not impressed all logicians,[25] let alone the many British draftsmen who nowadays resort to double (i.e. reflexive) entrenchment of constitutional provisions; so we propose to ignore the argument here. More pertinent was Ross's argument that where a constitutional clause governing constitutional amendment is amended in accordance with its own rules, the new amending clause cannot be regarded as derived from the old, or as valid because derived from it. 'Any such derivation presupposes the validity of the superior norm and thereby the continued existence of the same, and by derivation cannot be established a new norm which conflicts with the source of the derivation.'[26] Hart replied that there is no conflict if a rule of amendment is amended in accordance with its own provisions, for the original rule and the amended rule

---

[21] H. W. R. Wade, 'The Basis of Legal Sovereignty' [1955] Cam.L.J. 172, at p. 196.

[22] Alf Ross, *On Law and Justice* (1958), p. 83; cf. below p. 64, n. 48. Similarly, on a practical level, Beadle C.J. reasoned (in the case on the status of the revolutionary Rhodesian Government) that after a complete change from one constitution to another, the position of a judge who was appointed under and accepted the earlier constitution is the same when the change was effected in defiance of the rules of change in the earlier constitution as when it was in accordance with them. In either case, the earlier constitution is 'completely gone' and 'non-existent' 'for all purposes'; so the judge must simply make a free option to accept or not to accept the new constitution: *Madzimbamuto* v. *Lardner-Burke* 1968 (2) S.A. 284, 328–9.

[23] Ross, *On Law and Justice*, p. 81.

[24] Ibid., p. 81; see also Ross in 78 *Mind* (1969) 1, at pp. 7–17, and below p. 63, n. 48.

[25] See Hart, 'Self-Referring Laws', at p. 316.

[26] Ross, *op. cit.*, at p. 82.

relate to different periods of time.[27] This reply is correct as far as it goes; but, as we have already remarked, it fails to recognize that for Ross the source of the difficulty was that (on any view other than his own) the original rule *remains* in some way 'in force' as a source of the validity of the amended rule—so that, as Ross insisted, it is hard to see why an amendment of the amended rule should not rely for *its* validity, too, on the original rule rather than on the former amended rule[28], in which case there would indeed be a conflict, though perhaps not precisely the conflict indicated by Ross.

A consideration of Hart's *Concept of Law* reveals why he displayed little sympathy for Ross's difficulty, and why he summarily dismissed as 'questionable' Ross's 'statement that a derivation of a new norm pre-supposes not only the validity of the superior norm but its continued existence after the creation of the new norm'.[29] For in Hart's analysis of legal system the transtemporal validation of basic rules, relied on by Kelsen and recognized as troublesome by Ross, is simply and silently omitted.

Is this purported by-law of the Oxfordshire County Council valid? Yes: because it *was* made in exercise of the powers conferred, and in accordance with the procedure specified, by a statutory order made by the Minister of Health. . . . Finally when the validity of the statute has been queried and assessed by reference to the rule that what the Queen in Parliament enacts is law, *we are brought to a stop in inquiries concerning validity*: for we have reached a rule which . . . is . . . unlike [the intermediate statutory order and statute] in that there is no rule providing criteria for the assessment of its own legal validity.[30]

For Hart, the existence of a rule of recognition is simply a present matter of fact. Likewise, the question whether a legal system retains its identity or has become two legal systems is simply a question of fact (though it *can* also be regarded as a question of law within a given system of law),[31] and the answer to the question is in no way affected by the way in which this matter of fact came about. The result is the same, whether

[27] Above, p. 53, n. 20.   [28] Ross, *op. cit.*, at p. 83.
[29] Above, p. 53, n. 20.
[30] Hart, *Concept of Law*, pp. 103–4 (emphasis added).
[31] Ibid., p. 118.

the parent legislature 'retire[d] from the scene by removing legislative power over the former colony', or whether there was a revolutionary 'break' by violence: in either case 'the ultimate rule of recognition now accepted and used [no longer includes], among the criteria of validity, any reference to the operations of legislatures of other territories.'[32]

But can we accept Hart's escape from the problem of the temporal dimension of legal rules and systems? We can, only if we stifle legitimate questions. I shall devote the rest of this section of this essay to raising and evaluating two particular lines of questioning.

(i) In the first place, can we accept that, after a change of rule of recognition, the new rule of recognition 'no longer includes *any* reference to the operation of legislatures of other territories'? Suppose that in Australia the rule of recognition changed, in 1942, from 'What the Westminster Parliament enacts is law' to 'What the Canberra Parliament enacts is law',[33] and suppose (for the time being) that no questions are raised about the basis of the latter rule; there remain urgent questions about the basis of the *present* validity of the whole set of legal rules in force in Australia immediately *before* the change. It seems that the new rule of recognition must indeed contain a clause identifying as law all those rules, not since repealed, that were valid immediately before the change; and such rules can only be identified compendiously as those valid by virtue of enactment by the Westminster Parliament before 1942 or 1939. Thus the new rule of recognition must indeed include a clause referring to the operations of a foreign legislature, albeit to operations in the past. In a later work, Hart has said:

In any full description of the criteria used by the courts after [a] revolutionary break in ascertaining the law, the old legislation would have to be specifically mentioned *eo nomine*. Had there been no revolution, it would have been identified by reference to the general provision qualifying the unbroken succession of legislators. After

---

[32] Ibid., pp. 117–18.

[33] Cf. Statute of Westminster Adoption Act 1942 (Comm. of Aust.), bringing the Statute of Westminster 1931 (Imp.) into force in Australia as from 3rd September 1939. Of course, the real rule of recognition in Australia may be thought of as changing in 1942, 1939, 1931 or even earlier or even later.

the revolution, therefore, the validity of the old legislation comes to rest on a different rule of recognition from before.[34]

Hart is not here considering the problem of colonial independence. But how would his remarks apply to that problem? After Australian independence, *however attained*, the Australian courts will accept a rule specifically mentioning the old legislation '*eo nomine*'. True, and can we not go on to say that, if independence was attained by virtue (at least indirectly) of an Act of the Westminster Parliament the old legislation can still be identified 'by reference to the general provision qualifying the unbroken succession of legislators'? What is 'broken' about the succession from Westminster to Canberra Parliament, if that succession was regulated by a rule of succession of rules, in force at the time of the succession? Hart could reply, perhaps, that if the succession of legislators is not broken, nevertheless the succession of rules of succession of rules is broken because the rule of succession of rules in 1940 was 'Whatever rule of succession of rules the Westminster Parliament enacts is law', whereas after 1940 it is 'Whatever rule of succession of rules the Canberra Parliament enacts, with the approval of a referendum[35] is law'. But this reply would not suffice, since there seems no reason to call this change from one rule of succession of rules to another 'a break', except the assertion that rules of succession of rules cannot be regarded as reflexive. This assertion would indeed save Hart's opinion, in the *Concept of Law*, that the rule of recognition in a newly independent territory is not affected, in nature, content or jurisprudentially recognizable *raison d'être*, by its mode of creation.[36] But of course it would not cohere with his insistence, as against Ross, that the ultimate rules of succession of rules in a system can indeed be reflexive. For what would be the point of insisting on the reflexive capacity of a rule of succession of rules (rule *A*) if one at the same time insisted that the legal validity of any successor (rule *B*) to rule *A* would be legally unquestionable *whether or not* rule *B* had been created in accordance with the reflexive provisions of rule *A*? Yet Hart does

---

[34] Loc. cit. above, p. 49, n. 12.

[35] cf. Constitution of the Commonwealth of Australia 1900, s. 128. Note, incidentally, that this Constitution was promulgated as a Schedule to an Imperial Act, 63 and 64 Vict. c. 12.   [36] Above, p. 56, n. 32.

insist that no question can be raised about the legal basis of the rule of recognition, that here 'we are brought to a stop in inquiries concerning validity'.[37] And this provokes our second line of questions.

(ii) Is not the outlawing of further questions always an occasion of suspicion in theoretical study? And in this context, is it not particularly dubious? Hart's 'rule of recognition' is a complex of disparate elements. One of these elements is a power-conferring rule (i.e. rule of competence) qualifying, here and now, a rule-making body to create rules.[38] But we have seen that there is another element, viz. a rule of identification, which is not a rule of competence since it confers no powers on any existing body, but which identifies, and validates, *eo nomine* and for the present, the rules created in the past by a rule-making body that then was, but now perhaps is not, qualified (by a rule of competence) to create those rules. And this present rule of identification does not itself rest on, nor is it identified by reference to, any existing rule of competence. Hart wishes to say that, as with the existing basic rules of competence, its existence is a matter of fact, viz. the fact of 'the rule of recognition', which is to be counted as one rule because, notwithstanding their multiplicity, the rules of competence and identification within it are 'unified by their hierarchical arrangement'.[39] But, to repeat, this hierarchical arrangement is one of 'relative subordination' *not* of derivation.[40] This is to say, the rule of identification supporting the pre-revolutionary or pre-independence law is not itself supported

---

[37] Above, p. 55, n. 30. Cf. also Kelsen: 'This final norm's validity cannot be derived from a higher norm, the reason for its validity *cannot be questioned*', *Pure Theory*, p. 195 (emphasis added).

[38] There are problems about this. Hart says that 'rules of the second type confer powers' (*Concept of Law*, p. 79), and the rule of recognition is of this second type. Moreover, a standard formulation of the rule of recognition is 'What the Queen in Parliament enacts is law' (ibid., pp. 104, 108, 112, 117); in this formulation the ambulatory present tense of 'enacts' suggests that the rule includes (a) a 'rule of change' qualifying the acts (including speech acts) of certain persons at time T_1 as authentic 'acts in the law' (i.e. valid *acts* of legislation), as well as (b) a rule of identification enabling the products of those acts of legislation to be recognized as valid *rules* at all times subsequent to T_1. On the other hand, Raz is confident that 'this [sc., that the rule of recognition is a power-conferring rule] is not Hart's intention, as he himself confirmed to me', but is rather a duty-imposing rule (*Concept of a Legal System*, p. 199). In short, the rule of identification also imposes a duty on officials to apply the rules it identifies.

[39] Hart (1965) 78 Harv. L.R. 1293.   [40] Hart, *Concept of Law*, p. 98.

by or derived from the rules of competence (although it is subordinate to them in so far as the present rule-making body is authorized to repeal the pre-existing law). It exists by virtue of the fact of 'official acceptance'.

Now if there is, in a system, a rule that does not depend for its existence on present rules of competence, one can raise the question whether perhaps there are other rules similarly independent, existing simply by virtue of the fact of their official acceptance. And one can raise the more radical question whether *any* rule need be regarded as dependent on present rules of competence. Perhaps all rules exist simply by virtue of the fact of their official acceptance?

It might be replied that the function of Hart's rule of recognition is to explicate the word 'official' in the phrase 'official acceptance'. But this reply would overlook the fact that, on Hart's own account, the rule of recognition may contain at least one element which is not a rule of competence indicating who is 'official': for it may contain a rule of identification indicating as valid all those existing rules that cannot be regarded as supported by existing rules of competence. And the radical question can be pressed by another route. If there is a set of rules which depend, not on any 'existing' rule of competence, but on a rule of identification incorporating 'past' rules of competence, why should this set be privileged and peculiar? Why should we not say of all the other rules of the system that, once created according to the then existing rules of competence, they no longer depend for their validity on those rules *qua* 'present' rules of competence, but rather depend on a 'present' rule of identification incorporating those rules of competence *qua* 'past' (i.e. *qua* 'present' at the relevant times, 'past', of their creation)? The drift of these questions is obvious: May it not be the case that revolutions of all sorts, disturbing only rules of competence, need not be regarded as disturbing any other rules of the system, since all these other rules can be regarded as based on rules of identification which the revolution may leave quite unaffected?

The questions just raised call for exploration even if one accepts, as I do not, that it is obvious that no questions can be raised about the legal basis of the rule of recognition in so far as it is a present rule of competence.

To recapitulate; we set about our examination of the theory of discontinuity by asking about the sufficient and necesssary conditions for a change in the identity of a legal system. Analysis of the *coup d'état* showed that, if any revolution accomplishes, *eo ipso*, a change in the identity of a legal system, a *coup d'état* must do likewise. But the second question, whether there are methods of changing the identity of a legal system otherwise than by revolution, proved more resistant to analysis. Standard discussions of the problem differ widely. At the root of the differences lies a disturbing obscurity about the very object of legal theory, the legal system. Kelsen considered that 'past' constitutions, if they have been replaced in accordance with their own reflexive provisions, are in some way a present part of the legal system which, as a whole, is validated by the present basic norm. Ross considered that past constitutions are wholly irrelevant to the present legal system since they cannot provide reflexively for their own replacement, and must therefore have been suppressed by the magic of a perhaps peaceful revolution, i.e. by evolution as opposed to lawful devolution. Hart saw no difficulty in reflexive provisions for constitutional replacement, but refused to grant that 'past' rules of recognition have any systematic relationship to the existence of 'present' rules of recognition. But this amputation of the past of the rule of recognition opened the way for embarrassing problems about the relevance of the present rule of recognition (*qua* rule of competence) to the admitted present existence of rules which, after all, were created in the past.

In short, Hart and Ross freed the 'present' legal system from the incubus of a mass of superseded constitutional rules, but at the price of suppressing relevant questions about the relevance of the upper levels of their hierarchical models of 'legal system'. Kelsen tackled these questions, and answered them in a lawyerlike fashion by accepting lawful devolution of ultimate constitutional rules. But this left Kelsen incapable of explaining how a legal system might divide into two independent systems by process of law. And, much more serious, Kelsen's analysis employed a concept of 'validity' (i.e. 'existence') incapable of distinguishing between the existence of a 'present' rule of competence and the existence of a 'past' rule of competence, lawfully superseded, but still somehow 'valid' and present as a source of the validity of the 'present' rules.

The question of the necessary conditions of change of identity of a legal system cannot, therefore, be answered until an attempt has been made to clear the analytical logjam that has developed.

III. WHEN DOES A RULE CEASE TO EXIST?

It will first be useful, in resolving the analytical confusion, to attain some caution and self-consciousness in using, for theoretical purposes, the practically serviceable lawyer's terms, 'valid', 'in force', and 'existence'. Very often, theorists use such terms as these as if they were univocal, clear in meaning, and self-explanatory. But in the law, their meaning is often a matter for debate and decision—and the decisions will vary according to context and purpose.

Consider the notion of repeal. Joseph Raz, with the confidence of the analytical jurist, offers three propositions about repeal and the existence of repealed and repealing laws:

P_1 'It is doubtful whether there is much point in regarding a repealing law ... as existing after the laws it repealed ceased to exist.'[41]

P_2 'There are good grounds to argue that ... norms are repealed not by repealing-norms but by repealing-acts.'[42]

P_3 'No termination of a norm legalizes offences committed while the norm was in force: offences committed while the norm existed can, of course, be punished later.'[43]

Now it happens that in England, prior to 1850, the common law notion of repeal included the rule that the repeal of a repealing Act revived the Act originally repealed. There is nothing conceptually odd about this notion of repeal; its practical inconveniences led to its supersession (see now Interpretation Act 1889 s. 11 (1) and s. 38 (2) (a)), but it is obvious that, where such a notion prevails (as it did for centuries in England and still does, perhaps, in other legal systems) propositions P_1 and P_2 would not be as intuitively persuasive as here and now they are. Proposition P_3 represents English law, subject to the important proviso that s. 38 (2) (c) of the Interpretation Act 1889, while adopting (in effect) proposition P_3, does so only

---

[41] Raz, *Concept of a Legal System*, p. 58.   [42] Ibid., p. 64, n. 2.
[43] Ibid., p. 64. I have inverted the order of sentences here.

'unless the contrary intention appears'. Since a 'contrary intention' does sometimes appear, and since s. 38 (2) (c) in any case replaces a common law rule of precisely opposite effect [44] the 'of course' in Raz's formulation P_3 must be rejected as suggesting an unwarranted claim to analytical necessity: indeed, the universality of proposition P_3 ('No termination...') is unfounded.

As with 'repeal', so with 'existence' and 'force'. Both the theorist (Raz) and the English rule (Interpretation Act 1889, s. 38 (2) (a)) speak of repealed rules being 'not in force or existing'. But, as we have just seen, the effect of repealing a rule need not be to obliterate it completely as if it had never been passed and had never existed. English law since 1889 agrees with P_3: persons for instance who aided escaping felons before 1 January 1968 can, and perhaps will, be punished years after the rules about misprision of felony and accessories after the fact were repealed from that date.[45] From the point of view of such persons, and of their legal advisers, the police, and the courts who must judge them, it is in many senses just not true that the repealed rules do not exist and are not in force. They do exist and they are in force! They are present guides to decision.

With this in mind, let us examine a related passage in Raz, where he takes up the more general issues discussed in the preceding section of this essay:

> By representing [laws conferring legislative powers] as conditions for sanctions enacted on their basis, Kelsen assumes that their effect is merely to establish the validity of laws already in existence. He overlooks the fact that they confer legislative powers which have not yet been exhausted, that new laws can yet be created on their basis. But this forward-looking aspect of these laws is their *real legal meaning*: by repealing a law conferring legislative powers the laws which have already been created on its basis are unaffected; the only change is that it [sc. the power-conferring law] cannot be used for creating new laws.[46]

Now, the notion of repeal used in the last sentence is only one

---

[44] On 'contrary intention' here see e.g. *Hosie* v. *Kildare C.C.* [1928] Ir.R. 47. For the old common law rule contradicting P_3, see *R.* v. *Swan* (1849) 4 Cox C.C. 108; *Bennett* v. *Tatton* (1918) 88 L.J.K.B. 313.

[45] Cf. *R.* v. *Fisher* [1969] 2 Q.B. 114.

[46] Raz, *Concept of a Legal System*, p. 117 (emphasis added).

among several legal meanings of the term 'repeal'[47]: if we find it the most attractive meaning, we ought to ask ourselves whether this is not precisely because it would be (usually) pointless and inconvenient if repeal were to entail consequences with respect to things already done and laws already enacted on the basis of the law repealed. And when thinking in terms of 'point' and 'pointless', we are thinking of what Raz calls the 'real legal meaning' of the laws in question (though he is speaking, not of repealing laws, but of power-conferring laws).

In any event, what Raz has said seems acceptable (if too rigidly expressed). Its consequences should now be explored. He has not argued from a denial of the Kelsenian premiss that power-conferring laws 'establish the validity' of laws created in the exercise of those powers. But he denies that the validity of the laws so created must, at every moment, rest on the continuing 'existence' of the appropriate power-conferring law. On what, then, does the validity of a law rest once its authorizing law has been repealed? Does it rest on the repealing law? Raz thinks not; indeed, there seems something extravagant in supposing that a repealing law is the basis of the validity of all laws created by virtue of the power-conferring law it repeals. And the supposition is not necessary. For it seems reasonable to suppose (and here we go beyond Raz) that there is a general principle of the practical and theoretical understanding of law which can be formulated as follows: A law once validly brought into being, in accordance with criteria of validity *then in force*, remains valid until *either* it expires according to its own terms or terms implied at its creation, *or* it is repealed in accordance with conditions of repeal in force *at the time of its repeal*.[48]

If this general principle is accepted, it is easy to see that the

---

[47] Indeed the English doctrine is that repeal of an enactment empowering rule-making *abrogates* rules already made thereunder, unless the repealing law expressly saves them (*Watson* v. *Winch* [1916] 1 K.B. 688). This case shows the doctrine to be a mere relic of the common law principle (not without exceptions in favour of completed transactions and vested rights) of obliterating repeal, itself largely abrogated by the Interpretation Act 1889 s. 38 (2). Saving clauses are common, and some legislatures (e.g. Ontario) have now adopted the policy of the Act of 1889, introducing the rule Raz takes for granted.

[48] Cf. Ross's newly invented 'basic norm' designed to resolve the puzzle of constitutional amendments without resort to 'magical acts'—'Obey the authority instituted by [the ultimate rule of amendment] until this authority itself points out a successor: then obey this authority, until it itself points out a successor, and so on indefinitely' (78 *Mind* at p. 24). The 'general principle' above generalizes Ross's 'legally unchangeable' basic norm.

repeal of the power-conferring law (rule of competence) by virtue of which a given rule was created *need* have no effect on the rule so created: the continuing and present validity of the rule, after its creation, rests on the general principle—and while the general principle refers to the power-conferring law as existing, this reference is to the existence of the power-conferring law *at the time* (past) of the creation of the rule in question. The general principle, by thus referring to the power-conferring law, makes it ever-presently relevant to the continuing existence of the rules once created on the basis of the power-conferring rule: in this sense, the power-conferring law can be said to be 'existing' and 'in force' even if it is no longer 'existing' or 'in force' in its 'forward-looking aspect', its 'real legal meaning' as a law conferring power to create *new* rules. It will be seen, too, that the 'rule of identification' which we identified earlier in this essay as a post-independence component of the 'rule of recognition', is only an instance of the general principle at present under discussion. And it is clear that if the general principle is recognized as the basis of the validity of present rules, one can accede to the lawyerlike demand for a root of title without imperilling the independence and autochthony of a new state or the stability of an *octroi* constitution: there can be no legally plausible appeal to this root of title *against* the present rules of succession of rules. Finally the effects of successful revolutionary assaults on certain rules of the legal system, even on the most basic power-conferring law, need not be regarded as entailing any effect on the rest of the system: for even the rules now valid 'by reason of' power-conferring laws which the revolutionaries have successfully eliminated are valid really 'by reason of' the general principle, which identifies and supports them by a reference to those power-conferring laws as being in force at the time of the creation of the rules; and this reference back need not be the object of revolutionary attack. A revolution, unless it deliberately seeks the total subversion of the order of society, does not challenge, even temporarily, the general principle. All that a revolution normally seeks to do is to modify the application of the general principle in one special respect, viz. in so far as this general principle is the present basis of *the rules of succession of rules*: the revolutionaries postulate new conditions of repeal, and on the basis of this postulate, they repeal (or modify) first the pre-existing rules of repeal and then (in accordance with the new rules of repeal) such other rules (if any) as they may wish to.

But why should we accept this general principle? Why does it 'seem reasonable to suppose' it? One might defend it simply as a purely 'analytical' explication of 'the ordinary man's point of view' or of a 'general consensus of lay and professional opinion'.[49] Certainly, it makes sense of the history and practice of legal systems and lawyers. But it seems to me that to rely on this defence of the principle would be evasive and incomplete. If we are prepared to discuss the *point* of power-conferring rules, or of repeals, in general and in particular forms, we ought to be prepared to say that the general principle presupposes, expresses, and realizes (or secures) the most general and basic *function* of 'the law'—namely, to relate the past to the present, by providing a present guide to actions which take place and have effect in the future (when this present will be in the past). Always what is wanted of 'the law' is a present guide, and always the action and decisions so guided will be in the future; but what is wanted is a guided response to a situation which *has been* brought about, often by men who were then relying on 'the law' to guide them; to shut one's eyes to their reliance would be a paradigmatic form of unfairness as well as a sowing of the whirlwind. This tension of 'the law' between past, present, and future is expressed in the very formulation of the general principle we have been discussing.

But the relation of 'the law' (the legal system) of 'now' with 'the law' of 'then' or 'then' presents further problems. In the present section I have been discussing the legal meanings of terms such as 'the law in force', in relation between one meaning and another, and the justification and point of adopting such meanings for practical and thence for descriptive and analytical purposes. But the problems of the existence of 'the law', the legal system, are not exhausted by an explanation of the senses in which particular laws do and do not, *as a matter of law*, exist.

IV. IS 'THE LEGAL SYSTEM' A SET OF RULES?

In modern jurisprudence, the legal system is commonly

---

[49] Cf. Raz, *Concept of a Legal System*, p. 200, n. 2; also p. 201 ('an explication of common-sense and professional opinion'); p. 103.

assumed to be a set of rules or principles. But it is further assumed that this set of rules has a duration, i.e. an identity through time. On this basis, finally, it is assumed that revolution, at least, can *put an end* to one legal system and *initiate* another.

Sometimes, indeed, it is asserted, as by Hart, that a legal system 'like a human being, may at one stage be unborn, at a second not yet wholly independent of its mother, then enjoy a healthy independent existence, later decay and finally die.'[50] Now such an appeal to organic analogy could never be made by Kelsen, though Hart (like Kelsen) offers to analyse the legal system as a set of rules ('union of primary and secondary rules'). But Hart's remark may focus the question which underlay the analytical 'to and fro' of the preceding sections: How can *a set of rules* be regarded as coming into being, lasting, and passing away?

No lawyer will deny that every rule in a legal system is equally valid. There are no grades of validity. No doubt the legal rule that contracts are not valid without consideration is more interesting and fecund than the legal rule that cars may not be parked outside the Oxford Town Hall on Fridays; but the latter is not less valid than the former. This being so it cannot be denied that 'English law' is *changing every moment* by the addition and subtraction of rules which, however trivial, particular and concrete, are just as valid—i.e. just as much members of the set—as the most long-standing and hallowed general rule. Thus, not only every time a local authority makes a by-law, but also every time a judge grants probate of a will, every time a contract is made, every time a judgment is entered, new rules are created, and one set of rules called 'English law' is replaced by a new set with different components.

Thus there is no escaping the conclusion that the set of rules called English law and loosely spoken of as subsisting with the same identity in 1970 as in 1900 is really a *sequence of sets*.[51] Thus our question about the duration of a set of rules resolves into the question: What is it about a sequence of sets of rules that entitles us to interpret it as an existing or subsisting system of rules with a lasting identity or duration?

Modern jurisprudence will incline us to reply to this

---

[50] Hart, *Concept of Law*, p. 109.
[51] See also Raz, *Concept of a Legal System*, pp. 35, 170.

question (which, however, is not usually raised in its present form) by asserting that what gives the sequence of sets continuity is the lasting constitution, or basic norm, or rule of recognition.[52] But can this form of reply bear critical scrutiny?

Bare reference to 'the constitution' will evidently not suffice. For 'the constitution', too, is a set of rules which range from the general and abstract to the concrete and particular. Every time one of these rules changes, we are obliged (since all rules are equally valid) to say that there is a new set of rules. Thus 'the constitution', like 'the legal system' as a whole, is a sequence of sets of rules, and the basis of the continuity of the sequence is what is in question.

To refer to 'the basic norm' will not suffice, **either.** Kelsen's basic norm is an overtly fictitious construction designed to suppress theoretical questions rather than to answer them. In reality, one can know the rules which the basic norm is said to validate, only when one already has answered all the questions which matter in jurisprudence, viz. all questions about the existence and *raison d'être* of those rules. Moreover, as we have already noticed, the basic norm is as much the basis of the validity of 'the historically first constitution' as of the 'present' constitution; there thus arise the embarrassing questions raised in section II of this essay and never answered by Kelsen, about whether a lawfully 'superseded' 'historically first constitution' is or is not still 'valid'.[53] Finally, it must be further noticed that the basic norm can give an appearance of unity to a sequence of sets of rules only because, in itself, it refers to an apparently unitary set, viz. 'the historically first constitution'. But one is entitled to assume that there is a single, identifiable 'historically first constitution' only if one already assumes the theory of discontinuity—i.e. if one assumes that a revolution necessarily makes a *tabula rasa* of the law of the constitution. For, unless this is one's assumption, it is clear that 'the historically first constitution' is, like the rest of the legal system, a 'set of rules', rules which originate at different moments of

[52] Cf. Hart, *Concept of Law*, p. 113.

[53] Note that for Kelsen, the 'temporal sphere of validity' of a norm is an element of its *content* and does not represent or account for the existence and duration of the norm-with-that-content: see *Pure Theory*, p. 13. Kelsen's wide-ranging attempt to replace the concept of *existence* with that of *validity*, throughout his legal theory, leads to many well-known problems.

time and which therefore constitute, in reality, a sequence of sets—the basis of whose continuity is what is in question.

To refer to 'the rule of recognition' will not solve the problem. In the first place, 'the rule', even considered synchronically as Hart usually considers it, is really a set of rules, some of them power-conferring and others mainly identificatory, some superior, and some subordinate. Even synchronically, these rules seem to have rather little in common with one another, other than that they are not derived from one another and that legal questions indeed 'cannot' be raised about this derivation. Even synchronically, then, the basis of the unity of the set is problematical. Diachronically, the problems are much greater. Hart has discussed the ways in which, standardly, a court has power, or assumes the power, to determine authoritatively and finally disputed questions about the content of the 'rule of recognition' (including questions about the powers of the courts, not excluding the power just mentioned).[54] Thus, from time to time, rules (whether general or particular) are added to and subtracted from 'the rule', and so the problem once more appears of the basis of the unity of the sequence of sets thus produced.

Is there *any* component of 'the rule of recognition' which is privileged in the sense that it lasts unchanged and thus unifies the sequence of sets of criteria of validity, and such that when it changes one is obliged to recognize that a new rule of recognition (and thus a new legal system) has come into being? It seems not. The only plausible candidate seems to be that offered by Alf Ross: the rule authorizing the amendment of the constitution, i.e. the ultimate rule of succession of rules.[55] The candidacy of this rule is dependent on Ross's very dubious assumption that this rule cannot be reflexive or self-referring and thus is immune from legal change.[56] Moreover, the proposal to base the unity of the legal system on a rule from which perhaps no other rules in the system are derived, and which is often (as in the U.K.) of the most ambiguous and disputable character (at least to the extent that virtually every concrete use of it must count as the determination or concretization of a new particular rule and thus as the creation of a new set in a

[54] Hart, *Concept of Law*, pp. 147–50.   [55] Ross, *On Law and Justice*, p. 80.
[56] Above, p. 54, notes 22–26.

sequence of sets . . .)—this proposal is so bizarre that one may suspect that its origins are ideological rather than purely theoretical.

This suspicion may, however, need qualification. For the theoretical implication of the arguments we have pursued in this section is certainly radical, and there need be no surprise at finding rather desperate measures adopted, on occasion, to avoid it. The implication is this: *the legal system, considered simply as a set of 'valid rules', does not exist,* since, considered simply as a set of rules, of interdependent normative meanings, there is *nothing* to give it continuity, duration, identity through time. As Eric Voegelin has pointed out, the existence in continuity of a legal system can no more be explained by reference simply to sequences of sets of valid rules than can motion, as Zeno discovered, be explained by reference to sequences of points.[57]

Still, if it is a basic phenomenon of legal experience that all valid rules are equally valid (and that was the starting-point in this analysis), it also is a basic phenomenon of such experience that legal systems do indeed exist and last. And if their existence cannot be grounded on any 'basic' rule or set of rules, there seems only one conclusion: the continuity and identity of a legal system is a function of the continuity and identity of the society in whose ordered existence in time the legal system participates. Hart has said that it is a defect of the pre-legal social rules that they had no common identity save that of the group of human beings which accepts them.[58] He offers the 'rule of recognition' as a remedy for this 'defect', but when the identity through time of this rule, *qua* rule, is critically analysed it becomes clear, as we have seen, that recognition of a 'rule of recognition' presupposes recognition of a continuing society whose lasting order can be interpreted as including that 'rule', as a matter of fact. This no doubt is why Hart and Ross embed their ultimate 'rules' in a matrix which provides those 'rules' with the substance and duration that the 'rules' alone fail to provide for 'the legal system' as a whole. For Ross, the lasting substance underpinning the legal system is 'a dominant

[57] Eric Voegelin, *The Nature of the Law*, an unpublished paper (available at the Institut für Politische Wissenschaft, University of Munich) to which I am much indebted in this section of the essay.

[58] Hart, *Concept of Law*, p. 90.

ideology'[59]; for Hart it is a 'shared official viewpoint' accompanying a 'complex congruent practice' amounting to 'acceptance' from an 'internal viewpoint' of common standards of action.[60]

Legal, like pre-legal, social rules have no common identity or basis of existence in time save that of the group of human beings which accepts them. In times of crisis, the lawyer is obliged to admit that his judgments rest on a critical assessment of the identity of an object which normally he regards as 'artificial and anomalous' and legally barely intelligible—viz. the great 'unincorporated society' in which he lives.[61] As soon as the Rhodesian judges had decided that Rhodesia was, as a matter of 'fact', a distinct society with its own accepted power structure and intelligible commonweal, not merely a fragment of imperial power and commonweal, their decision (if not their reasoning) became almost inevitable.[62] The reason for this inevitability was expressed, as we saw, by lawyers of Edward IV: 'it is necessary that the realm should have a king under whose authority laws should be held and upheld.'[63]

It is indeed possible to speak of a legal system growing, flourishing and withering away—but only if one considers it as something importantly more than a set of rules, however profoundly analysed.

V. REFLECTIONS ON METHOD IN JURISPRUDENCE

By a route similar but not identical to that followed in this essay, Joseph Raz has reached like conclusions. He has dis-

---

[59] Ross, *On Law and Justice*, p. 83.

[60] Hart, *Concept of Law*, p. 114.

[61] Cf. *Leahy* v. *A.-G. for New South Wales* [1959] A.C. 457, 477, per Viscount Simonds: '... the artificial and anomalous conception of an unincorporated society which, though it is not a separate entity in law, is yet for many purposes regarded as a continuing entity and, however inaccurately, as something other than an aggregate of its members.'

[62] I have discussed these cases at greater length in [1967] A.S.C.L. 89–95; [1968] A.S.C.L. 108–13; [1969] A.S.C.L. 71–78. Discussion of other Commonwealth judicial decisions in which appeal was made to the theory of discontinuity will be found in [1967] A.S.C.L. 82–84 (Uganda); [1968] A.S.C.L. 73–75 (Pakistan). See also *Sallah* v. *A.-G. for Ghana* (unreported: Judgement no. Const. S.C.8/70; comments by T. and F. Tsikata (1970) U. Ghana L.J. 192), in which two of the judges were unwilling to accept the theory of discontinuity, one considered it irrelevant to the issue, and one accepted it, and see Elias in (1971) 5 Nigerian L.J. 129.

[63] Above, p. 46, n. 7.

tinguished between momentary and non-momentary legal systems, and has remarked that the crux of the problem of the continuity of non-momentary legal systems is the question of continuity, viz. the problem of deciding whether two given momentary systems belong to the same legal system.[64] Like me he holds that

> ... neither the 'constitutional continuity' of the new laws nor their content are necessary or sufficient conditions for establishing the continuity or lack of continuity of legal systems. Legal systems are always legal systems of complex forms of social life, such as religions, states, regions, tribes, etc. ... The identity of legal systems depends on the identity of the social forms to which they belong. The criterion of identity of legal systems is therefore determined not only by jurisprudential or legal considerations, but by other considerations as well, considerations belonging to other social sciences.[65]

He adds that, since he does not wish to 'trespass on other fields', he will confine himself to the problem of the identity of momentary systems, but he stresses that it should *not* be assumed that momentary systems can be analysed independently of the (non-momentary) legal systems to which they belong—for the identity of a momentary system can be determined only by reference to other momentary systems *of the same legal system*[66] (in our terminology, by reference to rules of competence and rules of succession of rules in force at some earlier time).

But if the analysis even of momentary systems depends on an understanding of non-momentary systems, and if this understanding is not to be had without reference to 'other social sciences' than law and jurisprudence, it seems worth while to ask what these other 'social sciences' may be.

The original master of the philosophy of human affairs, Aristotle, has carried out an analysis of our problem from the other end—starting not with the identity of the legal system or constitution but with the identity of the society which has the system. Embarrassingly enough, he reached the opposite conclusion: that the identity of the *polis* changed every time the constitution (*politeia*) was changed by revolution.[67] This

[64] Raz, *Concept of a Legal System*, p. 187.
[65] Ibid., pp. 188–9.   [66] Ibid., p. 189.
[67] Aristotle, *Politics*, III. 1: 1275 b34–1276 b15; a convenient translation and paraphrase is Ernest Barker, *The Politics of Aristotle* (1946), pp. 97–100.

conclusion was forced on Aristotle by his procedure in carrying over to the analysis of human society the theoretical apparatus ('matter' and 'form') which he had devised for the analysis of organisms, artifacts, and purposive actions.[68] Thus he considered the citizens of a *polis* to be its matter, and its constitution to be its form; and change of form entails change of identity. This plainly is unsatisfactory (though we cannot here unravel the reasons for the 'obvious technical derailment'),[69] and Aristotle recognizes this. For as soon as he has reached his conclusion that there is a new *polis* with every revolutionary change of *politeia*, he adds: 'Whether a *polis* is bound in justice to fulfil its engagements when it changes its *politeia* is another question.'[70] In this sentence, the *polis* is a subject that retains its identity through the changes of constitution and 'legal systems'—it is a subject that has a *history* which embraces, and is not ended by, revolutions; and it is a subject that has or may have *ethical* obligations unaffected by revolutions.[71]

'History' and 'ethics' (the latter subsuming much of political philosophy) are the 'social sciences' concerned with the identity of the societies and legal systems with which jurisprudence is concerned. It is not possible here to undertake any full discussion of the theoretical situation which unfolds when any jurisprudential analysis is pushed to its limits, and which can be indicated in the proposition: Analytical jurisprudence is intrinsically subalternated either to history or to ethics or to both, and cannot be an independent discipline, with a viewpoint of its own. A few summary remarks must here suffice.

On the problem for history—What is the relevant unit which has an identity and thus a history?—we can say very little. The nature of the problem with which Hegel grappled (not least in his *Philosophy of Right*), can be indicated by Eric Voegelin's remarks on the impasse into which Aristotle, as we have seen, was led in his analysis of the *polis*.

... the society in the whole extension of its historical course, with its cycle of constitutional sub-forms, was well established [for Plato and Aristotle] as a unit of inquiry. Moreover, since it was recognized

---

[68] See the outstanding analysis and commentary by Voegelin in his *Order and History*, vol. III, *Plato and Aristotle* (1957), pp. 325–6, 331–6.

[69] Voegelin, op. cit., p. 332.   [70] *Politics* III. 1: 1276 b14.

[71] Voegelin, op. cit., p. 326.

that the cycle of forms applied not only to one particular polis, e.g. Athens, but was typical within a range of variations for all Hellenic poleis, even the single polis was already superseded as the ontological unit and had given way to the Hellenic society, organized as a manifold of poleis, as the unit of empirical inquiry . . . the process was well under way in which the object of inquiry expands from the order of the concrete societies to civilizations which belong to the same type of order, and ultimately to the order of history of a mankind which is no finite unit of observation at all as it extends indefinitely into the future.[72]

The problem for ethics—What is the relevant society to which I owe allegiance and with whose collective debts I am concerned?—is more immediately germane to jurisprudence. For as Hart has shown, a 'view' of a 'legal system' as a 'social phenomenon'[73] is 'realistic'[74] only if it *reproduces* the way in which the rules function as rules'[75] in the lives of those members of society who voluntarily accept the rules as common standards of behaviour, who have an 'internal' attitude to the rules.

Now this 'internal attitude' calls for further analysis before it can be used with precision as a criterion of relevance in jurisprudence. On Hart's account, the man with an internal attitude to the law is willing to do what is legally required; he wishes to arrange his affairs predictably;[76] he could see no reason for allegiance to a set of laws that provided no restrictions on the free use of violence, theft, and fraud or that did not back its restrictions with sanctions.[77] Indeed, Hart does not allow that the internal viewpoint is consistent with every sort of motivation whatever; for example, to regard the law as a reason for acting simply out of one's short-term self-interest in avoiding sanctions is precisely *not* to have the internal attitude.[78] But despite all this, it seems that Hart would deny that the internal attitude must standardly be based on the communal or civil friendship (*philia politike*) that Plato, Aristotle, and Aquinas were inclined to identify as the standard motivation of law-making and law-maintenance in its central forms.[79] Hart

---

[72] Ibid., p. 334.   [73] Hart, *Concept of Law*, p. 197; cf. pp. vii, 205.
[74] Ibid., p. 197.   [75] Ibid., p. 88.   [76] Ibid., p. 39.
[77] Ibid., pp. 89, 189, 193.   [78] Ibid., pp. 88, 111–13, 197.
[79] See e.g. Plato, *Rep.* 462; *Statesman* 311; *Laws* 627–628, 693, 701, 743, 757; Aristotle, *Eth Nic* IX, 6: 1167 b3.4; IX, 1: 1155 a23: Aquinas, *Summa Theol.* 1a 2ae, 99, 2c.

does indeed list 'disinterested interest in others' as one of the possible motives for allegiance to the law; but he insists that 'mere wish to do as others do' or 'an unreflecting inherited or traditional attitude' or 'calculations of long-term self-interest' will suffice.[80]

Doubtless these motives do all suffice. But is there any reason not to apply to the philosophical concept of the 'internal viewpoint' those philosophical techniques applied by Hart in his philosophical analysis of 'law'—viz. the identification of a central or standard instance among other recognizable but secondary instances?[81] And in fact the listed types of reason for accepting law as a reason for action do not seem all equally appropriate as standards of relevance in philosophically determining the criteria of law as a specific type of reason for action. Both 'traditional attitudes' and 'desire to conform' seem derivative from, and thus secondary to, the attitudes of others (forebears and fellows) who have adopted the internal viewpoint for other reasons. Moreover, to accept law simply out of respect for tradition or, especially, out of long-term self-interest (in the narrow and colloquial sense of that term) would be to have no reason for obeying or applying it in a strictly legal fashion—for tradition and self-interest do not provide any sufficient reason for 'taking seriously'[82] the policy—so central to the 'internal viewpoint' and allegiance to law—of applying in different cases, and against competing pressures and attractions, 'the same general rule, without prejudice, interest, or caprice'.[83]

In short (though the matter cannot be fully argued here),[84] we are led to adopt the position Hart was concerned to reject when he advanced his list of possible sufficient motivations for allegiance to law: the position that law can only be fully understood as it is understood by those who accept it in the way that gives it its most specific mode of operation as a type of reason for acting, viz. those who accept it as a specific type of moral reason for acting. Once one abandons, with Hart,[85] the bad man's concerns as the criterion of relevance in legal philosophy,

---

[80] Ibid., pp. 198, 226.   [81] Cf. ibid., pp. 15, 79, 234.

[82] Cf. ibid., p. 156.   [83] Ibid., p. 157.

[84] I have argued it a little more fully in 'Reason, Authority and Friendship in Law and Morals', in Khanbai, Katz, and Pineau (eds.), *Jowett Papers 1968–1969* (1970), p. 101.

[85] Ibid., p. 39.

there proves to be little reason for stopping short of accepting the morally concerned man's concerns as that criterion. In this way we can bring together those disparate figures whose apparently varying standards of relevance haunt the works of analytical jurists—for example, Kelsen's 'jurist' who sometimes seems to be within and sometimes without society; or Raz's 'ordinary man' and his 'judge faced with the question "which law ought to be recognized?"'[86] Analytical jurisprudence rejoins the programme of philosophizing about human affairs, the programme whose conditions have been identified by Aristotle: 'We hold that in all such cases the thing really is what it appears to be to the mature man [the *spoudaios*].'[87] If Aristotle is asked for what purposes he draws a theoretical distinction or elaborates a theoretical concept, he will answer that he is seeking to show forth the concerns and self-understanding of the *spoudaios* and the categories relevant to the *spoudaia polis*.[88] There is no distinct 'theoretical purpose' of the 'scientific observer' which could be set over against the 'practical purposes' that the *spoudaios* has in drawing the boundaries of concepts by using them in his life in society. The concepts thus differentiated for analytical use are the relevant 'standard cases' (e.g. of repeal, of power-conferring rule, of law, of legal system); secondary or deviant cases are not banished to other disciplines, but are recognized and dealt with by this discipline as secondary (i.e. as being best understood in the light of the analysis of the primary, standard cases).

To say this is not to provide an answer to any concrete problem about the identity of any society or legal system. It is simply to say that the problem for the jurist is the same as the problem for the historian or for the good man wondering where his allegiance and his duty lie. From neither perspective is the thesis of discontinuity, as expressed by Kelsen, persuasive or acceptable. A revolution is neither a necessary nor a sufficient condition for anything that should be described as a change in the identity of the state or the legal system.

The historian will be inclined to say that rules exist because of a continuing willingness to recognize them as standards for action in the present. This willingness is more fundamental

---

[86] Raz, *Concept of a Legal System*, p. 200, n. 2.
[87] *Eth. Nic.* X, 5: 1176 a17.   [88] *Politics* VII, 2: 1332 a33.

than the act(s) of will which originally put forward the rule, in
its determinate form, for acceptance by officials and citizens as
a standard for action. And with respect to the vast bulk of rules
in a system, the historian finds that revolutions rarely affect
that continuing willingness.

This is not surprising. For it is (ethically) reasonable to shape
one's willingness to recognize posited rules as standards for
one's action by referring to compendious rules or principles
of identification, for the sake of maintaining coherence of
action-in-society through time. (For everybody's life has to
be lived as a project in time.) Hence it is usually reasonable to
accept the new rules of competence and of succession of rules
proposed by the successful revolutionaries who have made
themselves masters of society and thus responsible for meeting
the contingencies of the future. And by the same token it is
reasonable to adhere to the 'general principle' (put forward
towards the end of the preceding section) as providing a
reason, unaffected by the revolution, for the validity of the
remaining bulk of the legal system. In both cases this 'reasonableness' is the reasonableness of justice and *philia politike*, which
demand legal coherence and continuity and respect for acquired rights.

Of course, justice has other demands. So sometimes the
character of a revolution is such that allegiance to the revolutionary order of society is unreasonable. Citizen, judge, and jurist
should, in such cases, say that the legal system is no longer the
one they recognized previously (except in some secondary senses
of 'same legal system'). But it is only in such extreme cases that
the elements of discontinuity are more significant for analysis
(moral, legal, jurisprudential) than the principle of continuity.

IV

The Common Law and Legal Theory

A. W. B. SIMPSON

I. INTRODUCTION

In ENGLAND and in those parts of the world where the English legal tradition has been received the characteristic type of law is common law, as contrasted with statute law. Common law in this sense has of course been modified by equity, but then equity is just another form of common law. The common law has in its time been given a variety of classifying titles which reflect different views as to its distinguishing or characteristic feature—for example 'case law', 'judiciary law', 'judge-made law', 'customary law', and 'unwritten law'. Names such as these reflect theories as to the nature of the common law, and it would be easy enough to cull from legal writings the expression of very divergent views of the institution. It seems to me however that to date no very satisfactory analysis of the nature of the common law has been provided by legal theory; indeed the matter has received remarkably little sustained attention by theoretical writers. What has been the subject of much writing is the doctrine of precedent or *stare decisis*; indeed a search of the literature for discussions of the nature of the common law tends to locate only accounts of the working of this doctrine, which is itself I suppose 'part of' the common law. To a historian at least any identification between the common law system and the doctrine of precedent, any attempt to explain the nature of the common law in terms of *stare decisis*, is bound to seem unsatisfactory, for the elaboration of rules and principles governing the use of precedents and their status as authorities is relatively modern, and the idea that there could be binding precedents more recent still. The common law had been in existence for centuries before anybody was very excited about these matters, and yet it functioned as a system of law without such props as the concept of the *ratio decidendi*, and functioned well enough.

Nor does the common law appear to have wholly altered its character over the years, and a theory of the common law, if it is to seem satisfactory, must cater for this continuity. It must accommodate the common law of the seventeenth century as well as the common law of the twentieth, or at least provide a view of the common law which will serve to explain whatever changes have occurred in the general character of the institution. One such change is indeed the increased importance attached to authority, in particular quoted judicial opinions, in the working of the system.

In the sense used here a theory or general view of the common law represents an attempt to provide an answer to the question whether the common law can be said to exist at all—and this has been seriously doubted—and if so in what sense. Put rather differently, such a theory will seek to explain how, if at all, statements in the form 'It is the law that . . . ', such as 'It is the law that contracts require consideration', can meaningfully be made, when such statements are conceived to be statements of the common law. Such an explanation is essential to the understanding of the workings of the judicial process, which is conducted upon the assumption that the common law (we are not concerned with statute) always provides an answer to the matter in issue, and one which is independent of the will of the court. What may be called general theoretical propositions of the common law, which are the stuff of legal argument and justification, take a variety of forms. Sometimes they are said to state *doctrines* of the common law (the doctrine of offer and acceptance), sometimes *principles* or *general principles* (the principle of 'volenti non fit iniuria') sometimes *rules* (the rule in *Rylands* v. *Fletcher*), sometimes *definitions* (the definition of conversion), and this is by no means an exclusive list of a diversity which is recognized more generously in the language of lawyers than in the writings of legal philosophers. Some attempts have been made to differentiate these concepts; thus Bingham,[1] and more recently Dworkin,[2] have sought to distinguish *rules* from *principles*. For present purposes these distinctions are not important, and all legal propositions may be

---

[1] J. W. Bingham. 'What is the Law?' (1912), 11 Mich.L.R. 1 and 109 at p. 22.
[2] R. M. Dworkin. 'Is Law a System of Rules?' *Essays in Legal Philosophy* (1968), ed. Summers, p. 25 at p. 34 ff.

considered together, and merely distinguished from propositions which purport only to be *about* the common law. An example would be such a statement as 'The common law does not favour self-help.' Put forward in a different form, for example like this, 'It is a principle of the common law that self help is to be discouraged', this would in my scheme rank as a general theoretical proposition of the common law; it would then purport to state the law rather than pass an observation about the law. It is primarily with propositions of law that I am here concerned.

In passing it is however important to notice that in legal reasoning propositions which are neither propositions *of* law nor propositions *about* law feature prominently. For example, when Lord Devlin said in the course of his judgment in *Behrens v. Bertram Mills*,[3] 'If a person wakes up in the middle of the night and finds an escaping tiger on top of his bed and suffers a heart attack, it would be nothing to the point that the intentions of the tiger were quite amiable', he was not making a legal observation, but justifying a decision on the law governing liability for dangerous animals by an appeal to common-sense. No doubt these non-legal justificatory propositions could be further divided—some for example refer to moral considerations, others to expediency—and they are used to claim for a decision a rationality which is not based upon the artificial reason of the law; though not themselves legal propositions they may be used to support the contention that this or that is the law. In the common law system no very clear distinction exists between saying that a particular solution to a problem is in accordance with the law, and saying that it is the rational, or fair, or just solution.

If, however, we confine attention to specifically legal propositions, how are they to be explained? The type of answer given to this question will depend upon the particular theoretical viewpoint adopted, for there appear to me to be a number of different possible conceptions of the nature of the common law. The predominant conception today is that the common law consists of a system of rules; in terms of this legal propositions (if correct) state what is contained in these rules. I wish to consider the utility of this conception, and to contrast it

[3] [1957] 2 Q.B. 1 at p. 17.

with an alternative idea—the idea that the common law is best understood as a system of customary law, that is, as a body of traditional ideas received within a caste of experts.

II. POSITIVISM AND THE COMMON LAW AS A SYSTEM OF RULES

The idea that the common law is a set of rules, in some unusual sense forming a system, is intimately associated with the movement known as legal positivism. Though purporting to be an observation, it is best viewed as a dogma, which derives basically from viewing all law in terms of a model of statute law. In its purest form legal positivism involves two basic assumptions, which will be found, variously elaborated, or sometimes merely covertly adopted, in very many theoretical writings. The first is that all law is positive law, and what this means at its simplest is that all laws owe their status as such to the fact that they have been laid down. In the curious and archaic language of Austin, laws properly so called are laws *by position;*[4] they are set, or prescribed, and human law at least is laid down by humans to humans. Blackstone, though inconsistent in his positivism, thought that municipal law was prescribed by what he called the supreme power in the State,[5] whilst Gray thought that laws were rules of conduct laid down by the courts.[6] Both assumed that laws must have been laid down by somebody or other to rank as laws, and to this extent were positivists. When in a modern book on the doctrine of precedent Professor Cross[7] writes, 'Such a rule (one derived from a precedent or series of precedents) is law "properly so called" and law *because it was made by the judges,* [my italics] and not because it originated in common usage, or the judges' idea of justice and public convenience', he is expressing the first basic assumption of positivism. In an uneasily modified form the same assumption is writ large in Kelsen:[8] 'Law is always positive law, and its positivity lies in the fact that it is created and annulled by acts of human beings, thus being independent of morality and other norm systems.' The insistence that all

---

[4] J. Austin, *The Province of Jurisprudence Determined,* ed. Hart (1954), xliii.
[5] W. Blackstone, *Commentaries on the Laws of England* (1809 ed.), p. 44.
[6] J. C. Gray, *The Nature and Sources of the Law,* 2nd ed. (1948), p. 84.
[7] Rupert Cross, *Precedent in English Law,* 1st ed., p. 23.
[8] H. Kelsen, *General Theory of Law and the State* (1961), p. 114.

law is positive law originally stood in opposition to the claim that some laws, or all laws, owed their status as such to the fact that they were in accordance with or sanctioned by nature. Pure positivism thus involves the notion that there is only one possible alternative basis for law to that provided by natural law theories. The most obvious point at which difficulty is encountered in maintaining the thesis that all law is posited is when dealing with custom, which common sense would suggest is not laid down; customs, we know, grow up. Kelsen runs into difficulty over this; though admitting custom as a possible type of law (to be contrasted with statute law) he is at pains to insist that even the norms of customary law, in a system which admits custom as 'a law-creating act', are *positive*. To preserve the dogma the notion of laying down or prescribing law has to be emasculated until it means only that the norms of customary law are the products of acts of will, even though these acts of will are not directed to the making of law at all. 'Since custom is constituted by human acts, even norms created by custom are created by acts of human behaviour, and are therefore like the norms which are the subjective meaning of legislative acts—"posited" or "positive" norms.'[9] This is hardly convincing, but my point is only to illustrate the basic *credo*.

The second basic assumption is less easy to state with precision. It involves conceiving of law as a sort of code. The law, including the common law, is identified with a notional set of propositions which embody the corpus of rules, principles, commands, norms, maxims, or whatever, which have, at any given time, been laid down. For present purposes nothing turns upon distinctions between rules, principles, maxims, et cetera, so this second assumption can be put thus: the law exists as a set of rules, the rules being identical with and constituting the law. Combining these two assumptions of positivism the common law must be conceived of as existing as a set or code of rules which have been laid down by somebody or other, and which owe their status as law to the fact that they have been so laid down. We are to conceive of the common law, somewhat perversely, as if it had already been codified, when we all know it has not. And if communication by words is the manner

[9] H. Kelsen, *The Pure Theory of Law* (1967), p. 9.

in which the action of laying down the law takes place, then the words used will constitute the law. In terms of such a model the general theoretical propositions of the common law can be thought of as stating rules of the common law, if 'correct', or as putative statements which may or may not be correct.

Around these two basic assumptions cluster various ideas either derived from them or at least intimately associated with them. Thus if all laws are laid down, all laws must have an author, for someone must have performed the act of positing the law. Secondly, there must be some test or criterion for identifying the lawmaker or lawmakers who have authority to lay down the law, or entitlement to do so, for it would be absurd if anyone who cared to do so could lay down law; the primary ground for saying that this or that is the law will be the fact that the right person or group laid it down. Thirdly, if law is by definition laid down, all law must originate in legislation, or in some law-creating act. Fourthly, law so conceived will appear as the product of acts of will, and the law which results as the will of the lawmaker. Fifthly, if laws owe their status to their having been laid down by the right author, it cannot be a necessary characteristic of law that it should have a particular content, for its content will depend upon the will of the law-maker, who may be devil or angel or something in between— hence the separation of law and morals. And sixthly, if law consists of what has been laid down, then what has been laid down, conceived as a code, is exhaustive of the law at any given moment, so that where nothing has been laid down, there is no law; the law is conceived of as in principle a finite system. And unless one admits the possibility of the existence of a number of co-existing common laws, which seems absurd, there must at one moment be one unique set of rules constituting the common law.

This may be called the 'school-rules concept' of law, and it more or less assimilates all law to statute law. In recent times there have been advanced what may be called weaker versions of positivism, which have gone some way towards abandoning the first assumption whilst retaining the second: law continues to be conceived of as a set of rules, but their status as law does not necessarily depend upon their having been laid down. Examples are to be found in the legal theories of Kelsen (who, as we have seen, still maintains that all law is positive in a peculiar sense) and Hart.[10] Such theories[11] are committed to giving some explanation of how one is to tell whether a putative rule belongs to the club or not. The answer given is that membership depends upon the satisfaction of tests provided by some other higher or basic rule or rules, sometimes called power-conferring rules or rules of competence, in absent-minded conformity to the idea that all law originates in legislation. Those which qualify are characterized as valid—valid meaning 'binding' or 'existing as a rule of the system'—and the corpus of rules possessing the quality of validity, together with the basic rule or rules (grundnorm, constitution, rule of recognition) constitute the legal system. A legal system is conceived not as an institution, but as a code of rules, systematic only in the peculiar sense that the contents of the code satisfies the tests. Although it might seem consistent with such an approach to admit the possibility that some rules might qualify because of their content (the rule possessing some supposed quality, such as being in accordance with the will of God or the principle of utility) both Kelsen and, less clearly, Hart seem to have in mind criteria dealing with the mode of origin of the rule, or, as Dworkin has put it, with the 'pedigree'[12] of the rule, rather than content. All law is like statute law in that its authority is independent of its content.

As applied to the common law such weak versions of positivism could in principle no doubt cater for the possibility that it consists of rules which are not necessarily of legislative origin, nobody having ever laid them down. Kelsen does not really develop the application of his theory to the common law. In his *General Theory of Law and the State*[13] he conceives of law, in the form of general norms, as originating either in custom or legislation, statutory law and customary law being the two fundamental types of law. In so far as the common law derives from judicial precedents he apparently conceives of it as statutory; in so far as it is based upon the long practice of the courts it is customary law. Hart too does not devote more than a small

---

[10] H. L. A. Hart, *The Concept of Law* (1961).

[11] There are of course very considerable differences between Kelsen's theory and Hart's.

[12] Dworkin, op. cit., p. 28.   [13] See pp. 114 and 149–50.

part of *The Concept of Law* to the detailed application of his theory to the common law. But he envisages the possibility that in a complex legal system the criteria for the validity of rules may include reference to 'customary practice', 'general declarations of specified persons', and 'past judicial decisions' in addition to reference to an 'authoritative text' or 'legislative enactment';[14] such criteria no doubt are included to cater for the common law. Elsewhere he seems to regard the activities of courts as sometimes legislative in character; like Kelsen, Hart perhaps conceives of the common law as a medley of rules of different character. But in the absence of a rather more full treatment of the subject it is not at all easy to see quite how the common law fits into the scheme of things.

III. DEFECTS OF POSITIVISM

But both in its strong and weak forms positivism seems to me to present a defective scheme for understanding the nature of the common law. In its strong form, as presented by Austin, it claims that the common law consists of rules which owe their status as law to the fact that they have been laid down. Now the plausibility of claiming that the common law has been posited— presumably by the judges, there being no other obvious candidates for the honour—turns largely upon the offering of a choice between the devil and the deep blue sea. Austin presented his hearers with the alternative of either agreeing that the common law was laid down by the judges, or believing in the childish fiction (as he called it) that the common law was 'a miraculous something made by nobody, existing, I suppose, from eternity and merely declared from time to time by the judges'.[15] Confronted with this crude choice it is natural to prefer the former view. But difficulties arise if an attempt is made to apply Austin's view to a specific instance. Consider, for example, the rule that parole contracts require consideration (I choose this example because nobody would, I think, deny that this is a rule of the common law). Austin tells us 'there can be no law without a legislative act'[16] and the legislative act here must be a judicial decision, if one is to be found. Now it is well known that this rule has been on the common

---

[14] Hart, op. cit., p. 97.
[15] Austin, *Lectures*, 5th ed. (1855), ii, 655.   [16] Austin, *Lectures*, ii, 216.

law scene since the sixteenth century, and some hundreds of reported cases would seem to a historian to be relevant to the understanding of the history and evolution of the rule. There would be no difficulty whatever in citing *authority* for the existence of the rule—that is to say acceptable warrants for the contention that there is such a rule. One might for example cite *Eastwood* v. *Kenyon*,[17] decided some three centuries after the rule had, as we say, emerged, or perhaps *Rann* v. *Hughes*,[18] a little earlier, or perhaps a statement by a modern text-writer. No doubt the best possible authority would be a recent case in the Lords applying the rule. No such case in fact exists, but let us suppose there is a decision, reported in the Appeal Cases for 1970. It would seem to me to be absurd to identify such a case with an act of legislation, conferring the status of law on the rule. For we know that in some meaningful sense the rule has been law for centuries before this. The point is that the production of authority that this or that is the law is not the same as the identification of acts of legislation. Conversely what might plausibly rank as an act of judicial legislation will not necessarily rank as good authority. Suppose that one was able to find a case, decided say in 1540, where the assembled judges ruled that consideration was necessary in parole contracts, and there was every reason to suppose that this was the first case in which this ruling was given. Not only would it seem wrong to say that the rule derived its status as law today from this antique decision, but the decision would not even rank as particularly good authority for the rule. We may contrast the case of a rule which is of legislative origin—by way of example take that jurisprudential old chestnut, the rule that a will requires two witnesses. Here we can identify the act of legislation which conferred the status of law on the rule as the Wills Act of 1837, and this enactment (granted certain presuppositions) is the reason why today wills do require two witnesses for effective attestation. The statute is both the only reason and a conclusive reason for saying that this is the law. The notion that the common law consists of rules which are the product of a series of acts of legislation (mostly untraceable) by judges (most of whose names are forgotten) cannot be made to work, if taken seriously, because common law rules enjoy whatever status they

[17] (1840) 11 A. & E. 438.   [18] (1778) 7 T. R. 350, 4 Brown P. C. 27.

possess not because of the circumstances of their origin, but because of their continued reception. Of course it is true that judges are voluntary agents, and the way in which they decide cases and the views they express in their opinions are what they choose to express. Their actions create precedents, but creating a precedent is not the same thing as laying down the law. The opinions they express possess in varying and uncertain degree authority, as do opinions expressed by learned writers, but to express an authoritative opinion is not the same thing as to legislate. There exists no context in which a judicial statement to the effect that this or that is the law confers the status of law on the words uttered, and it is merely misleading to speak of judicial legislation.

Weaker versions of positivism escape the difficulty involved in the claim that all the rules of the common law are the product of judicial legislative acts. They share however with pure positivism the claim that the law—and this includes the common law—consists of a set of rules, a sort of code, which satisfies tests of validity prescribed by other rules. Such theories suffer from defects which have their source in the confusion of ideals with reality. Put simply, life might be much simpler if the common law consisted of a code of rules, identifiable by reference to source rules, but the reality of the matter is that it is all much more chaotic than that, and the only way to make the common law conform to the ideal would be to codify the system, which would then cease to be common law at all.

It is firstly central to such theories that there exist rules setting out the criteria which must be satisfied by other rules for them to belong to the system. These rules exist either in the sense that they are used and accepted by those concerned— roughly by the caste of lawyers—as the proper way of identifying other rules, or in the sense that they are the necessary presuppositions which make the identification of other rules possible. Either way it seems we must locate these supposed rules by considering the way in which legal propositions are justified, and legal argument conducted. Now it is quite true that in relatively recent times in the long history of the common law growing attention has been devoted, both by the judiciary and by legal commentators, to the formulation of rules governing the use of authorities in legal argument. Such rules constitute attempts to state the proper practice over such questions as what courts are bound by what decisions, how one is to distinguish authoritative statements of law from statements of no authority, what law reports should be used and what difference, if any, it makes if a writer is dead or alive. It is all a very theological world, with mysteries similar to those which surround the doctrine of papal infallibility. These rules governing the proper use of authority and the reverence due to it are notoriously controversial, and we all know both that the practice of the courts is not at all consistent in these matters, and that judicial views as to the proper thing to do both differ and change. One moment the House of Lords or the Court of Criminal Appeal is absolutely bound by its own decisions, the next moment it is not. All is reminiscent of the smile on the face of the Cheshire cat. Such rules as are advanced are commonly vague or qualified by escape clauses (the *per incuriam* doctrine, for example), and on very many matters no rules can be said to exist at all. For example, what is one supposed to do with a House of Lords decision where they all say different things? And what is the authoritarian pecking order between a decision of the American Supreme Court, dicta by the late Scrutton L.J., and an article by Pollock? There are no rules to deal with conundrums of this sort. Furthermore arguments to the effect that this or that is the law are commonly supported by reference to ideas which are not specifically legal—expediency, commonsense, morality, and so forth—as in the example of Lord Devlin and the errant tiger; they are supported by reference to reason and not authority. And nobody, I think, would claim that rationality in the common law can be reduced to rules. These familiar facts form the background to the notion of tests of validity, which involves a claim that legal reasoning and justification is governed by rules to an extent which it is not; legal life is far too untidy. Only if it were the case both that the use of authority in the law was wholly rule-governed, and all legal argument based upon authority, would such a theory correspond with reality.

A second objection to the notion of the common law as a system of rules turns upon the contrast between the essentially shadowy character of the common law and the crisp picture of a set of identifiable rules. Consider for example contexts in which a common lawyer might well talk of rules—the rule in *Rylands* v. *Fletcher*,[19] the rule in *Shelley's Case*,[20] or the rule in *Hadley* v. *Baxendale*.[21] These I take to be paradigm cases of rules of the common law, and to say that the common law consists of rules suggests a system of law in which such rules are the norm rather than the exception. Now one obvious characteristic of these rules is that their text is fairly well settled, though even in the cases where this is so the text is not utterly sacrosanct; the rule in *Rylands* v. *Fletcher* might for example be reformulated or more elegantly stated without the heavens falling; furthermore there may exist exceptions to these rules which are not included in a statement of the rule. But the general position in the common law is that it lacks an authoritative authentic text; as Pollock put it, the common law '... professes ... to develop and apply principles that have never been committed to any authentic form of words.'[22] It consequently distorts the nature of the system to conceive of the common law as a set of rules, an essentially precise and finite notion, as if one could in principle both state the rules of the common law and count them like so many sheep, or engrave them on tablets of stone.

IV. IS THE COMMON LAW A FICTION?

Indeed in an important sense it is in general the case that one cannot say what the common law is, if its existence is conceived of as consisting of a set of rules, and if saying what the law is means reporting what rules are to be found in the catalogue. The realization that this was so led Jeremy Bentham into the most powerful attack ever made upon the idea that the common law could be meaningfully said to exist at all, and it is no accident that this attack was made by a positivist. Although his view of the matter wavered, his extreme and characteristic opinion was that the existence of the common law was 'a fiction from beginning to end', and belief in its existence no more than 'a mischievous delusion'.[23] Of the expression 'common law' he wrote: 'In these two words you have a name pretended to

---

[19] 1866 L.R. 1 Ex. 265, L.R. 3 H.L. 330.
[20] (1581) 1 Co. Rep. 936.   [21] (1854) 9 Exch. 341.
[22] F. Pollock, *A First Book of Jurisprudence*, 3rd ed. (1911), p. 249.
[23] J. Bentham, *Collected Works*, IV, 483.

be the name of a really existent object:—look for any such existing object—look for it till doomsday, no such object will you find.'[24] The common law was 'mock law', 'sham law', 'quasi-law', and in consequence the exercise of the judicial function an example of 'power everywhere arbitrary'.[25] It is instructive to see what drove Bentham into this scepticism. What he perceived very clearly was the existence of an incompatibility between the 'school-rules concept' of law and the thesis that the common law could be regarded as existing in any real sense. His thesis is perhaps most clearly stated in the *Comment on the Commentaries*: '*As a system of general rules*, the common law is a thing merely imaginary'.[26] The italics are mine, the point being that Bentham's scepticism leaves open the possibility that in some other sense the predication of existence to the common law might be meaningful. Bentham's scepticism depends mainly upon the fact that rules can only be stated in a language—if somebody asks me to tell him one of the rules of chess I have to *say* something or *write* something in reply. But it is a feature of the common law system that there is no way of settling the correct text or formulation of the rules, so that it is inherently impossible to state so much as a single rule in what Pollock called 'any authentic form of words'. How can it be said that the common law exists as a system of general rules, when it is impossible to say what they are?

Bentham's point depends upon the familiar fact that if six pundits of the profession, however sound and distinguished, are asked to write down what they conceive to be the rule or rules governing the doctrine of *res ipsa loquitur*, the definition of murder or manslaughter, the principles governing frustration of contract or mistake as to the person, it is in the highest degree unlikely that they will fail to write down six different rules or sets of rules. And if by some happy chance they all write down (for example) 'killing with malice aforethought' an invitation to explain what *that* means will inevitably produce *tot jurisprudentes quot leges*. Again we all know that no two legal treatises state the law in the same terms, there being a law of torts according to Street, and Heuston, and Jolowich and James and the contributors to Clerk and Lindsell, and we buy them all

[24] Ibid., p. 483. [25] Ibid., p. 460.
[26] J. Bentham, *A Comment on the Commentaries*, ed. Everett (1928), p. 125.

because they are all different. And what is true of the academics is true perhaps even more dramatically of the judges, who are forever disagreeing, often at inordinate length. When, after long and expensive argument the Law Lords deliver themselves *ex cathedra* of their opinions—and this is the best we can do— they either confine themselves to laconic agreement or *all say different things, and this even when they claim to be in complete agreement.* It would hardly be worth their while to deliver separate opinions if this were not so. Nor does the common law system admit the possibility of a court, however elevated, reaching a final, authoritative statement of what the law is in a general abstract sense. It is as if the system placed particular value upon dissension, obscurity, and the tentative character of judicial utterances. As a system of legal thought the common law then is inherently vague; it is a feature of the system that uniquely authentic statements of the rules which, so positivists tell us, comprise the common law, cannot be made.

Such extreme scepticism as Bentham's seems to me to carry us too far, for at any given moment in time there appear to me to be many propositions of law which would secure general agreement amongst expert lawyers as being correct, and if there are wide differences in the way in which propositions of law are formulated there is at the same time a very considerable measure of agreement as to the practical application of the law in actual cases. If the common law is a fiction from beginning to end, and the exercise of judicial power everywhere arbitrary, it is difficult to see what explanation can be given of this. Now one way of explaining this cohesion of thought is to say that in spite of a certain degree of vagueness and uncertainty the source rules of the common law do not work at all badly. Hart, for example, says: 'The result of the English system of precedent has been to produce, by its use, a body of rules of which a vast number of both major and minor importance, are as determinate as any statutory rule. They can only be altered by statute.'[27] I doubt this explanation. If we look back into the history of the common law before there were doctrines of precedent and articles on the *ratio decidendi* of a case the same phenomenon—a cohesion of ideas—is to be found; indeed I suspect (though this is not capable of strict proof) that there

[27] Hart, op. cit., p. 132.

was a much greater degree of cohesion in say the fifteenth century than there is today. The explanation for this cannot be the use of tests of valid law. Furthermore it seems to me that the contemporary rules for the use of authority in the common law are as we have seen vague, uncertain, changing, and in any event incapable of settling the correct formulation of legal rules. Nor does it seem to me to be true, as positivists must have us believe, that once a rule satisfies the tests it can only be altered by legislation. The reality of the matter is that well settled propositions of law—propositions with which very few would disagree—do suffer rejection. The point about the common law is not that everything is always in the melting-pot, but that you never quite know what will go in next. Few in 1920 would have doubted that manufacturers of products were immune from the liability soon to be imposed upon them, or in 1950 that the House of Lords was bound by its own decisions. Who ever heard of family assets in 1900?

V THE COMMON LAW AS CUSTOMARY LAW

If however we abandon the positivist conception of the common law, in terms of what other conception can the institution be more realistically depicted and its peculiar characteristic explained? Positivists take as their basic model of law an enacted code, but a better starting-point, if we are concerned with the common law, is the traditional notion of the common law as custom, which was standard form in the older writers. Hale[28] for example divided the law of England into the *lex scripta* and the *lex non scripta*. The former comprised statutes 'which in their original formation are reduced into writing, and are so preserved in their original form, and in the same stile and words wherein they were first made'. In contrast the *lex non scripta* comprised 'not only general customs, or the common law properly so called, but even those particular laws and customs applicable to certain courts and persons'. Blackstone[29] too adopted much the same view:

The unwritten or common law is properly distinguishable into three kinds: 1. General Customs, which are the universal rule of the

---

[28] Sir Mathew Hale, *The History of the Common Law*, 2nd ed. (1716), p. 22.
[29] Sir William Blackstone, *Commentaries on the Laws of England*, pp. 66 ff.

whole kingdom, and form the common law, in its stricter and more usual signification. 2. Particular customs which for the most part affect only the inhabitants of particular districts. 3. Certain particular laws; which by custom are adopted and used by some particular courts, of pretty general and extensive jurisdiction.

This view of the common law has today fallen almost wholly out of favour, and the reason for this, or at least one predominant reason, is not far to seek. By a custom we commonly mean some practice, such as drinking the health of the Queen after dinner, which is regularly observed and has been regularly observed for some time in a group, and which is regarded within the group as the normal and proper practice. It is also integral to the idea of a custom that the past practice of conformity is conceived of as providing at least part of the reason why the practice is thought to be proper and the right thing to do. Clearly the common law as an institution is in part customary in this sense. If however one considers general theoretical propositions of the common law—for example the rule against perpetuities, or the doctrine of anticipatory breach, it is perfectly absurd to regard propositions stating such rules and doctrines as putative descriptions of the customary practices of Englishmen. It may be true that such parts of the common law reflect, or are based upon, or consistent with, ideas and values which either are or once were current in the upper ranks of English society, or in society generally, but this does not make them into customs.

Writers such as Hale and Blackstone were perfectly well aware of this point. Thus Blackstone[30] points out that there are some (I suspect he had in mind Sir John Fortescue and Christopher St. Germain)[31] who have

divided the common law into two principal grounds or foundations;
1. Established customs ;such as that, where there are brothers, the eldest brother shall be heir to the second, in exclusion of the youngest; and,
2. Established rules and maxims: as, 'that the king can do no wrong', 'that no man shall be bound to accuse himself,' and the like.

[30] Blackstone, p. 68.
[31] Christopher St. Germain, '*Doctor and Student*', Dialogue 1 c. 8, Fortescue, *de Laudibus Legum Anglie* (ed. Chrimes) (1942), p. 21.

Fortescue, for example, conceived of the law as being derived from principles (*principia*), these being certain universals called maxims, which are not demonstrable by reason; a similar Aristotelian doctrine is found in St. Germain, and both writers distinguish these maxims or principles from other grounds of law. Blackstone rejects this distinction as irrelevant to his theme, 'For I take these to be one and the same thing. For the authority of these maxims rests entirely upon general reception and usage; and the only method of proving, that this or that maxim is a rule of the common law, is by showing that it hath been always the custom to observe it.' Hale[32] makes a similar point:

> But I therefore stile those parts of the law, *leges non scriptae* because their authoritative and original institutions are not set down in writing in that manner, or with that authority that Acts of Parliament are; but they are grown into use, and have acquired their binding power and force of laws by a long and immemorial usage, and by the strength of custom and reception in the Kingdom.

Thus in characterizing the common law as custom these writers were primarily concerned to make a point about the contrast between the basis for the authority of statute law and common law. A proposition derived from statute counts as law because Parliament in the exercise of its law-making power has so prescribed—wills require two witnesses because Parliament so provided in 1837. Contracts on the other hand require consideration because as far back as anyone can remember this has been accepted as necessary. As Blackstone[33] puts it,

> ... in our law the goodness of a custom depends upon its having been used time out of mind, or, in the solemnity of our legal phrase, time whereof the memory of man runneth not to the contrary. This it is that gives it its weight and authority; and of this nature are the maxims and customs which compose the common law, or *lex non scripta*, of the kingdom.

Nobody today would, I think, wish to express himself in quite this way. In the first place for the reasons given custom seems an inappropriate term for abstract propositions of law; laws are not customs simply. We need rather to conceive of the common law as a system of customary law, and recognize that

---

[32] Hale, p. 23.   [33] Blackstone, p. 66.

such systems may embrace complex theoretical notions which both serve to explain and justify past practice in the settlement of disputes and the punishment of offences, and provide a guide to future conduct in these matters. In the second place we are rather more conscious of change in the law—we know for example that although the doctrine of consideration is old, it is not of immemorial antiquity, and that there are recently evolved doctrines too; some come and go, like the deserted wife's equity, and others survive. With these modifications however it seems to me that the common law system is properly located as a customary system of law in this sense, that it consists of a body of practices observed and ideas received by a caste of lawyers, these ideas being used by them as providing guidance in what is conceived to be the rational determination of disputes litigated before them, or by them on behalf of clients, and in other contexts. These ideas and practices exist only in the sense that they are accepted and acted upon within the legal profession, just as customary practices may be said to exist within a group in the sense that they are observed, accepted as appropriate forms of behaviour, and transmitted both by example and precept as membership of the group changes. The ideas and practices which comprise the common law are customary in that their status is thought to be dependent upon conformity with the past, and they are traditional in the sense that they are transmitted through time as a received body of knowledge and learning. Now such a view of the common law does not require us to *identify* theoretical propositions of the common law—putative formulations of these ideas and practices—with the common law, any more than we would identify statements of the customs observed within a group with the practices which constitute the customs. And this, as it seems to me, disposes of Bentham's main difficulty in admitting the existence of the common law. Formulations of the common law are to be conceived of as similar to grammarians' rules, which both describe linguistic practices and attempt to systematize and order them; such rules serve as guides to proper practice since the proper practice is in part the normal practice; such formulations are inherently corrigible, for it is always possible that they may be improved upon, or require modification as what they describe changes.

VI. THE ACHIEVEMENT OF COHESION IN A CUSTOMARY SYSTEM

It is no doubt impossible in principle to attach precision to such notions as acceptance and reception within the caste of lawyers, and the definition of membership of this group is essentially imprecise. Nevertheless it seems to me that the point made by Hale and Blackstone is correct—that the relative value of formulated propositions of the common law depends upon the degree to which such propositions are accepted as accurate statements of received ideas or practice, and one must add the degree to which practice is consistent with them. Now a customary system of law can function only if it can preserve a considerable measure of continuity and cohesion, and it can do this only if mechanisms exist for the transmission of traditional ideas and the encouragement of orthodoxy. There must exist within the group—particularly amongst its most powerful members—strong pressures against innovation; young members of the group must be thoroughly indoctrinated before they achieve any position of influence, and anything more than the most modest originality of thought treated as heresy. In past centuries in the common law these conditions were almost ideally satisfied. The law was the peculiar possession of a small, tightly organized group comprising those who were concerned in the operation of the Royal courts, and within this group the serjeants and judges were dominant. Orthodox ideas were transmitted largely orally, and even the available literary sources were written in a private language as late as the seventeenth century. A wide variety of institutional arrangements tended to produce cohesion of thought. The organization of the profession was gerontocratic, as indeed it still is, and promotion depended upon approval by the senior members of the profession. The system of education and apprenticeship, the residential arrangements, the organization of dispute and argument—for example the sitting of judges *in banc* and the existence of institutions such as the old informal Exchequer Chamber—all assisted in producing cohesion in orthodoxy and continuity. So too did such beliefs as the belief that the common law was of immemorial antiquity, and the belief that if only the matter was considered long enough and with sufficient care a uniquely correct answer could be distilled for every problem. The combination between institutional arrangements and conservative dogma is well illustrated in Blackstone's description of 'the chief cornerstone' of the laws of England:[34] '. . . which is general immemorial custom or common law, from time to time declared in the decisions of the courts of justice; which decisions are preserved amongst our public records, explained in our reports, and digested for general use in the authoritative writings of the venerable sages of the law.'

Even more striking is this passage from Hale.[35] The context is that Hale is explaining the wisdom of holding jury trials mainly before justices who are selected from the twelve men in scarlet who sit in Westminster Hall. He says:

It keeps both the Rule and Administration of the law of the kingdom uniform; for those men are employed as justices, who as they have had a common education in the study of the law, so they daily in term-time converse and consult with one another; acquaint one another with their judgements, sit near one another in Westminster Hall, whereby their judgements are necessarily communicated to one another, and by this means their judgements and their administrations of common justice carry a consonancy, congruity and uniformity one to another, whereby both the laws and the administrations thereof are preserved from the confusion and disparity that would unavoidably ensue, if the administration was by several uncommunicating hands, or by provincial establishments.

In such a system of law as the common law the explanation for the degree of consensus which exists at any one time will be very complex, and no *general* explanation will be possible, and this remains true today. For example, it is very generally agreed today that there are no legal limitations upon the legislative competence of Parliament. The explanation for this is very largely connected with the fact that the basic book and the best written book, is Dicey, and it is around Dicey that nearly all lawyers study constitutional law. This has been so for a long time now. Dicey announced that it was the law that Parliament was omnicompetent, explained what this meant, and never devoted so much as a line to fulfilling the promise he made to demonstrate that this was so. The oracle spoke, and came to be accepted. Again, a wide measure of consensus is apparent in magistrates' courts on very many points of law.

[34] Blackstone, p. 73.   [35] Hale, p. 252.

Part of the explanation of this is that all clerks rely on Stone as a sort of holy writ. Settled doctrines, principles, and rules of the common law are settled because, for complex reasons, they happen to be matters upon which agreement exists, not, I suspect, because they satisfy tests. The tests are attempts to explain the consensus, not the reason for it.

To study such a system, whether one is concerned with it at present, or in the past, involves, amongst other things, an attempt to identify what ideas are or were current at any particular period, and what ideas received or acted upon. What is involved is basically an oral tradition, still only imperfectly reduced to published writing. No clearer modern illustration is provided than D. A. Thomas's *Principles of Sentencing*, which publishes in comprehensive literary form the customary laws of the criminal appeal in England for the first time; as Mr. Thomas says with a slight air of puzzlement, 'It is almost true to say that the policies and principles of the Court [of Criminal Appeal and its successor] have developed as an oral tradition amongst the judges who sit as the Court, and the high level of consistency achieved is all the more remarkable for this reason.'[36] A historian is confined to the use of written sources—records, note books, legal writings, and indeed any document which throws light on the matter; his interest is not limited to a search for authorities. From such sources it is within limits possible to show that the doctrine of offer and acceptance was not a going idea in 1800, though by 1879 when Anson published his book on contract law it had come to be orthodoxy. Opinions as to what ideas were current, and what ideas generally accepted, are necessarily imprecise; there cannot in principle be a catalogue of such ideas, and in any event different and incompatible doctrines and views can co-exist. This seems to me to be just as true today as it was in the past. To argue that this or that is the correct view, as academics, judges, and counsel do, is to *participate* in the system, not simply to study it scientifically. For the purposes of action the judge or legal adviser must of course choose between incompatible views, selecting one or other as the law, and the fiction that the common law provides a unique solution is only a way of expressing this necessity.

[36] p. xlvi.

When there is disagreement within a customary system there must, if the system is to function, be some way of settling at a practical level which view should be acted upon—for example for the purpose of directing a jury or determining an appeal. This problem is solved by procedures, and these may take a wide variety of forms, though all will involve vesting a power of decision in some person or persons. In a system which lays claim to rationality—and the common law did—it will be supposed that differences can be resolved rationally by argument and discussion, and that the method adopted to solve disputes at a practical level is in principle capable of producing in general a correct solution to the general question—What is the law? In a tightly cohesive group there will exist a wide measure of consensus upon basic ideas and values as well as upon what views are tenable. Argument and discussion will commonly produce agreement in the end, and so long as this is the case there will be little interest in how or why this consensus is achieved. There is no *a priori* reason for supposing that just because agreement is commonly reached this is because there in fact is a rational way of deciding disputes. When however cohesion has begun to break down, and a failure to achieve consensus becomes a commoner phenomenon, interest will begin to develop in the formulation of tests as to how the correctness of legal propositions can be demonstrated, and in the formulation of rules as to the use of authorities—that is to say warrants or proofs that this or that is the law. This is the phenomenon of laws of citation, and it has really struck the common law only in the last century. It seems to me to be a symptom of the breakdown of a system of customary or traditional law. For the only function served by rules telling lawyers how to identify correct propositions of law is to secure acceptance of a corpus of ideas as constituting the law. If agreement and consensus actually exist, no such rules are needed, and if it is lacking to any marked degree it seems highly unlikely that such rules, which are basically anti-rational, will be capable of producing it. It is therefore not surprising to find that today, when there is great interest in the formulation of source rules in the common law world, the law is less settled and predictable than it was in the past when nobody troubled about such matters. In a sense this is obvious. There is only a felt need for authority for a legal proposition when there is some doubt as to whether it is correct or not; in a world in which all propositions require support from authority, there must be widespread doubt. The explanation for the breakdown in the cohesion of the common law is complex, but it is easy to see that the institutional changes of the nineteenth century, and the progressive increase in the scale of operations, had much to do with the process. In place of the twelve men in scarlet there are now (according to my most recent count) ninety-eight. How far it has proceeded may perhaps be brought home by comparing the current state of affairs with the fact that during the thirty years during which Lord Mansfield presided over the Court of King's Bench it is said that there were only twenty dissenting opinions recorded. In the period 1756–65 not a single decision was given which was not unanimous.[37]

How then are we to view the positivists' notion of the common law as a body of rules, forming a system in that the rules satisfy tests of validity? We must start by recognizing what common sense suggests, which is that the common law is more like a muddle than a system, and that it would be difficult to conceive of a less systematic body of law. The systematization of the common law—its reduction to a code of rules which satisfy accepted tests provided by other rules—is surely a programme, or an ideal, and not a description of the *status quo*. (Indeed even in the case of law of statutory origin common law judges shrink from identifying the law with the text of the statute, which they rapidly encrust with interpretation—consider the fate of the definition of diminished responsibility, no longer to be simply read out to the jury as 'the law'.) It is the ideal of an expositor of the law, grappling with the untidy shambles of the law reports, the product of the common law mind which is repelled by brevity, lucidity and system, and it is no accident that its attraction as a model grows as the reality departs further and further from it. It is, I suspect, a rather futile ideal; the only effective technique for reducing the common law to a set of rules is codification, coupled of course with a deliberate reduction in the status of the judiciary and some sort of ban on law reporting. But to portray the common law as actually conforming to this ideal is to confuse the aspirations of those who are attempting to arrest the collapse of a degenerate system of customary law with the reality.

[37] See C. H. S. Fifoot, *Lord Mansfield* (1936), p. 46.

V

Legal Obligation and the Imperative Fallacy

D. N. MacCORMICK

THERE are some statements which seem to bear their truth so shiningly upon their faces as to defy denial. 'Thou shalt not kill' plainly does not mean the same as 'You ought not to kill', nor does 'Go to Hell' mean 'You ought to go to Hell'. Section I of the Wills Act (1837) says: 'No will shall be valid unless it shall be in writing and executed in the manner hereinafter mentioned . . .', thereby making informal wills invalid; but making such wills invalid is not the same as saying that they ought to be invalid. 'No will shall be valid . . .' has a different meaning from 'No will ought to be valid . . .' or even from 'No will ought to be enforced . . .'. The praetor appoints a judge by saying 'Titius shall be judge' (*Titius index esto*), but he who says 'Titius ought to be judge' does not thereby make an appointment, even if he is praetor; he advocates an appointment or justifies one which has been made.

To put the matter mildly, the evident undeniability of these statements should put us on our guard against legal or ethical theories which appear to involve contradicting them. In a celebrated passage, Hume professes himself 'of a sudden surpriz'd to find, that instead of the usual copulations of propositions *is* and *is not*, I meet with no proposition that is not connected with an *ought* or an *ought not*[1] (in arguments purporting to base ethical theses on the proof of God's existence). We are entitled to be equally surprised, or even amazed, to find juristic or philosophical theses which suggest that imperative utterances either entail or mean 'propositions . . . connected with an *ought* or an *ought not*', or vice versa. It is by no means evident that 'ought' is derivable from 'shall' or 'shall' from 'ought'.

Yet confusion between the imperative and the normative is

---

[1] David Hume, *A Treatise of Human Nature*, III. 1.1, *sub fin.*

one of the perennial and persistent fallacies in legal philosophy. If it needs a name, it could well be called the Imperative Fallacy. To show how and why it is wrong to confuse the imperative and the normative is a principal object of this essay. The task is not a merely negative one, since its successful performance involves giving a positive account of norms, and particularly of those norms which impose obligations, in a manner which does not present them as deriving from commands or other imperatives. Since the notions of obligations under the law and of the obligatoriness or binding force of the law are fundamental to the understanding of law, this task is obviously worth while.

The errors of earlier and more primitive versions of the command theory of law are now so well established that we need not rehearse them. A more recent and complex, yet none the less gross form of the imperative fallacy is to be found in Kelsen's *The Pure Theory of Law* , in which almost impenetrable obscurity is caused by his insistence that 'acts of will' mean 'oughts', as we see in the following passage:

'Ought' is the subjective meaning of every act of will directed at the behaviour of another. But not every such act has also objectively this meaning; and only if the act of will has also the objective meaning of an 'ought' is this 'ought' called a 'norm' . . . The ought which is the subjective meaning of an act of will is also the objective meaning of this act, if this act has been invested with this meaning, if it has been authorized by a norm which therefore has the character of a 'higher' norm.[2]

Earlier, he has said in elucidation of the word 'norm', that

By 'norm' we mean that something *ought* to be, or *ought* to happen, especially that a human being ought to behave in a specific way. This is the meaning of certain human acts directed toward the behaviour of others. They are so directed if they, according to their content, command such behaviour, but also if they permit it, and—particularly—if they authorize it.[3]

What kind of conduct is denoted by the words 'act of will' may not be entirely clear, but certainly legislating and commanding are included. Of the latter he says: 'The command

---

[2] H. Kelsen, *The Pure Theory of Law* (tr. M. Knight, 1967), p. 7. There is no trace of this doctrine in *General Theory of Law and the State* (1945).

[3] Ibid., pp. 4–5.

of a gangster to turn over to him a certain amount of money has the same subjective meaning as the command of an income tax official, namely that the individual at whom the command is directed ought to pay something.'[4]

Before embarking upon criticism of these remarks, I must at once concede that in part at least their obscurity is the fault of the translator, and in particular that the German *sollen* is wider in its usage than the English 'ought', a fact which is not happily brought out anywhere in the translation. Nevertheless, both translation and original are wrong in two ways, first, in that it is wrong to assert that commands and other 'acts of will' mean 'oughts'; and secondly, in that it is wrong to assert that all norms are necessarily derived from acts of, or acts akin to, commanding (a view which leads to the extraordinary conclusion that the basic norm is the content of an imaginary act of will).[5] In what follows, I shall try to show why these views are mistaken (a) by explaining commands; (b) by discussing legislation and the ways in which it differs from commanding; and (c) by showing that the use of rules or norms can and must be explained in different terms. Finally, I shall give an account of the crucially important class of rules which generate obligations or duties in an effort to explain the obligatoriness and binding force of law without committing the imperative fallacy.

Although Kelsen is taken as the primary target for criticism, it should be observed that the argument is in some degree applicable against such other contemporary jurists as Olivecrona[6] and Ross.[7] It is also applicable against Professor Hare's 'prescriptivist' thesis[8] in ethics, which, in insisting that 'evaluative' 'oughts' entail 'imperatives', may justly be said to commit the converse error to Kelsen's, at any rate if 'imperatives' are taken as being 'commands' in the proper sense of the word shortly to be explained; and if 'imperatives' are not commands, prescriptivism loses much of its distinctive interest.

I. COMMANDING

In this section and the next, what has to be explained is the nature of commanding, not the meaning of any particular

---

[4] Ibid., p. 8.   [5] Ibid., pp. 9–10.
[6] K. Olivecrona, *Law as Fact* (2nd ed., 1970); see esp. chs. 5 and 8.
[7] Alf Ross, *Directives and Norms* (1968); see esp. chs. 3 and 4.
[8] R. M. Hare, *The Language of Morals* (1952); see esp. ch. 11.

command. To elucidate Lady Macbeth's 'Stand not upon the order of your going, but go at once' by pointing out that she meant the assembled dignitaries who were her guests to leave immediately without assorting themselves into the correct order of precedence, would be nothing to our purpose. For when Kelsen tells us that 'ought' is the subjective meaning of every command he is presenting a thesis about the nature of commands as such, not about the meaning of this or that command.

Commanding or ordering (I shall treat the terms as equivalent) being a specific kind of act, albeit a 'speech act', it will be helpful in this legal context to separate it into the traditional legal elements of *actus reus* and *mens rea*; although commanding is no crime, it would be a pity to let such useful concepts rust unused on grounds of mere infelicity, for it is indeed essential that we take account both of the observable conduct and of the intention behind it which together constitute the act of commanding.[9]

The *actus reus* is simple enough, consisting in the utterance by speech or writing of words capable of being understood as an express direction to another person or persons to do or refrain from some act or acts; for example, by displaying the notice 'No smoking' or by saying 'Stop smoking'. Express directions should be distinguished from statements which may indirectly induce the addressee to act, such as 'Your house is on fire and your children are inside.' The normal grammatical form of express directions is the imperative mood, but this is not essential as 'No smoking' and 'Spitting prohibited' show. Necessarily, a command makes reference to some kind of future action or refrainment by the addressee. Thus a meaningless utterance cannot be a command; 'Jones, be quadrilateral' is absurd, even if 'Don't be a square!' is good slang. This reference to action takes place in the context of an utterance which has imperative force.

To understand what is meant by 'imperative force' (and thus to see how any utterance could be understood as an 'express direction') we must look beyond overt acts, and

[9] Cf. P. F. Strawson 'Intention and Convention in Speech Acts' 73 *Philosophical Review* (1964) 439, esp. 455. See also J. L. Austin, *How to do Things with Words* (1962) and J. Searle, *Speech Acts* (1969).

consider the intentions behind them. *Actus non facit imperatorem nisi mens sit imperans*, one might almost say. There is an old joke about a Frenchman travelling on the night boat from Dover to Calais who regrettably took as a command the words 'Look out!' uttered by the Englishman in the upper bunk the moment before he was overwhelmed with *mal de mer*. The point is, of course, that the latter intended these words as a warning, not as an order. The words 'Give us this day our daily bread' might be an order if uttered to a baker; but in the context of prayer they are clearly not intended as such— and *because* they are not so intended, they are not an order. Likewise, requests or pleas and the like are distinguishable from orders by reference to intention.

There is some risk of confusion here, as between the object which one intends to achieve by giving an order, and how one intends the other person to understand one's utterance. It will be convenient to call the former 'ulterior intention', and the latter 'internal intention'.

To deal with ulterior intention first, it is obvious that *normally* A does not order B (for example) to leave the room unless he (a) desires B to leave the room, and (b) intends by his utterance to induce B to leave the room. But this alone is neither a necessary nor a sufficient condition of commanding. That it is not necessary is shown by the story of God's order to Abraham in Genesis 22:2. God told Abraham to take his son Isaac and offer him for a burnt offering; but his objective in doing so was only to test Abraham's obedience. So far from intending or desiring the incineration of Isaac, God intervened at the last minute through the agency of an angel and called off the sacrifice. Moreover, this ulterior intention would not be a sufficient condition for distinguishing commands from requests, prayers, or pleas. For equally one's purpose ('ulterior intention') in these activities is normally to get another to perform some action. We must therefore look to 'internal intention' not 'ulterior intention' in explaining commands.

True though these observations are, it is nevertheless the case that any command, and any request, prayer, plea, or the like, purports to be an expression of a wish of the speaker to get the addressee to do some deed, and of an intention on his part to (try to) get him to do it. God's trial of Abraham's obedience could only be effective as such if Abraham actually thought that God wanted and intended him to make a burnt offering of Isaac. Conversely, expressions of desire may readily be taken as orders in appropriate circumstances. Even if Henry II of England did not in fact want his knights to kill Thomas à Becket, he must have, or should have, realized that they were likely to take his saying 'Will no man rid me of this turbulent priest?'[10] as expressing a desire of his that the knights should kill Becket, and an intention to get them to kill Becket. Thus, when they did so, Henry was justly to blame since it was a reasonable interpretation of his act that he wished to bring about the murder by expressing an intention that the knights should commit it.

From this follows an understanding of one essential element of the 'internal intention' necessary to commanding. *B* cannot understand an utterance of *A*'s addressed to him as being a command unless he takes it as signifying that *A* wishes him to do *x*, and intends to get him to do it in virtue of his recognizing that intention of *A*'s. Therefore *A* must intend[11] *B* to take his utterance 'Do *x*' as disclosing a wish that *B* do *x* and an intention to get *B* to do *x* in virtue of his recognizing that intention. This is a necessary condition of *A*'s utterance being a command. It is not, however, a sufficient condition since it plainly applies also to requests, prayers, pleas, and the like. Yet, it does enable us to see in what sense it is 'normal' that commanders desire the performance of the deed commanded. There is no logical incompatibility between saying that *A* does not desire *B* to do *x* and saying that *A* intends *B* to take an utterance of his as disclosing a wish that *B* do *x*. But his utterance is in that case insincere,[12] and it is a general truth that all insincere utterances are effective only to the extent that the addressee fails to perceive the speaker's undisclosed as distinct from his purported intention. Thus, insincerity is apt to become self-defeating, as the tale of the boy who cried 'Wolf!' warns us.

---

[10] No claim of historical accuracy is made in relation to this quotation.

[11] As the case of Henry II indicates, it is sufficient if *A* knows, or ought to realize, or thinks it likely that *B* will take him to have the relevant intention. This qualification should be borne in mind throughout the following passages.

[12] Cf. J. L. Austin, op. cit., pp. 15–18, 38–44; J. Searle, op. cit., pp. 60–2.

2. THE CONTEXT OF COMMANDING: SUPERIORITY AND AUTHORITY

What is next required is to find the element which distinguishes orders and commands from other acts, such as requests, which also involve the intention to be understood as intending to get the addressee to do some act. The key to this is the fact that somebody who commands is necessarily calling for *obedience* on the part of his addressee, whereas to make a request is to appeal to the kindness or courtesy of the other. To 'call for obedience', in the sense here intended, involves asserting one's superiority over another. There are certain relationships, relationships of superiority and inferiority, which may exist between persons, such that the inferior is in one sense or another required to comply with the expressed wishes of the other in relation to his conduct. One person is properly said to obey another if he complies with the other's expressed wishes, willingly or unwillingly, in recognition that he is required to do so in virtue of their relationship.

This leads to the crucial observation that there are only certain relationships in which commanding is appropriate, and that these differ from the relationships in which requesting is appropriate. Commanding is only appropriate in a context of superiority, whereas requesting is appropriate (though not only appropriate) between people who acknowledge each other as equals, provided that they are on friendly or at least courteous terms with each other. If your neighbour dislikes you, and you know that he does, it is inappropriate and almost certainly pointless to ask him for a loan of his lawnmower. Conversely, the bank clerk has cause to dislike the robber whose gun menaces him, but the robber's order to him to hand over money is neither inappropriate nor indeed pointless. The robber has at least momentary superiority in point of force.

It behoves us further to investigate superiority; what does it mean to say that 'the inferior is in some sense or another required to comply with the expressed wishes of the other'? There are two essential sorts of 'requirement', coercion and obligation. To take coercion first: as in the bank robber's case, A has physical [13] power to, and is prepared to, inflict undesired

---

[13] Of course, not all forms of coercion involve the threat of the immediate application of physical force; cf. the bank manager's 'power to sack' below.

harm on *B* without present risk of equal or similarly undesirable retaliation; there is at least some range of acts which *B* is prepared to do, however unwillingly, in order to avoid suffering the harm which *A* can inflict; and *A* and *B* both know all this, or at least suppose it to be the case. This type of relationship may be called 'coercive superiority', and may be contrasted with legitimate authority.

The latter is the type of relationship in which one person has a duty or obligation to conform with the expressed wishes of another, in relation to some range of acts or activities. Let us take as a paradigm the relationship of a bank clerk, not with a bank robber, but with his bank manager. Within the normative structure of the bank's organization, the roles of clerk and manager are such that the clerk has a duty to comply with the manager's instructions so far as concerns the business of the bank. Thus if the bank manager tells the clerk not to cash Mrs. Jones's cheques, the clerk has, in virtue of the manager's authority, a duty not to cash them. In addition, since the manager has power to have him dismissed from his job, he may well regard it as prudent to comply. Here, therefore, there is an element of coercive power as well as of legitimate authority, though the power is founded on legal competence rather than physical superiority. If an inferior does not acknowledge the duty of obedience upon which his superior's authority depends, its being backed by coercion becomes essential, as in the case of an unwillingly conscripted soldier. Where there is disagreement as to the 'legitimacy' of 'authority', coercion comes into its own. Nevertheless, it should be observed that authority may well exist albeit backed by no coercive power of any sort. For example, two friends on a sailing holiday in a jointly hired yacht might take it in turns to act as skipper. Whoever is for the moment skipper has a right to be obeyed by virtue of the principle underlying their arrangement, so if he says 'slacken the jib', the other ought to slacken it. His only motive for obedience is respect for the principle tacitly or expressly adopted. His companion has no other power over him, though doubtless respecting the principle is important in ensuring the safety of both of them. Legitimate authority does not necessarily depend on coercive power, though they are very often associated with each other.

It would be wrong to proceed from the observation that commanding is only *appropriate* in such relationships to the conclusion that it is only *possible* in a context of coercive superiority or legitimate authority, or both. Every schoolboy knows that King Canute commanded the rising tide to turn back, and every parent knows that small children frequently address the plainest and most imperious (and not always reasonable) orders to their parents. Again, it is one form of rudeness for one person to give orders to another having no authority over him—for example if one diner in a restaurant walks to another's table and loudly says 'Give me that salt-cellar'. Yet it could not be rude to give one's equals orders if it were logically impossible to give them orders. On the contrary, it is rude precisely because in so doing one implicitly assumes some superiority to exist which does not exist in fact. What is constitutive of the command is not the existence of superiority, but the assumption of superiority which the speaker evinces.

The conclusion which follows is, again, that it is the speaker's 'internal intention' which is vital. When *A* says 'Do *x*' to *B*, his utterance is a command (as distinct from a request and the rest) only if he intends [14] *B* to take it as disclosing an intention to get *B* to do *x* *in recognition of A's superiority over him*, and in virtue of *B*'s recognizing that intention. It is perfectly possible to evince such an intention even if one does not have any actual superiority or authority over one's addressee, just as it is possible to do so even when one does not want him to do *x*. A good way of picking a fight with a stranger in a bar is to order him to go and jump in the river, though it is doubtless unwise if he has the superior physique, even supposing that one actually desires him to jump in some adjacent river.

Our conclusion calls for an amendment of Bentham's 'A parole expression of the will of a superior is a command';[15] a command is an utterance which the speaker intends his addressee to take as expressing a will that the addressee do some act in recognition of the speaker's superiority. A command is sincere and appropriate ('felicitous') only if the commander

---

[14] Or if he knows or thinks it likely or should realize that *B* will so take it. Cf. p. 105, n. 11, above.

[15] J. Bentham, *A Fragment on Government* (ed. W. Harrison, 1948), p. 39, n. 1.

does wish to get the deed done and only if he is in fact superior to his addressee in respect of the act commanded. Moreover, it is essential that the speaker's internal intention be successfully communicated to his addressee, otherwise the command is incomplete. Ordinarily, the context of the utterance and the speaker's tone of voice will make this clear enough. But, by virtue of the meaning of the words 'command' and 'order', the speaker can make his intention clear beyond a peradventure by the use of some explicitly declaratory phrase, as in 'I command you to leave the room' or 'No smoking. By Order of the Senate.' Such declaratory phrases operate upon a principle analogous to estoppel; one who uses them, unless clearly in jest or otherwise unseriously, is debarred from denying that he intended his utterance as an order, nor can he to whom they are addressed say that he did not know he was being commanded. They settle conclusively questions of intention when other evidence might be equivocal.[16]

3. COMMAND AND 'OUGHT'

It is now possible to anatomize the error which Kelsen commits in saying that 'ought' is the subjective meaning of every command. It is perfectly clear that no command is normally involved when one person tells another what he ought to do; for example, when a solicitor advises his client that he ought not to defraud the Inland Revenue by making a false tax return, or that he ought to have his will signed by two witnesses. That is not an assertion of superiority. Conversely, it would be highly unusual, though not quite impossible, to give a command by using the auxiliary 'ought'. It may be admitted, for example, that a tutor might say to his pupil, 'you ought to write an essay on Austin this week' intending that as a command, not as the expression of an educational value judgment for discussion with his pupil. The pupil, if he knew his tutor well enough, would take it as an order, fully realizing that it would be deemed an act of gross impertinence if he pretended otherwise. But that utterance is an order because the context and authoritarian character of the tutor make his intention sufficiently clear; it is an order *in*

---

[16] I believe this to be the proper explanation of the operation of all forms of 'explicit performatives', but we cannot go into that question here.

spite of the fact that the use of 'ought' is ordinarily inadequate to convey an intention to command. This is an odd use of 'ought', not one which discloses on its face the essence of commanding.

In contrast, a quite normal use of sentences about what people ought to do is to *state* principles or rules which are taken to be guides to conduct and standards against which to criticize it, or to *appeal* to such rules and principles. Thus I may tell you that you ought to go to Jennifer's wedding because you promised to. That is to *appeal* to a certain principle, which may be *stated* thus: 'People ought to keep their promises.' Such a speech act is not an order, but conversely I might order you to attend the wedding without believing that there is any principle under which you ought to go, or even under which you ought to obey me, as we have seen.

There is of course a relationship between command and 'ought', of which relationship authority is the nexus. To take an earlier example, the bank manager, by commanding the clerk not to cash Mrs. Jones's cheques, makes it true that the clerk ought not to cash them. But for the command, the clerk would have no duty to refrain from cashing the cheques—he would indeed have on other grounds a duty to cash them. Let it be observed however that this is not because the command 'means' an 'ought'. There is a principle—or rule—implicit in the organization of the bank that clerks ought to do what managers (acting within their ostensible competence) order them to do. In terms of, and by virtue of, that principle, the fact that the manager orders the clerk to 'Do *x*' entails that the clerk ought to do *x*. But this is a simple syllogism the major premiss being an ought-statement (stating a rule) and the minor a statement of fact. The 'ought' in the conclusion is therefore plainly derived from the major; and, in short, to aver that 'Do *x*' means '*x* ought to be done' is simply to commit the mistake of overlooking the major premiss in the argument. It is to treat deductive inference as though it were immediate entailment.

A further observation which follows is that in such a case, the manager in giving the order 'Do *x*' may be supposed to intend the clerk to take his order as making *x* an act which he ought to do. That is indeed a logically entailed element of any commander's 'internal intention' in commanding, whenever the superiority in virtue which he intends to get his addressee to act is legitimate authority.

That observation may be set up in partial defence of Kelsen's thesis. At one point in *The Pure Theory of Law*, he says of a would-be testator who makes a formally invalid putative will that 'the subjective meaning of this act is a testament'.[17] From this it appears that an agent's 'subjective meaning' in relation to some speech act is his intention as to how his act is to be understood by others. If this reading is correct, it follows that 'subjective meaning' in Kelsen's terminology is equivalent to 'internal intention' in mine. So, at least in the case of relationships of legitimate authority, it can be said in defence of Kelsen that the commander's 'subjective meaning' or 'internal intention' includes or entails an intention to be taken as making *x* an act which the recipient ought to do.

It is not much of a defence, however; ' "ought" is the subjective meaning of every act of will directed at the behaviour of another' says Kelsen; but (1) in our benevolent interpretation of the statement it can only apply to some, not to all, commands; and (2) it is of no use in explaining norms, since we have to assume the existence of norms conferring legitimate authority in order to show how some commands can be said to disclose 'ought' as their subjective meaning.

Perhaps the first of these objections could be avoided by saying that even in the case of commands, like the bank robber's, which are intended to be taken as invoking coercive superiority alone, the robber manifests an intention to be taken as making it the case that the clerk ought in prudence to hand over the money. Perhaps also Canute could be said to have evinced an intention to be taken as making it the tide's duty to turn. But even if such rather implausible suggestions were accepted, they do not save Kelsen's thesis, for the second objection is the crucial one, and it is ineluctable. No amount of discourse about commands as such can assist us to understand the operation of such rules or principles as those upon which legitimate authority is founded, for these are presupposed by some commands and explained by none. Kelsen

---

[17] Op. cit., p. 3. No better hint is anywhere given as to the meaning of 'subjective meaning'.

in effect concedes this in saying that only those acts which have the 'objective' as well as the 'subjective' meaning of 'ought' are acts which create norms. But he tries to have it both ways in insisting that all norms derive from acts of will, and this leads him into the obscurity of a basic norm which is not 'posited' but 'postulated' as the content of an imagined act of will.

All this confusion can only be avoided if we start from the clear realization that commands are one thing and statements about what ought to be are quite another thing. 'Ought' is no more derivable from 'shall' than from 'is'.[18]

4. LEGISLATION AND THE LEGAL 'OUGHT'

We may now take up more explicitly legal questions. The central point which has been established is that commanding is an authoritative act, in that it involves an assertion of superiority or authority; while in contradistinction the language of 'ought' is not normally appropriate to convey an assertion of authority by one person over another. The simplest level at which this distinction appears in law is the difference between making the law and using the law. Legislating is closely analogous to commanding in that it is an authoritative act. To legislate is to lay down what rules *are to be used* as law in a community. No doubt in a well-ordered community this act of legislation will be preceded by thorough discussion of the question what ought to be the law. But the act of laying down a rule as law neither is nor necessarily presupposes the normative judgment that the rule in question ought to be law. What it does entail is a presumption of authority on the part of the legislator; the presumption that if he enacts rule x, the fact of that enactment makes x a rule of law. Whether or not x ought to be law, it is hereby made law, and ought to be taken as such according to the norm tacitly presumed to exist by the very act of laying down the law.

The other side of the coin is to be found by asking what it is to 'take a rule as law'. Let us take as a concrete case Section 9 of the Wills Act 1837:

No will shall be valid unless it shall be in writing and executed in

[18] Indeed, it would be less so if Searle were correct. See 'How to derive "ought" from "is"' 73 *Philosophical Review* (1964), 43–58, and *Speech Acts*, ch. 8.

the manner hereinafter mentioned; (that is to say) it shall be signed at the foot thereof by the testator . . . and such signature shall be made or acknowledged by the testator in the presence of two or more witnesses present at the same time, and such witnesses shall attest and shall subscribe the will in the presence of the testator.

To take that enactment as law is to use it as providing a standard for the guidance of testators and for the evaluation of attempts at will-making. Thus a solicitor will advise his client that he ought to have his will signed by two witnesses, and the client will then have it so witnessed because he believes that at law he ought to. To use the enactment as law is to accept that informal wills are invalid (i.e. that they are instruments which ought not to be, or at least need not be, enforced) and that certain formalities ought to be followed. A perfectly natural way of putting this is to say that the Wills Act means that wills ought to be witnessed etc.; but to avoid the trap into which Kelsen falls, we must observe that this does not justify the assertion that 'shall be signed' *means* 'ought to be signed'. All that the sentence does, is express what ought to be done on the assumption that the enactment is a valid act of a duly authorized legislator.

To use enactments as law is to take them as providing rules about what we *ought* to do, but to make enactments is to lay down what shall be done and what shall be the consequences of failure to do it. If we wish to understand the legal 'ought', and the sense in which the law is 'obligatory' or 'binding' we cannot do so by reference to the act of norm-creating, the 'act of will' which is legislating. Legislating is like commanding in that it is authoritative: it *makes* rules, as commanding imposes tasks. Therefore legislation no more '*means*' 'ought' than does commanding. It creates 'oughts' only if some 'ought' rule already exists conferring legislative authority. How such 'ought' rules are to be explained is a question which must detain us further, since the theories which seek to explain them on the basis of authoritative 'acts of will' have been shown to be inadequate. However, before embarking on that topic, I shall digress briefly to discuss the differences between commanding and legislation.

5. COMMANDING AND LEGISLATING

The crucial similarity between these two is as we have seen that they are authoritative acts. To do either is to issue directions as to what shall be or what shall not be done. Thus, for example, it is pure nonsense to ascribe truth-value to either. To use such expressions as: ' "No will shall be valid unless . . ." is false', or ' "Go to bed" is true', is to talk sheer nonsense. On the contrary, however, one can quite accurately ascribe truth-value to ought-propositions, such as 'A bishop ought to be moved diagonally' (true) or 'You ought to have your will signed by one witness' (false).

These are two quite simple cases in which 'ought' is used in reporting the content of existing rules. That they are reports does not preclude them from also having the distinctively normative function of guiding action. If I as a chess player or would-be testator receive advice in those terms, and believe it to be true, I shall follow it—in the one case to my advantage, in the other to my detriment. Equally—to take a case from criminal law—it is both true, and a useful guide to action, if you tell me that in driving on British roads I ought not to, indeed may not, drive at more than seventy miles per hour. Of course, the ultimate normative questions (in the cases mentioned) whether I ought to play chess, or whether I ought to commit myself to conforming with the law, are not susceptible of true or false answers, unless subsumed under some superior norm to which I am already committed. But that is not a good or sufficient reason for saying that all ought-propositions are unverifiable.[19] The fact is that some normative utterances have truth-value, while no authoritative utterances do.

But it is not accurate wholly to identify commanding with legislating. (And to do so by stipulative definition is to create needless confusion.) There are two principal differences, firstly that legislation is normally a formal act, and secondly, that legislation is concerned with making rules.

1. Even in what is conceptually the simplest case of legislating, that of the single all-powerful legislator (*quod principi placuit legis habet vigorem*), some criteria ('rules of recognition'[20])

[19] See, e.g. Alf Ross, *Directives and Norms*, p. 102.
[20] H. L. A. Hart, *The Concept of Law* (1961), ch. 6.

are in practice highly desirable for identifying his law-making acts from his private orders and expressions of desire. Otherwise all despots would be reduced to an unhappy condition not unlike that of Midas. And wherever the constitution is in any degree more complex, requiring a collective act of two or more people for the enactment of legislation, it is necessary, *in principle* and not merely for practical convenience, to adopt some criteria as to what counts as enacting a law; in particular, criteria identifying the persons whose co-operation is necessary, and prescribing the procedures which they must adopt in order that their pronouncements may be accounted legislation. But if such criteria are in use among the citizens of a state, or at least among the executive and judiciary, then *necessarily* any act which fulfils the conditions laid down is *for that reason* legislation. It is not inconceivable that one such criterion may be that no act is legislative unless intended as such by all members of the legislature—though in practice such a rule would give rise to formidable problems of proof. Clearly it is not necessary that there be a rule requiring intention to legislate over and above such other rules as for example the British rules about three readings in both Houses and so on.

In this sense, then, legislation is a formal act: the acts of certain conventionally identified persons which conform with conventionally prescribed criteria thereby count as legislation; there is no *necessary* reference to the intention or will of the legislator(s). Conversely, commanding may be an informal act: whenever I use words capable of being understood as a direction to you to do something, *intending* them as a command, I am properly said to 'command'.[21] It may therefore be observed that Bentham's and Austin's notion of 'tacit commands' is nonsense as an explanation of the persistence of law. In the case of true commands, 'tacit commanding' is not inconceivable. But 'tacit legislation' is necessarily absurd. How can you have a criterion which specifies what legislators must abstain from doing, in order tacitly to enact old laws, unless it be that they pass no abrogating legislation? But if that is the criterion, we end up by assuming what we started out to explain, viz. that old laws remain laws until formally revoked.

---

[21] J. L. Austin appears to have thought that all 'performative utterances' are conventionally defined. This is certainly not true of commanding, as is (I hope) clear from the foregoing argument. See *How to Do Things with Words*, *passim*.

It also follows that Kelsen's description of acts of legislation as being acts of will (whose content is *therefore*—if you please—a subjective 'ought') is necessarily wrong. It is hard to imagine Parliament accidentally passing a law,[22] and no doubt *somebody's* intention or will lies behind whatever is enacted. But these are matters of fact, not of logic. (Moreover, the notion of the 'intention of parliament' as a guide to statutory interpretation is absurd, unless in the sense of 'presumed intention', in which case we ought to ask upon what basis intentions are to be imputed to legislators. That is not a question of fact, and unlike questions of real intention is in no way comparable with inquiries into the state of the legislative digestion.)

2. The main function of legislation is to make rules. If a particular act is accepted as being legislative in a community, then the citizens of that community will use it as providing a rule about what ought to be done. But commands function as a means of making people do things, and where *A* commands *B* to do one particular act, e.g. 'Shut the door', this does not entail any creation of or reference to a rule. No doubt an order may be taken as laying down a rule—thus a secretary may take her employer's order to her to open the mail every morning as making it a rule that she ought to do so. But this is not a necessary feature of commanding as it is of legislating (leaving out of account arguable exceptions such as Acts of Attainder).

This further reinforces the point that it is impossible to elucidate the function of ought-language in a legal context without reference to the use of rules as standards for conduct. The connection between ought-language and legislation is to be found in the *rule*-making nature of legislation; in this context the analogy, such as it is, between commanding and legislating is confusing, not helpful. An examination of legislating as an authoritative activity does not explain, it presupposes, the use of rules about what we ought to do; to which topic I now turn.

6. THE USE OF RULES

Let us initially take up again for discussion the rule, 'Wills ought to be signed by two witnesses.' In enunciating that rule

---

[22] But Lord Denning was of opinion that it did change the law accidentally in the case of s. 56 (1) of the Law of Property Act 1925. See *Beswick* v. *Beswick* [1966] 1 Ch. 538 at p. 556 *overruled* [1968] A.C. 58.

one is stating a standard by which wills may be judged. By reference to it, a will signed by only one witness is a bad will, an incorrectly made will—one might perhaps say that it is not really a 'will' at all. 'Ought-language' is thus used in enunciating the general rule. But it may also be used in passing particular judgments with reference to it, as when the solicitor advises his client, 'You ought to have this signed by two witnesses.' Yet it is neither here nor there that we may formulate such rules, and state the conclusions which follow from them in particular cases, unless someone actually *accepts* the rule. Only if someone *accepts* the rule, will anyone actually use it as a standard for judging his own and others' attempts at will-making, or take the rule as providing a motive for acting in a particular way. One 'accepts' a rule if and only if one takes it as a guide to conduct, and to the criticism of one's own and others' conduct.

There is a number of kinds of reason why one may accept a rule, of which the following seem to be the most significant. First of all one may accept it on rational grounds, such as, in the present case, the utilitarian one that it is important to be sure of the authenticity of documents purporting to be wills. Secondly, one may accept a rule simply in imitation of members of one's social group; fellows of Oxford colleges wear gowns at dinner, and have a rule that this ought to be done; a newly appointed fellow accepts the rule simply because it's the done thing, and there are no strong utilitarian arguments against it, even though there are none for it. Thirdly, one may accept a rule on grounds of 'legitimate' authority—because it is laid down by persons whose rulings ought to be accepted. Fourthly, one may accept a rule for prudential reasons, because it will be the worse for oneself if one does not conform to it.

In the case of legal rules, such as the rule that one ought not to commit murder, or that wills ought to be witnessed, a man might accept the rule, that is use it as a guide to action and as a standard of judgment, for all four reasons. Rationality, imitation, authority, and prudence might all co-operate as factors in his acceptance of the rule. But it is only in the case of a rule expressly enacted by someone enjoying legitimate authority that the rule must necessarily have been created by an 'act of will' in Kelsen's sense. And to speak of accepting a rule because of the authority of the maker is to presuppose that there is some rule to the effect that the maker's ordinances ought to be accepted. Plainly to avoid an infinite regress we must assume that such rules as to authority are accepted ultimately upon rational, imitative or prudential grounds only.

To accept or adopt a newly formulated rule upon rational grounds is plainly in some sense an 'act of will'; an example might perhaps be found in Lord Atkin's speech in *Donoghue* v. *Stevenson*.[23] Equally plainly one may accept a rule imitatively without anything which could reasonably be called an act of will being involved; very few people can ever have taken a conscious decision to accept the rule that promises ought to be kept—rather, it would call for an act of will to reject it. Unless we are prepared to believe in the existence of rules which nobody ever decided to adopt, it follows that the use of rules in social life is explicable only in terms of 'acts of will' of rational beings. But obviously this does not mean that in every enunciation of a rule that such and such ought to be done, the speaker is indulging in an 'act of will', or *a fortiori* that every judgment passed in terms of a rule is an 'act of will directed at the behaviour of another'.

In consequence we may conclude, not only that it is false to claim that ' "Ought" is the subjective meaning of every act of will directed at the behaviour of another', but also that not every 'ought' directed at the behaviour of another is an act of will, or presupposes any such act on the part of the speaker.

We are confronted with the simple fact, so well brought out by Professor Hart,[24] that people do have and use standards for judging conduct and other things, and that these standards can be enunciated as rules. The use of 'ought-language' is simply the linguistic manifestation of this activity of judging and rule using. That such judgments provide us with motives for action is obviously true; and so indeed do commands provide us with motives for action. But this can scarcely justify us in treating the two as being even prima facie closely related since beliefs about facts can also motivate action.

[23] [1932] A.C. 562.
[24] See H. L. A. Hart, *The Concept of Law*, chs. 1–6, *passim*.

7. THE VARIETY OF RULES: OUGHT AND OBLIGATION[25]

It is of the greatest interest to observe that there is a variety of kinds of rule which we characteristically use. Of particular interest is the difference between rules of obligation and others. Not all rules generate obligations. As Professor Hart has pointed out, for example, it is wrong to say 'you was', but it would be improper to speak of this in terms of 'a duty' not to say 'you was'. On the other hand, it is not only wrong to tell lies; one has indeed a duty to tell the truth. Why do we speak of some rules in terms of 'obligation', but not of others? This distinction between rules of obligation and others is of high importance in legal theory, in that we must seek to understand the concepts of obligations or duties under the law, and of the obligatoriness of the law itself.

Professor Hart's criterion for distinguishing between them appears to be inadequate. He says: 'Rules are conceived and spoken of as imposing obligations when the general demand for uniformity is insistent and the social pressure brought to bear on those who deviate or threaten to deviate is great.' [26]

This is surely neither a necessary nor a sufficient criterion. The parable of the good Samaritan is plainly intended to imply that the Samaritan had an obligation to assist the Jew. This is not a self-contradictory nor a linguistically improper use of the word 'obligation'. But we know that there were at that time very heavy social pressures against co-operation between Jews and Samaritans. So Hart's criterion is not a necessary test of obligation. On the other hand, there is heavy social pressure in an Oxford common room that men should wear trousers, not shorts or skirts, yet clearly it would be inaccurate to speak in this context of having a duty to wear trousers. There is simply a rule about the correct way to dress. So Hart's criterion is not sufficient either.

The precise deficiency of his test is, to use his own invaluable distinction, that it is a criterion specified in terms of the

---

[25] In the following passage, I treat the words 'duty' and 'obligation' as being synonymous, and use one or the other simply for stylistic variation. Such differences of nuance and usage as exist between the words does not here concern us.

[26] *The Concept of Law*, p. 84. Further criteria are mentioned on p. 85. See below, pp. 124–5.

'external point of view'. It provides a test for distinguishing obligations from other rule governed acts from the point of view of the social observer. From this perspective, no doubt, it might be a useful rule of thumb for distinguishing those social rules conceived of by the members of the society as imposing obligations from other rules. But even at this level it would not be wholly satisfactory as the (hypothetical) case of the transvestite don illustrates. To discover the true significance of the word 'obligation' we must look at it from the internal point of view. What special force is there in the judgment that a particular act is a duty, from the point of view of the person who makes the judgment?

Let us re-examine the type of case which Hart uses to demonstrate that not all cases of breach of rules are cases of breach of duty. A small boy says to his mother, 'Honestly I were at school today', when in fact he has been playing truant. In one utterance he has two wrongs for the price of one. But the rule against lying is one under which duties arise, whereas no duty arises under the rule that 'I was' is the correct form of the first person indicative of the past tense of the verb 'to be'. Wherein lies the difference? Leaping lightly over the superficially attractive but fundamentally question-begging explanation that the former rule is moral and the latter grammatical, we may make a highly useful initial observation by taking note of a clear difference in types of criticism which breaches of the two rules may properly evoke.

We can criticize the boy for telling a lie by saying that he 'has done wrong' or 'acted wrongfully' or 'committed a wrong', but none of those types of criticism is apposite to his grammatical error—as to that, he has 'spoken incorrectly', 'expressed himself wrongly', 'declined the verb improperly', and so on. It is not accurate (unless it is simply question-begging) to *explain* this difference by saying that the former class of criticism is more 'serious' than the latter. However harshly and heavily we react to errors of expression (one schoolmaster of the writer's habitually administered corporal punishment for errors of spelling in English composition) we do not thereby commit ourselves to regarding them as 'wrongs', and conversely no contradiction exists between adopting a lenient attitude to 'white lies' and 'little fibs' while continuing to regard them as genuine misdeeds. The difference is one of *kind* not of *degree*.

To understand this difference of kind, let us contrast two abstract and generalized examples: 'Doing *x* is doing wrong' and 'doing *x* in manner *m* is doing *x* wrongly'. The former of these is appropriate to expressing a criticism of *what* somebody did, the latter to expressing a criticism of *how* somebody did (or tried to do) something or other, leaving open the question whether doing *x* in these circumstances is or is not open to criticism in itself. The former (let us say) expresses *substantive* criticism, the latter, *procedural* criticism. But if such different types of criticism are properly used in applying different socially recognized rules to human acts, it must follow that the rules which are applied are themselves recognized as being of different types. This difference is one of function: some rules function as substantive guides to conduct, guiding us as to *what* ought or ought not to be done, others as procedural guides, laying down in what manner this or that ought to be done.

This is certainly a real enough distinction (and not necessarily the only one which could be drawn), though it may appear at first sight to depend on mere verbal accidents of how people may on occasion chance to express themselves. Let me substantiate it with some examples of rules which would count as 'procedural' in the admittedly wide sense in which I am using that word. First, table manners: although it may be easier to eat garden peas by scooping them into one's mouth with a knife than to eat them with a fork, it is widely regarded as being wrong to do so, but it is 'wrong' simply because, and only in the sense that, there is a conventional standard stipulating how to eat peas in the company of others. Second, language: there is nothing in the nature of the words 'I were' as against 'I was' which makes the latter more desirable as a mode of self-expression; there is simply a conventional rule under which 'I was' is the correct formation of that mood and tense of the verb. Third, other forms of communication: a car driver wishing to turn left who extends his right arm out of the driver's window and holds it straight has given the wrong signal; by the existing convention, the correct way to signify an intention to turn left is by revolving the right arm, not by holding it straight. Fourth, games: the right way to move a bishop at chess is diagonally, and so on with all the other pieces, such conventions being constitutive of playing the game, though in a case in which two players ignored or altered or misunderstood only one or two such rules we should rather say that they were not playing properly than that they were not playing chess at all. Fifth, legal cases: the only way in which *A* can transfer the legal property in Blackacre to *B* is by executing a deed of grant, that is by following certain legally stipulated procedures.

Such diverse rules exhibit many differences of type between themselves, which would indeed be worthy of further study. Nevertheless, it is a genuinely common element in all that they establish a standard mode of performing some activity which is at least sometimes permissible in itself. The justifying reasons for having such rules or conventions may differ. Sometimes having them and observing them (most of them most of the time) is essentially constitutive of an 'institution' which we wish to maintain, as in the case of rules of language, or of other forms of communication (e.g. traffic signals); likewise rule-defined games. Sometimes, as in the case of rules governing the valid exercise of legal powers, the procedures stipulated may be thought desirable in ensuring authenticity and publicity, though here again, that some particular obligation can be created or cancelled by certain specified acts, or that ownership can be invested and divested by certain procedures, is essentially constitutive of the 'legal power' in question. In the case of table manners, the justification of the conventions can only be in terms of the desirability of having *some* shared practice to be adopted in eating meals with others—it cannot be said that the conventions are constitutive of the activity of eating in company; thus in such a case, the wrongness of the non-conforming act can only be explained in terms of the existence of some convention which it is thought desirable to have even if there is nothing intrinsically preferable in the procedure required (e.g. eating peas with a fork) as against other possible methods (e.g. eating them with knives or fingers).

This whole group of rules exhibits an interesting similarity with 'instrumental norms' which specify what one must do or ought to do in order to achieve some purpose. 'To keep one's car radiator from freezing, one ought to drain it or to put in anti-freeze.' But whereas in this type of case the appropriateness of the procedure is determined by its *efficacity* in producing the proposed result, the appropriateness determined by 'procedural rules' is essentially *conventional*. That others observe the convention in question may however have the result that the adoption of improper (conventional) procedures may *also* be inefficacious. If you want to indicate an intention to turn your car left, you must use the proper signal or you will be misunderstood, and if you wish to convey Blackacre you will not achieve your objective unless you follow the legally appropriate procedures.

By contrast, substantive rules of conduct are conceived of as indicating permissible and impermissible forms of behaviour, not as indicating steps to be taken in order to achieve some goal or another, though the effects of the behaviour prescribed or proscribed may be relevant to the justification of the rule. There cannot, indeed, be a clearer way of indicating the nature of such rules than by considering how their maintenance has to be justified, if justification be demanded. One can justify the maintenance or introduction of a rule against doing *x tout court* if and only if one seriously believes (whether on good or on bad grounds) that for some reason doing *x* is undesirable, and would remain so even if there were no conventionally observed rule against doing it. It may indeed be the case that demanding money with menaces is conventionally regarded as an inappropriate procedure for obtaining money from others: but there is more to it than that, for the act of menacing people with a view to gain is widely regarded as undesirable both in itself and in the consequences which would result from its toleration. The justification of maintaining the rule against it is not solely in terms of the need for *some* convention about valid modes for the transfer of money, but rather in terms of the conceived evil nature of the proscribed behaviour. The obligation to pay taxes certainly involves prior decisions as to methods of raising money for state purposes, and as to the proper rates of tax; but given such decisions, general refusal to pay would clearly have adverse consequences, and the toleration of individual refusals to pay would be grossly unfair.

If the people who have and wish to keep some rule of conduct consider the justification for having and keeping it to be that deviant behaviour is undesirable in itself or because of its

· consequences or both, and not simply because it deviates from a convention in relation to an activity to which having some convention is either essential or useful, then for those people that rule has—'from the internal point of view'—the function of guiding conduct in a 'substantive' way. If they regard the deviating behaviour as being undesirable in the strong sense of deserving blame and non-toleration,[27] rather than simply the withholding of praise, the substantive guidance of the rule is guidance as to a minimal standard of acceptable conduct. These are the features which combine to constitute that particular type of rule of which the people who themselves accept and endorse it are accustomed to speak in terms of 'duties' and 'obligations' imposed by the rule. It is upon this 'internal' usage that all more detached and sociological, anthropological, or simply dissentient usages depend. It is these features which some rules of law, some social rules of positive morality, and some personal standards of individual morality all share, and their sharing them shows why 'duty' and 'obligation' are not simply punning homonyms when severally prefixed by the qualifications 'legal', 'social', 'moral'—in contrast to the use of the word 'duty' in the phrase 'excise duty'.

Thus we can properly grasp the meaning and range of uses of the normative words 'duty' and 'obligation', and together with them such converse terms as 'wrongful act', 'wrong', 'misdeed', 'crime', 'delict', and 'sin' only by understanding the nature of rules as standards of conduct, and of that particular type of rule which function for those who use it as a *substantive*, minimal, standard of conduct. It is false, misleading, and quite unnecessary to suppose, with Kelsen[28] and others that 'delict' can only be explained in terms of 'sanction', and 'duty' only as being the converse of 'delict'.

Professor Hart mentions two further criteria[29] for identifying duty-imposing rules in addition to the one earlier criticized, namely: (1) that such rules are considered essential to the preservation of highly prized or essential features of social life; and (2) that conformity with them may sometimes conflict with

---

[27] It should be observed how similar this requirement is to Hart's requirement of serious social pressure. Clearly, the present thesis is no more than a modification (and perhaps refinement) of Hart's. See also p. 125 below.

[28] Op. cit., pp. 111–18.   [29] Op. cit., p. 85.

individuals' desires. These are fundamentally correct, but require modification. As to the first, it can hardly be said that the maintenance of a common language does not deserve to be accounted a highly important feature of social life, yet the rules of languages impose no obligations as Hart himself points out. The point is, rather, that sharing standards for the suppression and discouragement of undesirable forms of conduct is *one* essential prerequisite of social life, but not a *unique* one. As to the second, conforming with some procedural requirements may sometimes conflict with an agent's desires, as for example if a testator should wish to make some secret provision for an illegitimate child without the publicity which a will involves.[30] The point is rather, that the *applicability* of procedural rules ordinarily depends upon the agent's choosing to engage in some optional or permissible activity to which some procedural standard is annexed, in contrast to substantive rules which apply willy-nilly. Here, as in the rest of the present passage, what is offered is rather extension and amendment of Hart's suggestions than radical rejection and displacement of them.

In any consideration of the jurisprudential application of this thesis, two essential observations must be borne in mind. First the distinction here drawn between 'procedural' and 'substantive' standards of conduct does not exactly correspond to the traditional legal distinction between 'substantive law' and 'procedural law'. For *inter alia* all rules relating to the proper exercise of legal powers count as 'procedural' in the present classification, whereas 'the law of procedure' comprehends only those rules which relate to the power of instituting litigation in Court. Secondly, and much more important, it is possible, and perfectly legitimate, to adopt jurisprudential 'principles of individuation of laws'[31] in the light of which procedural rules count only as *parts* of laws, not as laws in themselves. Some illustrations will elucidate this point.

Suppose that a rule of road traffic law imposes upon drivers a duty to give traffic signals when performing such manoeuvres as turning or stopping in heavy traffic. Is this a case of two rules, one imposing a duty to signal in heavy traffic, the second

---

[30] Cf. H. G. Hanbury, *Modern Equity* (9th ed., 1969, by R. H. Maudsley), pp. 155–70.

[31] See J. Raz, *The Concept of a Legal System* (1970), pp. 70–7, 140–6, 157–8.

laying down how to indicate an intention to make the various manoeuvres, or is it a case of one single rule of the form: 'In heavy traffic, before stopping or turning left or right, drivers of vehicles must signify their intention to do so by making the following signals . . .' The answer is that for some theoretical purposes, and for such practical ones as teaching a person to drive, it may be more useful to treat the case as one of two separate but mutually related rules, (1) *how* to signal, and (2) *when* signalling is obligatory, the former being legally relevant only given the existence of the latter. For the purpose of analysing the structure of a legal system postulating as few normative entities as possible, the case is better treated as being of one single rule. Similarly, in the case of the procedure laid down in the Wills Act for making a legally valid will, or of the procedures required for the constitutional enactment of valid legislation, we may—and do for some educational purposes—consider these as sets of procedural rules whose conjoint observation is essential to the creation of obligations upon executors and judges in the former case, or upon judges and citizens in the latter. For any other purposes we may rightly wish to represent all these elements as constituting two single but complex power-conferring laws.

The present purpose has been to indicate the special characteristics of those rules, both legal and non-legal, under which obligations are properly said to exist. For that purpose it is essential to see the difference in function between procedural and substantive standards of conduct. Though it is as true, and as much a guide to conduct, that Englishmen ought to make their wills in writing as that they ought not to assault and murder each other these legal rules have very different functions. In law and in morals, the concepts 'duty' and 'obligation' are only to be grasped by appreciating that difference of function between procedural and substantive standards.

8. THE OBLIGATORY CHARACTER OF THE LAW

What remains to be explained is the conception of the 'bindingness' or 'obligatoriness' of the law as such. A step upon the road to that final elucidation may be taken by adverting to a further advantage of the approach adopted in the last section. Legal theory from Bentham and Austin down to

Kelsen has been bedevilled by the recurrent habit of defining duty in terms of 'sanction'. The best illustration of the absurdity of any such theory is that in the case of such officials as judges we are debarred from ascribing to them a legal duty to impose the sanction which the law lays down. Thus Kelsen is driven into asserting that in the last resort the sanction is only 'authorized' not 'commanded'. But this is surely nonsense. Whether or not a sanction may be directed against a judge who wrongfully acquits or convicts, or who imposes a sentence less or more than that for which the law provides in case of some specific offence, surely it is proper to say that judges have an obligation to apply the law honestly to the disputes which are brought before them. Surely it is proper to call that obligation a 'legal obligation'.

The present thesis certainly indicates why it is proper to say that. The point is that citizens and judges alike treat the standards of proper judicial conduct as being substantive standards annexed to the legally defined office of judge. Deviation from them is indeed misconduct, not merely incorrect procedure. Equally, in the case of ordinary citizens' duties under the law, the present thesis enables us to see the sanction as simply the distinctively legal means for securing compliance with substantive rules of conduct, not that which is the logical precondition of the existence of 'duties' at all.

From this, we may go on to observe what is the really significant difference between citizens' duties and officials' duties as such. Citizens' duties are duties under the law, defined by law. But at least some of the duties of officials, and especially of judges, are duties *in respect of* 'the law'. That is, the officials are under obligations to *apply* the law properly. Section 9 of the Wills Act does not impose a duty on the would-be testator; it defines the legally correct procedure for making a will. But because Section 9 is a rule of law, a judge is obligated to apply it according to its terms and to enforce any will made in accordance with it. Section 1 of the Drugs Act 1964 makes it an offence to be in possession of certain specified drugs. A citizen in possession of one of those drugs commits that offence. But the judge who disingenuously directs the jury to acquit him does not commit that offence. He is in breach of a different obligation, a distinctively official, indeed judicial, obligation; the obligation to respect and apply all those rules which are 'rules of law'. (For present purposes I am content to assume that the 'rules of law' in a particular system are identified by reference to criteria of recognition as suggested by Professor Hart.[32])

It seems clear that the working of a legal order depends upon a general acceptance by the great majority of the officials of the system that they are under duties to respect the valid rules of law, and to direct their actions towards securing the regular and uniform application of those rules, whether the rules in question be themselves substantive or procedural *vis à vis* citizens. These obligations are obligations upon officials only, but they are recognized by citizens too, and form the basis of citizens' expectations as to the conduct of officials.

Herein lies the key to the binding character of law. I as a citizen may or may not be disposed to accept each and every law in itself and for itself. I may deeply disapprove of the content of particular laws, but insofar as the majority of citizens continue to accept that the law can only be made or changed by settled procedures, and in so far as the officials who administer it continue in fact to acknowledge and honour a duty to apply it scrupulously, the law binds me whether I like it or not. I cannot change bad or inconvenient laws, and the officials are not free to apply them or ignore them according to my likes and dislikes, or according to their own. The law, because it is the accepted law of the community, must be applied by the officials. That is the duty of their station. So long as that duty is generally honoured by them, the legal system will remain a working order. If they cease to honour that duty the system will break down into a wilderness of arbitrary power. Alternatively the system may be smashed by a successful revolution. Until that moment comes, the citizen is bound by the law, in that he must like it or lump it.

This explains the minimal sense in which we may speak of the law as 'being binding' or 'having binding force'. Just as the conclusion that some contract is 'binding' implies minimally that each of the parties must fulfil it according to its terms, which they may not unilaterally change whether they like them or not, and that this is so because the agreement made is adjudged to conform with certain rules which provide

[32] Op. cit., ch. 6.

for the formation of contracts and for the application of sanctions to contract breakers; so the conclusion that some specific law is 'binding' implies that its applicability to a particular citizen is not affected by his likes or dislikes, because it qualifies as a law which ought to be enforced against him according to its terms. Likewise the law as a whole is binding in that it will be applied and may not be changed *ad hoc* to suit individual convenience. As long as the law survives, with the willing or unwilling acquiescence of the majority of citizens, so long is it prudent for each citizen to guide his conduct in accordance with the law. For it is brute fact that the law will be applied against him. But even that brute fact depends upon the interlocking obligations of the officials of the system, and upon their honouring them as such. Even the crudest notions of the binding force of law cannot wholly divorce themselves from the concept of obligation.

In this minimal sense, even the most odious legal systems may be said to be binding, so long as they survive. But although sometimes the notion of the 'obligatoriness' of law may be watered down and taken as meaning no more than this, the judgment that law as such is obligatory normally implies something more than that we have Hobson's choice of conforming or suffering the pains of non-conformity. It signifies that there is at least a prima facie moral obligation to conform to law. This prima facie obligation is not unrelated to the fact of the bindingness of the law. However evil laws may be, that they are binding in the minimal sense mentioned, implies that they secure the existence of some sort of order in society. And on the whole order is morally preferable to disorder. The promotion of disorder is prima facie a moral wrong. This is not the place in which to enter into the debate about what considerations ought to be taken as overriding that prima facie obligation, though they are doubtless many and diverse. It is sufficient that we should observe how the obligatoriness of law is related to, and in some sense follows from, its binding force, which in turn can only be explained in the light of an adequate theory of norms and obligations.

CONCLUSION

I have tried here to show that the 'ought' in law cannot be derived from commands or imperatives as such. Instead, we must seek to understand the use of rules and standards as guides to conduct and its judgment. Only then can we fully understand commanding, legislating, and other 'norm-creating' acts. The concept of obligation in the law and elsewhere can then be explicated by reference to a specific type of rule, differentiated from others by the function which it fulfils for those who use it. Yet it is not the existence of obligations under the law, but rather the obligations of officials *towards* the law as such which enables us to grasp the binding nature of the law.

VI

Sanction Theories of Duty[1]

P. M. S. HACKER

I. INTRODUCTION

THE concept of a sanction plays a dominant role in many philosophical analyses of duty. Any theory which specifies an analytic connection of some sort between failure to perform an obligatory[2] act and a consequent sanction may be called a sanction theory of duty. The specific nature of the nexus is of course a matter of controversy. Three different views may be distinguished. According to one theory the connection is predictive and probabilistic. According to another, the connection is imperatival, i.e. the sanction is commanded in the event of non-performance of the act in question. According to the third view the failure to perform the relevant act is a reason or ground for the sanction.

An alternative kind of analysis of duty approaches the problem from an investigation of the requirement to perform the act which is said to be a duty. Here too at least three distinct kinds of analysis have been suggested to explain the nature of the requirement to act analytically involved in the concept of duty. According to one theory a duty is an act commanded under certain circumstances. Such an account may be termed imperatival. According to an alternative theory a duty is an act the performance of which is required by a rule of a certain kind. This account may be termed normative. A third approach suggests that the requirement to perform the duty act must be explained by reference to certain kinds of justifying reasons (other than a prospective sanction) which support the doing of

---

[1] I should like to acknowledge my indebtedness and gratitude to Professor H. L. A. Hart and Dr. Joseph Raz.

[2] Like Bentham I shall treat duty and obligation as synonymous. In fact obligations are best construed as a subclass of duties, namely those duties that are contractual or quasi-contractual with correlative rights *in personam*. This distinction is of no importance for present concerns.

the act in question. This kind of analysis may be termed justificative.

The two different angles of approach are often combined to form modified sanction theories. Thus an imperative approach to the problem of the nature of the requirement to perform a duty has been combined with either a predictive sanction theory or with an imperatival sanction theory. Similarly a normative analysis of the requirement to do the duty has been combined with the third kind of sanction analysis to yield the claim that a duty is an act the performance of which is required by a rule or norm of a certain kind, and the non-performance of which is a reason or ground for sanctions of certain sorts. A justificative analysis may similarly be modified by combination with the third kind of sanction theory. Other less plausible combinations are, of course, possible too.

Since the concept of duty fulfils an important role in discourse concerning a wide variety of kinds of standards of conduct, for example in law, morality, religion, social practices, etc., the various approaches to the problem of analysis must involve sufficient flexibility in their definitions of the general concept of duty to account for the different types of duty. This is typically done by specifying variations in the sources, nature, and character of sanctions analytically involved in the concept of duty, or alternatively by specifying *differentia* in the sources, logical form, or content of the requirement to perform the obligatory act, or both.

Cutting across these different classifications is a further notorious source of contention. The various theories of duty may be distinguished into social-fact or positivist theories on the one hand or non-positivist, more rationalist-inclined theories on the other. Social-fact theories conceive statements about duties to be statements about complex structures of social facts concerning patterns of behaviour, reactive and affective responses to behaviour, critical attitudes, and beliefs. The more rationalist-inclined theories will tend to lay stress not on actual behaviour, critical attitudes, and beliefs, but upon rational justifications for action, or for rules requiring the performance of certain actions, or for sanctions or censure. What people take as a reason must be understood not in terms of social facts *simpliciter*, but in terms of their beliefs, correct or incorrect, as to what is a reason or justification. The notion of reasons or justifications, the antipositivist will argue, cannot be analysed in terms of social facts, but only in terms of a rational system of values and principles.

This typology is by no means the only possible one for classifying philosophical analyses of duty. Nor is it suggested that all important theories of duty can be readily accommodated in it. All that is claimed is that this is one useful way of looking at many attempts to render an explication of the problematic concept of duty.

It should be noted that the notion of a reason for action, and the logically related notions of justifications and grounds for action, and of what ought to be done, occupy a central role in many philosophical analyses of the concept of duty. In the ensuing discussion the notion of a reason for action will be used extensively. No attempt will be made to provide a proper analysis of this philosophically problematic concept, but its use will, I trust, accord with our ordinary linguistic intuitions regarding the correct employment of the term. Nevertheless, a few clarificatory remarks are necessary.

Whenever an action ought prima facie to be done, then there is a reason for doing it. Conversely, whenever there is a reason for doing something, then it ought prima facie to be done. The notion of a reason for action is involved both in the explanation and in the justification of human action. When there is a reason for action then there is a justification of some kind for acting. Various kinds of factors are referred to as reasons, despite important differences in their roles in practical reasoning and justification. Sometimes we simply cite a fact as a reason. Thus the third type of sanction theory stresses that failure to do an obligatory act is a reason for a sanction-applying act. Here a past act of omission is held to be a reason. I shall refer to reasons of this kind, that is backward looking reasons, as 'grounds' for action. Equally we often refer to future facts, for example prospective sanctions, as providing reasons for action. Such citation of grounds or forward-looking reasons do not reveal in virtue of what further considerations such facts are reasons for action. But in many contexts we explain why certain facts are reasons by reference to justifying principles and values which members of a social group accept, or which are conceived of as having a rational foundation (or both). I shall refer to reasons of this kind as 'justifications', although in ordinary discourse the term 'justification' includes both what I call 'grounds' and also forward-looking reasons. I am not suggesting that there is any ambiguity in 'reason for action'; merely that the logical structure of practical reasoning is complex, and that in normal discourse different constituent elements are, depending upon the context, selected as appropriate to cite as reasons. It is instructive to bear in mind that similar considerations apply to identifying a factor as a cause. According to various principles of selection we pick one factor out of an array of jointly sufficient and individually necessary conditions for the occurrence of an event and refer to it as 'the cause'. In a different context and with different interests we could, with equal propriety, select a different factor. So too, analogously, with reasons.

The explanatory role of reasons for action is evident whenever we speak of a person acting for a certain reason. Here a person's conduct is explained by reference to his having a reason, in one sense of the phrase, for acting as he did, and acting on it. It seems plausible to think that the notion of there being a reason links the explanatory and justificatory aspects of reasons for action. For a person subjectively has a reason for acting,[3] one might claim, in so far as he believes, rightly or wrongly, that there is a reason for him to act thus. And a person's actions are explained in terms of reasons for action in so far as we explain that he did what he did because of his belief that there was a reason for him to do it. These crude distinctions between grounds, forward-looking reasons, and justifications, and between acting for a reason, having a reason, and there being a reason, are important in understanding the different theories of duty to be examined. The distinctions are relatively crude, and stand in need of much refinement and explication. But for the purposes at hand they will, I trust, suffice.

In this paper I shall undertake a historical and critical examination of two famous, predominantly sanction theories

---

[3] We also employ the phrase 'has a reason' or 'had a reason' objectively, i.e. such that it does not imply any cognitive attitude on behalf of the person who is said to have the reason. A person objectively has a reason for acting in so far as there is a reason which applies to him, i.e. a reason for him, to act thus or so.

of duty. I shall first examine Bentham's account, or rather accounts, of duty and obligation. Next I shall survey Mill's writings upon duty and its sanctions, paying particular attention to the relations between his theories and those of Bentham. Finally I shall briefly dwell upon Hart's contemporary modified sanction theory. The upshot of the analysis will be to direct attention to justificative analyses of the requirement to do the duty act, and to stress the different needs which the concept of duty meets in moral and legal discourse which suggests that however appropriate a positivist analysis of legal duty may be, an antipositivist analysis of moral duty is required.

II. BENTHAM ON DUTY

Bentham[4] had many reasons for lavishing special attention upon the philosophical analysis of the concept of duty or obligation. In the first place it is a salient concept in the descriptive language of legal theorists, designating a central feature of any legal system we can conceive. Secondly, being a substantive, it suggests the existence of some corresponding entity to which it refers. This suggestion is deceptive. A duty, Bentham claimed, is a fiction; it is, strictly speaking, a logical construction. That is, sentences in which the word 'duty' appears, while ostensibly about an objectively existing entity— a duty—are really about something else. Such sentences can be replaced by, or reduced to, logically equivalent sentences in which the word 'duty' does not appear. By applying a method of reductive analysis to the concept of duty a general method of reductive elimination of fictions can be exemplified. Thirdly, the concept of duty was frequently used by Bentham as a striking test case for his idiosyncratic and novel theory of definition. In Bentham's opinion *summa genera* and certain logical and grammatical connectives cannot be defined by *genus* and *differentia*. An alternative method is definition by

---

[4] In the following discussion Bentham's works are referred to as follows:

L.G.—*Of Laws in General. P.M.L.*—*An Introduction to the Principles of Morals and Legislation.* The editions employed are those of the *Collected Works of Jeremy Bentham* (University of London, Athlone Press 1970). *F.G.*—*Fragment on Government* in the Blackwell edition edited by Wilfred Harrison (Blackwell, Oxford, 1960).

Works—*Jeremy Bentham's Works* edited by Bowring (Tait, Edinburgh, 1843). *C.C.*— *A Comment on the Commentaries* edited by C. W. Everett (Clarendon Press, Oxford, 1928).

paraphrasis. Here we take a sentence or a sentential formula containing the word to be defined and substitute a logically equivalent sentence or sentential formula in which it does not appear. Paraphrastic definition, in Bentham's view, is not merely a novel and useful method of definition, but fulfils an important role in ontology, for it is uniquely suited for defining logical fictions, and peculiarly useful in reductive analysis. Fourthly, the concept of duty provided an impressive example of the subsidiary definitional process of archetypation. According to Bentham many terms, especially philosophically problematic ones have images or pictures etymologically built into them. These, if properly interpreted, can provide a clue to the the correct analysis of the terms in question. His favourite example for demonstrating the process of archetypation was the concept of obligation. Finally, Bentham's way of 'fixing' i.e. explicating, the concept of duty deliberately rendered the explicatum a peculiarly useful conceptual tool for a utilitarian censorial jurisprudence by reference to which we may 'rear the fabric of felicity by the hands of reason and of law'.

In the course of his voluminous writings Bentham delineates more than one analysis of duty and obligation. These are often divergent and occasionally incompatible. The most notorious is his predictive, probabilistic, sanction analysis. It is this which is most closely integrated with his theory of definition. One may distinguish the pure form of the predictive theory from its impure form. In the latter version it is combined ingeniously with Bentham's imperatival analysis of duty, a version hardly less notorious than the predictive theory.

The pure predictive theory is succinctly stated in Bentham's 'Logic'.[5]

An obligation (viz. the obligation of conducting himself in a certain manner) is incumbent upon a man (i.e. is spoken of as incumbent on a man) in so far as, in the event of his failing to conduct himself in that manner, pain, or loss of pleasure, is considered as about to be experienced by him.

The pain or loss of pleasure which results from the non-performance of the obligatory act is called a sanction. Bentham defines a sanction as a source of obligatory powers or motives,

---

[5] *Works*, Vol. VIII, p. 247; cf. 'Essay on Ontology', *Works*, Vol. VIII, p. 206.

that is pains or pleasures which operate, indeed are the only things which can operate, as motives for action.[6] A pleasure or pain consequent upon an act or omission which suffices to give 'binding force' to a law or any other rule of conduct qualifies as a sanction. Remunerative sanctions, that is rewards, do not suffice to generate obligations.[7] The above definition of obligation is a paraphrastic definition of the generic notion. The various species of duty or obligation so conceived are distinguished according to the agency constituting the source of the probable sanction. In the *Fragment on Government*[8] Bentham distinguishes three kinds of duty. Legal or political duty involves the application of a sanction by an assignable legal official. A religious duty is created by punishment expected from God, moral duty is created by the application of indeterminate sanctions from unassignable members of the public at large. Elsewhere[9] Bentham distinguishes a fourth kind of duty which he calls 'natural'. Here the agency is non-human nature, the sanctions being those pains likely to result from imprudent disregard of the likely causal consequences of naturally dangerous acts, for example walking along precipices, or on thin ice etc. Thus for any sentence in which the word 'duty' appears a logically equivalent sentence in which it does not appear may be substituted. Instead of '*A* has a moral duty to aid his brother' we may substitute 'In the event of *A* not aiding his brother he is likely to suffer indeterminate sanctions of opinion from unassignable members of the public'. The paraphrastic definition provides a method of translation and of reductive elimination of fictitious entities.

The generic concept of obligation has embedded within it two illuminating archetypes. We speak of being 'under an obligation' or of an obligation being 'incumbent upon us' and of duty being 'burdensome'. Here the emblematic image involved is that of a weight pressing upon us, necessitating us to act or refrain from acting in a certain way. Alternatively we speak of being 'duty-bound' or of the 'binding force' of obligations, of being obligated, and so bound to a course of conduct or person. The archetype here, clearly of etymological

[6] *P.M.L.*, p. 34.
[7] *L.G.*, pp. 289 f., although compare *L.G.*, p. 136 and note f.
[8] *F.G.*, p. 107 n.   [9] *P.M.L.*, pp. 35 f.

origin, is of a cord or rope tying us to a person or binding us to a course of action. Bentham interprets both archetypes as indicating the motivational necessitation of the probable sanction which, analytically, renders an action obligatory. It should be stressed, however, that the definition of duty which Bentham suggests is not a psychological one. It specifies nothing about the motives for which men *actually* fulfil their obligations. He does, misguidedly I believe, think that the *effectiveness* of obligations is wholly dependent upon men *having* as their reason for fulfilling their obligation the fact that they will probably suffer pain if they fail to do the act in question,[10] i.e. consciousness of the probable sanction is the standard motive for compliance with duty and hence a condition of its efficacy. But it is not a necessary condition for an act being a duty. Bentham's contention is that an act constitutes a duty because there *is* a certain forward-looking reason for performing it, namely the likelihood of sanction, whether anyone *has* this reason or whether anyone acts *for* this reason, is irrelevant.

We shall see later that in fairness to Bentham important qualifications must be introduced into this account of his sanction theory of duty which will serve, if not to deflect some of the standard criticisms, at any rate to soften the blows. Nevertheless this is the standard interpretation of his pure predictive theory and it is certainly not groundless. The theory is a 'naturalistic' one. It detaches the concept of duty from the notion of normativity. It is a social-fact theory, predictive and probabilistic. To assert a point of conduct to be a duty is to predict the conditional likelihood of a future sanction. The pure theory, narrowly interpreted as above, had a deep impact upon subsequent legal and moral philosophy. In an interestingly transmuted form it is one of the more popular currently debated analyses of duty. Before turning to its evaluation and elaborating Bentham's qualifications of it, it is necessary to give a brief outline of his pure imperative theory of duty.

In the *Fragment on Government* Bentham declares:[11] 'An act which is the object of a command, actual or fictitious; such an act, considered before it is performed, is styled a duty or a

[10] See footnote to the above definition of duty in his 'Logic', *Works*, Vol. VIII, p. 247 n.
[11] *F.G.*, p. 29.

point of duty.' Here the requirement to do the duty is explained, quite independently of the concept of sanction, by reference to the fact that the duty act is the object of a command. This analysis is reiterated in *Of Laws in General*:[12] 'Every legal command imposes a duty' and 'A law commanding or forbidding an act thereby creates a duty or obligation.' A similar analysis is to be found in 'View of a Complete Code of Laws':[13] 'To be subject to a certain obligation is to be the individual or other of those whom the law directs to perform a certain act' and 'To direct men to abstain from all acts which may disturb the enjoyment of others is to impose an obligation on them . . .'[14] In the *Principles of Morals and Legislation*[15] Bentham remarks that a law which commands or prohibits acts imposes duties. The matter becomes clearer, however, when, on the following page, Bentham clarifies his conception of legal obligations in particular by combining the pure imperative theory of the *Fragment on Government* with an imperative sanction theory:[16] 'What is it that constitutes a legal obligation in any case? A command, express or virtual, together with punishment appointed for breach of it.'

In 'Pannomial Fragments'[17] on the other hand, the pure imperative analysis and the predictive sanction analysis are combined in a definition which Austin clearly borrowed:

Obligation has place when the desire on the part of the superior, the obliger, being signified to the obligee, he understands at the same time that in the event of his failing to comply with such desire, evil will befall him, and that to an amount greater than that of any evil which he could sustain in compliance with that desire.

It should be noted that here consciousness of the likely sanction is specified as a necessary condition of an act being a duty.

How should one explain the coexistence of these distinct analyses and the varying combinations of imperative and predictive elements in Bentham's theory? The following conjecture may provide an analytic explanation, whether it is biographically correct or not. If one adopts an imperative theory of law rather than a normative one, as Bentham did, and

---

[12] *L.G.*, p. 58 and Appendix C, p. 293.
[13] *Works*, Vol. VIII, p. 181.   [14] Ibid., p. 159.
[15] *P.M.L.*, p. 206 n. (continuation of note e.2 from p. 205).
[16] Ibid., p. 207 f.2.   [17] *Works*, Vol. III, p. 217.

if one desires to propound a general theory of duty in which legal duty is viewed as a species of a wider genus, one is bound to find one's theory under strain. The imperatival features which appear to characterize law are wholly missing from morality (unless conceived as commands of the Deity) and while legal duties appear to be the product of the will of the legislator, moral duties cannot be so accounted for. However, a common feature does appear in respect of the consequences of not performing a duty. The legislator's volition trusts for its accomplishment 'to the expectation of certain events which it is intended such declaration should upon occasion be a means of bringing to pass',[18] and non-performance of moral duty can likewise be expected to result in certain unpleasant 'events' which have motivating force. Hence it is reasonable in one's general account of duty to seize upon this common feature of the probable outcome of non-performance of a duty act. But it is likely to prove irresistible to fill out this thin account of duty in general with a substantial addition of imperative theory when one deals with legal duty in particular. To be sure Bentham's analysis of legal duty is much more sophisticated than his general account would lead one to expect or indeed could warrant. Moreover not only is it often an impure predictive theory, having an imperatival admixture, it is often, as we have seen above, not even a predictive account at all. We shall return to this point below.

Before elaborating the defects of Bentham's sanction theory it is worth dwelling briefly upon its merits. The analysis has five central advantages. Firstly, it demystifies the notion of duty and stands opposed to any intuitionist or emotivist analysis. The existence of duties involves no mysterious transcendent realities, nor does the concept of duty allude to any psychological facts, cognitive or affective. The concept of duty is not logically tied to conscience or to a special moral sense, nor to feelings, attitudes, and emotions. The demystification is certainly desirable, although it is not obvious that this is the only way of achieving it. As we shall see below the severing of any conceptual nexus with conscience was subsequently to become a point of contention. The concept of duty is explained in terms of social (and other) *facts*. Secondly, Bentham provides

[18] *L.G.*, p. 1.

us with a perfectly *general* analysis of duty into which the various social types of duty, for example legal, moral, religious, etc., can, without undue strain, be systematically and uniformally explicated. It is a desideratum of an account of the concept of duty that the varieties of duty be generically related. However, it should also be borne in mind that there is no *a priori* reason for thinking that our concepts are so systematic. Analogical extension plays a central role in the evolution of language, and the price to be paid for a systematic generic explication may be excessive in terms of other criteria of adequacy for explications. Thirdly, Bentham identifies an important connection between duty and sanctions. Whether the sanctions he specifies are the right sort has been questioned. Is there an additional 'sanction of conscience' and is it not at the heart of our concept of duty? Is the nexus predictive and probabilistic at all? Indeed are Bentham and other philosophers who have rendered an analysis of duty and obligation in terms of a sanction right in thinking the nexus to be analytic at all? These questions will be examined below, but be the answers what they may it seems indisputable that there is a connection between duties and sanctions. Fourthly, Bentham's analysis of duty provides a basis for a fruitful analysis of other fundamental legal concepts such as powers, rights, liberties, liabilities, etc. This important feature is especially prominent when Bentham modifies his pure predictive theory by combining it with his imperative theory of law. The general theory of duty Bentham elaborates involves no reference to laws, either legal, moral, or religious, or to rules or norms. But his discussion of legal obligation frequently generates a concept of obligation which brings together elements of his imperative theory of law with a sanction theory of duty. Thus in the *Fragment* he writes:[19]

That may be said to be my duty to do (understand political duty) which you (or some other person or persons) have a right to have me made to do. I then have a duty towards you, you have a right against me.

What you have a right to have me made to do (understand a political right) is that which I am liable according to law, upon a requisition made on your behalf to be punished for not doing.

[19] *F.G.*, p. 106 n.

I say punished: for without the notion of punishment (that is of pain annexed to an act, and accruing on a certain account, and from a certain source) no notion can we have of either right or duty.

Here we have a sanction theory of duty put to revealing use in rendering an analysis of rights as a 'secondary fictitious entity'. It is interesting to note in passing that though Bentham's beneficiary theory of rights has acquired a certain notoriety, his 'choice' theory,[20] clearly specified here, has gone almost unnoticed. Bentham's sophisticated analyses of legal modalities stem from his grasp of the central position which the concept of duty occupies in this complex network of concepts. Related to this point is the fifth and final one worth emphasizing. This is Bentham's clear realization that legal fictions, as he called them, are merely reflections of the language we employ to describe the law and its operations, to classify aspects of legal situations and relations. He writes thus:[21] 'The affair of its being prescribed a duty and created an offence is only the language we use in speaking of what the law has done. They are different turns of expression of our own concerning what the law has done. . . .'

III. CRITICISMS OF BENTHAM'S THEORY

The most common criticism directed at Bentham's pure predictive sanction theory is to be found in Sidgwick;[22] in recent years it has been revived and extensively elaborated by H. L. A. Hart.[23] The likelihood of suffering a sanction is not a sufficient condition of an act being a duty. Moreover it is not even a necessary condition. Thirdly, as Sidgwick points out in a fashion similar to Moore's subsequent techniques, we can conjoin a statement of the likelihood of sanctions for non-performance with a statement that the act in question is obligatory, without any sense of redundancy or tautologousness.

---

[20] See H. L. A. Hart, 'Bentham on Legal Rights', below, p. 171.

[21] *C.C.*, pp. 97–8; cf. 'View of a Complete Code of Laws', *Works*, Vol. III, p. 159.

[22] H. Sidgwick, *Methods of Ethics*, Bk. I, ch. III (7th edition, 1907). On page 29 Sidgwick, while producing these forceful criticisms of Bentham's predictive theory of moral duty, mistakenly accepts the predictive theory of legal duty.

[23] H. L. A. Hart, *The Concept of Law* (1961), pp. 10–11, 81–8, and 'Il concetto di obbligo', (1966) 57 *Rivista di filosofia*, 125–40. It should be stressed that Hart's criticisms are directed at Bentham's pure predictive theory only (see 'Il concetto di obbligo', p. 133, note d).

Thus far Bentham's explication diverges profoundly from our ordinary concept. The error is to conceive of the concept as either predictive or probabilistic. To assert a point of conduct to be a duty is neither to assert that anything will certainly occur nor that it will probably occur. The nexus between duty and sanction is not predictive at all. Dereliction of duty, Hart points out, is a *reason* for suffering a sanction. It is true that sanctions for non-performance of a duty act are often predictable. But this is not a consequence of an analytic connection between non-performance and the probability of a sanction. It is a derivative consequence of the fact that failure to perform a duty is considered a ground or reason for applying a sanction. This connection between omission and sanction is analytic.

Was Bentham's theory as simple-minded as this powerful criticism suggests? It may be admitted that in some statements of the general pure predictive sanction theory Bentham's position is indefensible. But a closer examination of Bentham's numerous remarks on the subject reveal greater sensitivity to the issues involved.

The first point to examine is Bentham's elaborate discussion of sanctions. When explaining the legal or political sanction the existence of which creates a legal duty Bentham provides the following definition:

If at the hands of a particular person or set of persons in the community who under names correspondent to that of judge are *chosen for the particular purpose of dispensing it, according to the will of the sovereign* or supreme ruling power in the state it may be said to issue from the political sanction.[24]

Here it is quite clearly specified that the political sanction does not arbitrarily result from non-performance of a duty, but is applied according to the will of the sovereign. On the following page Bentham adds that the punishment that constitutes the political sanction happens to one by the *sentence* of the political magistrate. This suggests that Bentham is by no means oblivious to an extra-predictive nexus between non-performance of duty and sanction. The suggestion is reinforced by his subsequent remarks on the moral and religious sanction. A punishment of the religious sanction, he writes, is 'manifested *on account of*

[24] *P.M.L.*, p. 34, my italics.

some sin committed'. A punishment of the moral sanction is *occasioned* by the misconduct of the sufferer, it is done *out of* some dislike to his moral character. In all these cases it appears that Bentham views the consequential sanction as having the past misconduct as its ground or reason.

Is this conception of sanction integrated into the analysis of duty? Clearly not always. But when one examines Bentham's analyses of legal duty in particular, especially when the imperatival theory is being conjoined with the sanction (and allegedly predictive) theory, it is clear that the traditional strictures no longer apply. In the *Fragment* Bentham writes 'That is my duty to do which I am *liable* to be punished *according to law* if I do not do.'[25] In the *Principles* he writes 'What is it that constitutes a legal obligation in any case? A command, express or virtual, together with punishment appointed *for breach of it*,'[26] In Appendix A to *Of Laws in General* he writes 'Whatever business the law may be conversant about, may be reduced to one sort of operation, viz. that of creating duties. To make duties, in the first place it must define them: in the next place it must mark out the punishments to be inflicted for breach of them.'[27] To this passage Bentham appends a note as follows: 'When the law gives you a right, what does it do? it makes me liable to punishment in case of my doing any of those acts which would have the effect of disturbing you in the exercise of that right.' Though the analysis of rights here is neither correct nor representative of Bentham's more common view, it is clear that the term 'liable' is not to be interpreted predictively but as meaning 'legally liable'. This is clear too from the preceding quotations.

Of course it should not be surprising to discover that Bentham frequently stresses the liability to suffer a sanction for breach of duty and disregards the secondary and dependent feature of its predictability. For he conceives of law as a social technique for the control of human behaviour by means of a standard motivation. The standard of behaviour is established by the declaration of the volition of the sovereign and the standard motivation created by annexing a subsidiary law, a further command, requiring the application of sanctions for non-

---

[25] *F.G.*, p. 107, my italics; cf. *F.G.*, p. 106 n.
[26] *P.M.L.*, p. 207 f.2, my italics.   [27] *L.G.*, p. 249.

compliance with the primary law. It should be equally obvious that this dual imperative theory of duty cannot readily be carried through for the analysis of non-legal duty.

The standard criticism attacks Bentham's pure predictive account of duty because it allegedly misidentifies the nexus between duty and sanction. A deeper criticism, less easily deflected, attacks the theory not on the grounds of being predictive but on more general grounds. For what is less commonly noted is that Bentham's predictive sanction theory detaches the notion of duty from the notion of a course of action which ought to be followed. Acts which ought to be done are, according to Bentham, those acts which conform to the principle of utility, i.e. acts the tendency of which is to augment the happiness of the community. Only thus can 'ought' be given a meaning.[28] Duties, on the other hand, are acts the non-performance of which is likely to incur a sanction. Thus any coincidence of duties and acts that ought to be done is purely contingent. That something is a duty does not entail that it ought to be done, nor even that it ought prima facie to be done. To be sure, in an ideal, utilitarian, world the two will, up to a point, coincide, not by necessity, but by wise utilitarian legislation and enlightened public opinion. But what one ought to do and what is one's legal or moral duty to do are two quite distinct matters. Thus the legislators ought to legislate for the benefit of the community, but they have no legal duty to do so,[29] and, unless public opinion is utilitarian-minded, no moral duty to do so either.

Yet we do intuitively conceive of some logical link between duty and what one ought to do. If an act is a moral duty, then it seems, there is a moral reason or justification of a certain kind for doing it, and hence one ought, prima facie, to do it. Equally if an act is a legal duty then it is conceived of as an act for the performance of which a specific kind of legal justification can be adduced. As a result of his narrow conception of rationality,[30] his unduly restrictive conception of

---

[28] *P.M.L.*, p. 13. It should be stressed that there are other, subjectivist, analyses of 'ought' in Bentham's writings.

[29] *F.G.*, p. 107 n.

[30] See H. L. A. Hart, 'Bentham', (1962) 48, *Proceedings of the British Academy*, 316 ff.

what can constitute a reason or ground of action, and his monistic theory of justifying principles, Bentham never contemplated an important alternative to his analysis. This is the suggestion that the concept of duty in general be analysed in terms of an act supported by a justification of a specific kind. Accordingly duty, justification or reason, and what ought to be done are logically linked. Such an account of duty would treat the duty-sanction nexus as secondary and consequential. It is because a duty is an act supported by justifications of a peculiarly pressing kind that we take performance of the duty to be so important, and take violation of the duty as a ground for sanction. The sanction is a subsidiary, not a primary, feature.

Although Bentham denied any analytic connection between 'duty' and 'ought', it is interesting that he himself occasionally slips into this way of talking in spite of its being wholly inconsistent with his theory. In an autobiographical remark in the *Fragment*[31] he says: 'I learnt to see that utility was the test and measure of all virtue; of loyalty as much as any; and that the obligation to minister to general happiness was an obligation paramount to and inclusive of every other.' But the principle of utility tells us what we *ought* to do, not what we are likely to be censured for not doing; nor is it clear that it dictates that we ought always to be censured for not maximizing general utility. A similar backsliding occurs in Bentham's *Principles of the Civil Code*[32] in discussing need as a reason for action: 'The good Samaritan by relieving the wounded traveller saved his life. It was a noble action, a virtuous deed— nay, a moral duty.' But the pure predictive theory of duty clearly does not warrant such a use of 'moral duty'. Bentham's theory stands accused of two defects. It detaches 'duty' from 'ought' and it treats what is secondary as primary. We shall revert to these points subsequently.

So much for quite general criticisms of Bentham's account. Two brief points are worth making about the relation of the analysis to the sophisticated theory of definition. Firstly, though paraphrastic definition is useful and illuminating it is not obviously necessary. Bentham's pure predictive theory can be

[31] *F.G.*, p. 51.
[32] 'Principles of the Civil Code', in *The Theory of Legislation*, ed. C. K. Ogden (1931), p. 190.

phrased in a traditional definition thus: a duty is a kind of act non-performance of instances of which is likely to incur a sanction. Secondly, though the operation of archetypation is both interesting and valuable, it is not obvious that Bentham interprets the archetypes correctly. Clearly the pressing weight and binding cord are emblematic representations of necessitation. Bentham conceives the practical necessitation, the 'binding force', of duty to lie in sanctions. The justificative analysis previously hinted at would argue that this is a misconception of practical necessitation. Duty necessitates because of the pressing reasons for doing the duty act, independently of the sanction. In passing it is worth remarking that Bentham, rather surprisingly, fails to connect the binding-cord archetype of obligation with the archetype of a right. In giving the archetype of a right he stresses the notion of investiture[33] which is, perhaps, appropriate to his beneficiary or beneficiendary theory of rights. But the choice theory, above mentioned, can be attractively illuminated if the archetype of a right is conceived as 'a portion of matter', as he puts it, which is the loose end of the binding rope of obligation. Having a right, transferring a right, relinquishing a right, *releasing* a person from his obligation to one, etc. can readily be conceived as holding the ropes of practical necessitation and so possessing limited sovereignty over the person obligated.[34]

Finally a few comments on the specific accounts of duty. The concept of a natural duty is misguided. Bentham sees that elementary natural necessities provide a foundation for practical necessitations that are the subject of prudential reasoning. Given the desire to avoid falling then the fact that ice is slippery is a reason for walking carefully. If one does not walk carefully one is likely to fall and get hurt. Duty designates a normative necessitation and while the notion of a compelling reason for action is a connecting link between duty and practical necessitation, it is false that a prudential reason for acting which rests on the fact that non-performance of the act in question is likely to have untoward consequences makes the act a duty in any sense. Nor is the predictable unpleasantness rightly called 'a sanction' in the ordinary sense of this term, although Bentham

[33] *Works*, Vol. III, p. 217.
[34] See H. L. A. Hart, *The Concept of Law*, p. 85.

is right in suggesting that it has obliging (but not obligating) force. It is not intentionally applied by an agent on the grounds of non-performance of a required act.

The positivist concept of moral duty which Bentham elaborates may be well suited for anthropological and sociological purposes, but it is ill suited for moralists and moral philosophers. Rendering an analysis in terms of pressures of public opinion does not enable one to distinguish *mores* from morals, nor to assert without contradiction that although no evil consequences will be visited upon you for not doing so and so, nevertheless it is your duty. Bentham's concept of moral duty is analytically tied to social facts, namely affective and reactive behavioural responses to conduct. It is detached from any notion of a moral reason (of a certain kind), and so *a fortiori* from rational morality.

The pure predictive theory of legal duty is open to all the general objections already discussed. Substitution of an imperative sanction theory for a predictive sanction theory may avoid some of the defects of the predictive theory. Addition of an imperative analysis of a duty-imposing law doubtless avoids other difficulties. Though such an imperative theory is, for well-known reasons, unsatisfactory, it is arguably nearer the truth concerning the analysis of duty than any pure sanction theory. For it rightly associates the concept of a legal duty with the idea of a standard of conduct established by the legislator. The stress here is upon the requirement of conformity to a legally established standard rather than upon the legal consequences, whether predictable or commanded, of non-conformity to that standard.

IV. J. S. MILL'S ACCOUNT[35]

One of the main points upon which Mill recurrently criticized Bentham is the deficiency of his psychological theories. In his harsh, anonymously published paper 'Remarks on Bentham's Philosophy' he wrote:

As an analyst of human nature (the faculty in which above all it is necessary that an ethical philosopher should excel) I cannot rank

[35] References to Mill's ethical writings are abbreviated as follows:

R.B.P.—'Remarks on Bentham's Philosophy', B.—Bentham, *U.—Utilitarianism*. The edition employed is Volume X of *Collected Works of John Stuart Mill: Essays on Ethics, Religion and Society* (University of Toronto Press, 1969).

Mr. Bentham very high. He has done little in this department, beyond introducing what appears to me a very deceptive phraseology and furnishing a catalogue of the 'springs of action' from which some of the most important are left out.[36]

Purporting to describe the nature of man, Bentham has omitted all that makes us distinctively moral creatures. Although sympathy is included in his list of motives, Mill admits, the most significant ethical motives and emotions are neglected. An analyst of human nature who disregards conscience, the feeling of duty, the love of justice, the moral sense, who obscures the essential human capacity to do an act merely because it is right, has failed in his task.

Mill returns to the same theme five years later in his essay 'Bentham' written in 1838. Bentham's psychology, in particular his endeavour to explain all human conduct by reference to interest is condemned on the same grounds as before:

Man is never recognized by him [Bentham] as a being capable of pursuing spiritual perfection as an end; of desiring, for its own sake, the conformity of his own character to his standard of excellence, without hope of good or fear of evil from other source than his own inward consciousness. Even in the more limited form of conscience, this great fact in human nature escapes him. Nothing is more curious than the absence of recognition in any of his writings of the existence of conscience, as a thing distinct from philanthropy, from affection for God or man, and from self-interest in this world or the next.[37]

Given this persistent preoccupation it is interesting to note how the theme of conscience and its role in moral psychology reappear in *Utilitarianism*. The third chapter, entitled 'Of the Ultimate Sanction of the Principle of Utility', begins by posing a series of related questions. Regarding any moral standard we may ask—What is its sanction? What are the motives to obey it? More specifically, Mill continues, we may query—What is the source of its obligation? Whence does it derive its binding force? In the course of his complex reply to these questions, which he mistakenly takes to be identical, Mill argues that the sanctions of any morality, and so of the utilitarian morality too, are either external or internal. The external sanctions of morality are the Benthamite ones—the hope of favour and fear

[36] R.B.P., p. 12.   [37] B., p. 95.

of displeasure from our fellow creatures or from God; these are the external motives for observance of moral standards. But an account which mentions only these misses the most significant sanction, namely conscience—the internal sanction of duty:

The internal sanction of duty, whatever our standard of duty may be, is one and the same—a feeling in our own mind; a pain, more or less intense, attendant on violation of duty, which in properly cultivated moral natures rises, in the more serious cases, into shrinking from it as an impossibility. This feeling when disinterested, and connecting itself with the pure idea of duty, . . . is the essence of Conscience;[38]

The binding force of the idea of moral obligation, Mill continues,

consists in the existence of a mass of feeling which must be broken through in order to do what violates our standard of right, and which, if we do nevertheless violate that standard, will probably have to be encountered afterwards in the form of remorse. Whatever theory we have of the nature or origin of conscience, this is what essentially constitutes it.

The ultimate sanction of all morality, Mill concludes, is a subjective feeling in our minds.

On a superficial reading it may appear that Mill is trying to bolster up Bentham's predictive sanction theory of duty by the addition of the internal sanction of conscience. It may seem that Mill's recurrent criticism of Bentham's psychology comes to a head in the claims that Bentham lacked an adequate account of the sense of duty and that his account of the meaning of duty is defective for precisely this reason. Thus Mill has been interpreted as merely adding 'the "internal sanction" of conscience to Bentham's list of the sanctions which are "constitutive" of obligations'.[39] A proper account of conscience in terms of a 'subjective feeling in our minds', Mill is thus thought

---

[38] *U.*, p. 228.
[39] H. L. A. Hart, 'Bentham', loc. cit., p. 320; Alan Ryan, in *The Philosophy of John Stuart Mill* (1970), p. 209, argues, as Hart does, that Mill's theory of the sanction of conscience attempts to provide an analysis of 'duty'. Unlike Hart, Ryan does not see it as part of a predictive theory: 'He tends to analyse the notion of obligation as equivalent to feelings of discomfort at the thought of not doing an action. Thus "I am obliged to do X" is analysed as "the thought of not doing X causes me pain".'

to argue, will produce a satisfactory predictive sanction theory of duty. Duty is then analysed as an act the non-performance of which is likely to result in an internal sanction. It is, of course, unclear whether the idea of an internal sanction is conceived of as an element in the concept of any social type of duty, or only in that of moral duty.

Three questions arise: Is Mill's criticism of Bentham justified? Is Mill, in the course of his discussion of the ultimate sanction of utility, modifying Bentham's definition of duty or does he have some other target? Is Mill's account of the 'sanction of conscience' acceptable?

It is worth noting that Mill's most common accusations against Bentham on the score of conscience and the moral sense are not so much of conceptual error as of omission of fact. Bentham has left out of his account an important fact about human nature: 'The feeling of moral approbation or disapprobation properly so-called either towards ourselves or our fellow creatures, he seems unaware of the existence of.'[40] Consequently he fails to realize man's capacity for disinterested pursuit of spiritual perfection, 'without hope of good or fear of evil from other source than his own inward consciousness'. To this there are two replies. Firstly, in so far as one retains the utilitarian axiology then the fact that spiritual perfection is conceived of as an end of action can be readily accounted for as long as 'spiritual perfection' is interpreted in hedonic terms. What justifies its pursuit, the reasons for which men ought to aim at it, are the certain, pure, fecund pleasures which it affords. It is interesting to note that Mill believes that it is necessary to supplement the account of the justification for the pursuit of such ends (which he renders in eudaimonic rather than hedonic terms) by an account of motives, namely the hope of good or fear of evil from one's own inward conscience. The fact that Mill, like Bentham, takes for granted such a gap between justification and motivation is extremely important to the understanding of his views. Secondly, though Bentham's account of conscience is unquestionably defective, Mill was wrong to think that he never provided one. In the *Comment on the Commentaries*, which Mill probably never saw, Bentham briefly examines the notion of conscience in the course of a

[40] Mill, B., p. 95.

criticism of Blackstone.[41] Blackstone's notion of an obligation *in foro conscientiae*, Bentham argues, can either be accounted for in terms of the three external sanctions of obligation, or it is nonsense. For there is no other source of motives constitutive of obligations than the legal, moral, and religious sanctions. The will is governed by two motives, the idea of pain and the idea of pleasure. If one wishes to use the term conscience to speak of the faculty of the will in so far as it is determined by the prospect of pain derived from an invisible, divine source, one may do so. It is harmless as long as it is not conceived of as a novel source of obligation.

Would this account satisfy Mill? Clearly not. Bentham's theory of motivation, like his general theory of justification, is consequentialist. Sanctions, whether remunerative or punitive, are the sole source of motives, and they are necessarily prospective. In the 'Remarks on Bentham's Philosophy' Mill objects to this consequentialist account of motives.[42] To be sure pleasure and pain determine all our actions, Mill admits, but it is not only future pleasures and pains that do so, but also present ones which precede the contemplated act. If a man refrains from committing an offence out of fear of a likely social sanction, or even out of a desire to avoid the remorse he is likely to feel, he is not truly virtuous. The virtuous man recoils from the very thought of committing the act; the pain of contemplating himself as performing such an act determines his will and motivates his self-restraint. Such conduct is not determined by a deliberate conscious aim, but, Mill suggests, by an impulse or feeling which has no ulterior end. The virtuous act or forbearance thus becomes an end in itself.

Mill's riposte however seems to be directed at Bentham's theory of motivation rather than at his theory of value. We are not *moved* to action solely by prospective pains and pleasures, and in the case of acts done for their own sake, in particular virtuous acts, we are moved by our conscience, that 'mass of feeling' which is the product of socialization[43] and which can be utilized by the utilitarian pedagogue as much as by an intuitionist. Mill's criticism of Bentham in the matter of

---

[41] *C.C.*, pp. 55 and 95.   [42] R.B.P., p. 13.

[43] Mill's account of the phenomenology of conscience, as well as his theory of duty, is derived from Bain's *The Emotions and the Will* (1859).

conscience is not concerned with his theory of duty, nor indeed with his theory of justification, but with his moral psychology. Bentham, in Mill's opinion, cannot give an adequate account of acts done for their own sake, and hence fails to account for non-hedonic ends in themselves. This suspicion is confirmed in his essay on Bentham. For here again[44] he accuses Bentham of failing to recognize the possibility of pursuing any ideal end for its own sake, whether it be moral desire for perfection, or the quasi-aesthetic ideals of honour and dignity. Morality consists of two parts, Mill declares, an external and an internal part, social control and the training of the will and affections. Bentham's philosophy is concerned only with the former. But to omit the latter is to distort morality and to misconceive moral agency. The role of chapter III of *Utilitarianism* is to show that the classical theory of *motives* is incomplete, and must be supplemented by the addition of the sanction of conscience. It is thus not coincidental that in chapter IV Mill goes to great lengths to show that utilitarianism *properly interpreted* encompasses within the end of happiness (which is held to be the goal of all action) all goals pursued for their own sake. Mill's analytic account of the concept of duty appears only in chapter V of the book.

Before turning to that account some critical remarks on Mill's doctrine are in order. In the first place conscience cannot be conceived as a source of sanctions *stricto sensu*. A sanction is intentionally applied on the grounds of omission of a required act, in some cases with the intention of intimating a reason for future performance of such required acts. Conscience is conceived to operate in two ways, pangs of remorse subsequent to an offence, and powerful feelings of repulsion prior to a projected offence. In neither form is any suffering intentionally inflicted. In the latter case the unpleasant feelings of repulsion precede the act and do not have as their rationale the past commission of the offence. In the former case the remorse is felt on the grounds of having done an evil. Though not intentional, can prospective remorse provide a reason? Only in a secondary and derivative way. For if remorse is to be intelligible it necessarily involves the idea of violation of an accepted standard of conduct. Hence a primary reason for compliance is

[44] B., pp. 95 f.

necessarily the standard of conduct thus accepted and ultimately whatever reasons justify the standard. Prospective remorse could only constitute a sanction in a loose sense in those abnormal cases in which a conditioned remorseful response remains despite conscious and convinced renunciation of the previously accepted standard. Similar considerations apply to conscience when conceived of as involved feelings of repulsion at the thought of sinning. Although these powerful feelings may indeed play a causal role in one's self-restraint, they are essentially intensional, having as their intensional object the prospective offence. They cannot be conceived of as a sanction. They can be thought of as motives only if one employs, as Mill does, a misguided mechanical model of motivation.[45] But both these explanatory routes are redundant, for such feelings of conscience already involve a necessary reference to a reason for self-restraint, namely the thought of the prospective act as wicked.

Mill's difficulties arise because, *inter alia*, he adopts a so-called externalist[46] conception of the relation between obligation and motivation, assuming that there exists a gap between moral justification and motivation which needs to be filled in by a theory of sanctions. Hence he assumes that the question, regarding any moral standard, What is the source of its obligation? is identical both with What are the motives to obey it? and What is its sanction? This question, Mill argues, arises whenever one is called upon to adopt any moral standard. What he fails to realize, because of his externalist doctrine, is that *adopting* a moral standard is itself tantamount to generating such array of complex feelings and responses. They are not reasons for adopting the standard, but logical consequences of so doing. The questions that arise when one is called upon to adopt a standard are Why this standard rather than another? What is its justification? and not What is its sanction?

In chapter V of *Utilitarianism* Mill briefly outlines his own analytic account of duty. His purpose is to identify the domain of justice within the broader range of morality in general. The

45 See Mill, *System of Logic*, Bk. VI, chapter II.
46 See W. D. Falk, '"Ought" and Motivation', *Proceedings of the Aristotelian Society* 48 (1947–8); W. K. Frankena, 'Obligation and Motivation in Recent Moral Philosophy' in A. I. Melden, ed., *Essays in Moral Philosophy* (1958); T. Nagel, *The Possibility of Altruism* (1970), pp. 7–12.

concept of morality he employs is strikingly narrow, for he hives off a large segment of morality, allocating it to aesthetics—conceived unusually widely. The principles of Practical Reason may be distinguished into three groups:[47] prudential, ethical, and aesthetic, concerned respectively with the expedient, the right, and the noble or beautiful. The domain of morality in general is identified with that sphere of action which is right and omission of which is wrong. Such acts are moral acts. These Mill identifies with duty. Morality is essentially the doctrine of duty. He then provides the following analysis:

> We do not call anything wrong, unless we mean to imply that a person ought to be punished in some way or other for doing it; if not by law, by the opinion of his fellow creatures; if not by opinion, by the reproaches of his own conscience. This seems the real turning point between morality and simple expediency. It is part of the notion of duty in every one of its forms, that a person may rightfully be compelled to fulfil it. Duty is a thing which may be *exacted* from a person, as one exacts a debt. Unless we think that it might be exacted from him, we do not call it his duty . . . we call any conduct wrong . . . according as we think that the person ought, or ought not, to be punished for it.[48]

This brief account could readily be expanded. One may conceive of this as a fragmentary analysis of the generic concept of duty. The different social types of duty might then be analysed along Benthamite lines according to the source or sources and determinate or indeterminate nature of the sanction, the reason or ground for which is the non-performance of the duty. It is noteworthy that the notion of conscience is introduced into this analysis, but not as an expedient to avoid a defect in a predictive sanction theory. Rather it is introduced as an element of a theory which conceives of non-performance of a duty act as a ground for a sanction. It would appear, although Mill does not explicitly say so, to be intended as a distinguishing feature of moral duty. We conceive of an act as a moral duty in so far as we think that its omission *ought* to be 'punished' by the opinion of members of society and the reproaches of the agent's conscience.

Mill's fragmentary account (he stresses that he is indicating only part, presumably a necessary condition, of the notion of

[47] *System* of *Logic*, VI. xii. 6.   [48] *U.*, p. 246.

duty), like Bentham's main analysis, is a sanction theory. However it is neither a predictive nor an imperative sanction theory. The duty-sanction nexus is explained in terms of what *ought* to follow the non-performance of a duty, not in terms of what does, or is ordered, to follow. The reason or ground for the sanction is omission of the duty. How does Mill explain the notion of 'ought', or reason? Is non-performance of an act a reason for sanction if, and only if, people actually look upon it in a certain critical light and manifest their critical attitudes in conduct? Or is it rather a reason or ground if, and only if, certain kinds of rational principles justify the critical response? Is Mill's analysis positivist or antipositivist? Mill's position in *Utilitarianism* is not wholly clear. He gives a sociological-cum-genetic analysis of reactive responses which constitute an element of the sense of justice, and then gives a utilitarian account of the moralization of these responses. In *System of Logic*,[49] however, he clarifies his position explicitly. Indicative sentences in which words such as 'ought' appear, differ deeply from those in which only 'is' or 'will be' occur. The difference is not that the former fail, in some sense, to assert something. They affirm, according to Mill, that the act which ought to be done excites the speaker's approbation. But this is peripheral. The speaker's approbation is not a sufficient reason why others should approve, nor indeed is it a conclusive reason for himself. Rather it must be justified by reference to principles which will determine the *proper* objects of approbation. It is the task of the doctrine of Teleology to disclose such principles. The promotion of universal happiness, Mill declares, is the ultimate principle of Teleology.

What of the relation between 'duty' and 'ought', and of the nature of the requirement to do acts which are duties? In the fragmentary account of the concept of duty thus far examined, Mill seems quite oblivious to the important conceptual connection. Nor does he labour to clarify it elsewhere. It is, however, clear from the subsequent discussion of justice that, unlike Bentham, he connects the idea of justice, and so the obligations of justice, very closely to the notion of a rule, and so, in so far as this notion is connected with that of a reason, to the notion

---

[49] *System of Logic* VI. xii. 6 and 7.

of what one ought to do. 'Justice', Mill writes,[50] 'is a name for certain classes of moral rules, which concern the essentials of human well-being more nearly, and are therefore of more absolute obligation, than any other rules for the guidance of life.' It would not be unreasonable to infer from this and other like remarks that Mill did conceive there to be an analytic tie between 'duty', 'rule', and 'ought'. It would also appear that he did not analyse the notion of a duty-imposing rule by reference to social facts, but rather by reference to the requirements of the principle of utility. The introduction of the notion of a duty-imposing rule, and its analysis in terms of justifications for doing acts of the kind required by the rule, was an important modification of sanction theories. Mill, however, never developed the idea, nor sought to explore its ramifications. Nor is it wholly clear whether his antipositivist account of duties of justice is intended as a contribution to the analytic question 'What does "duty" mean?' or to the moral question 'What are our duties?'.

How does Mill put the notion of duty, thus explicated, to work? Morality has been identified with the domain of duty. The sphere of duty is the range of acts the non-performance of which is wrong and which ought to be punished or censured. Justice is concerned with that segment of morality which consists of duties of perfect obligation. These are duties to which there is a correlative right. Duties of imperfect obligation exhaust the remaining part of morality. These are duties which, 'though the act is obligatory, the particular occasions of performing it are left to our choice; as in the case of charity or beneficence, which we are indeed bound to practise, but not towards any definite person, nor at any prescribed time'.[51] The domain of worthiness, or, as Mill calls it in *System of Logic*, 'Aesthetics', is not part of morality. It is concerned with the desirable or laudable, the noble and beautiful. Performing worthy acts, it seems, is praiseworthy, but their omission is not blameworthy. Morality, as Mill conceives it, is concerned with the social minimum, with what may be *demanded* of men.[52]

---

[50] *U.*, p. 255.   [51] *U.*, p. 247.

[52] Cf. 'Thornton on Labour and Its Claims' in *Collected Works of John Stuart Mill*, Vol. V, pp. 650 f.

V. EVALUATION OF MILL'S THEORY

Mill's analysis of the concept of duty involves substantial advances over his predecessors. It has four desirable features. Firstly, in respect of the nexus between duty and sanction, Mill's suggestion comes very close to the truth. The connection between non-performance of duty and sanction is neither predictive nor imperative. It is rather that dereliction of duty is a ground or reason for sanction or censure. Secondly, Mill's undeveloped suggestion that a normative analysis of the requirement that the obligatory act be performed was a promising move. The concept of duty is thereby correctly associated with the notion of standards of conduct, and rightly allocated to the sphere of normative language. Thirdly, Mill's unclear suggestion that the concept of a duty-imposing rule should itself be analysed in terms of certain kinds of justifications or reasons for doing the duty act points beyond a normative analysis to a justificative one. I shall suggest below that this insight is worth developing. Fourthly, Mill's claim that the concept of moral duty is concerned, in some sense, with a social minimum, is, I think, correct.

These gains, however, on one interpretation of Mill's theory, are thrown away by an over-hasty insistence upon a necessary connection between the concept of duty and the principle of utility. This distorts both the analysis of the connection between duty and sanction, and the analysis, whether normative or justificative, of the requirement to perform the relevant act. While it is plausible to think that failure to perform a legal duty is a ground for a legal sanction and not merely a sign of its probability, it is highly implausible to think that only those acts whose non-performance would, *from a utilitarian point of view*, be justified grounds for sanctions are legal duties. *A fortiori* the claim that only legal rules justified by reference to the principle of utility are duty-imposing would be defective. This confuses expository with censorial jurisprudence and renders the important notion of legal duty useless for expository purposes. It would therefore seem *more* plausible to argue that the generic concept of duty is to be partly explicated as an act the non-performance of which is a ground for censure or sanction. Legal duty is then partly explained as an act the non-performance of which constitutes a legal ground for the application, by an appropriate organ, or a legal sanction (or, minimally, of legal, authoritative, censure). Moral duty would analogously be explained as an act the non-performance of which constitutes a moral reason for moral censure. Although this is insufficient, it is a move in the right direction. It needs supplementation by an analysis of the relation between duty and reasons or justifications for action. Moreover, this account of the generic concept fails to distinguish prudence from duty; for imprudent acts, to be sure, provide reasons for censure. Mill's introduction of the substantial element of the importance of acts that are duties to social well-being may serve to distinguish moral duties, according to utilitarian ethics, from mere prudence. But this is of no avail to remedy the weakness in the generic account. The modification provides a false analysis of legal duty. Furthermore it is not obviously correct for an analysis of moral duty unless, as Mill believed, duties of justice (and other moral duties) can be given a utilitarian rationale. If the notion of justification is to enter into the analysis of duty, it must do so in a more complex and flexible way than that suggested by Mill's rather crude theory.

A further point of criticism is that Mill mistakenly equates what one may exact from a person with what one may punish a person for not doing. Moreover he makes far too much of the idea of compulsion, whether by reference to exaction or to punishment. Such a rigorous account will not fit legal duty satisfactorily, and is inappropriate for moral duty (although, to be fair to Mill, he speaks loosely of being 'punished' by 'the opinion of his fellow creatures' or 'the reproaches of his own conscience'). The more flexible notion of censure needs to be invoked.

More specific criticisms than this are, given the incompleteness of Mill's account, pointless. But a few remarks upon his subsequent employment of the notion thus defined may be appropriate. Firstly, Mill's general conception of the domain of morality is unduly narrow. There is more to morals than avoidance of wrong and fulfilment of duty. There is the domain of self-sacrifice and heroism, of supererogation and favour.[53]

[53] See J. Feinberg, 'Supererogation and Rules' in his book *Doing and Deserving, Essays in the Theory of Responsibility* (1970).

There is also, as Mill points out in criticism of Bentham, the cultivation of moral virtues, not all of which are expressed in the fulfilment of duty, e.g. generosity, kindness, compassion, etc. Secondly, as a corollary of the first point, Mill's conception of the aesthetics of action is too wide. No doubt there is such a sphere. The less utilitarian the culture the larger it bulks. Concepts such as honour, dignity, and the like are quasi-aesthetic. But to identify the aesthetics of action with the domain of worthiness, and exclude the latter from the sphere of morality is misguided. Much that is worthy, laudable, and desirable in action, which is nevertheless not mandatory, belongs to morals. Such acts constitute part of the grounds for the assessment of the moral standing of a person, for the description of his virtues, character, and personality. The possession of such virtues as generosity, kindness, and compassion constitutes part of a moral, not aesthetic, ideal of life. Thirdly, Mill's conception of duties of imperfect obligation is defective. For if duty is identified with the contrary of wrong, and wrong conduct is that which ought to be punished, then it is unclear how charity and beneficence can be considered to be duties at all, for there can be, on Mill's account, no *specific occasion* of dereliction of duty which will be a ground for censure or punishment. To be sure one *ought to be* generous and beneficent. But the performance of acts of generosity is good and praiseworthy without their omission being wrong or (normally) censurable. Such acts belong to the domain of worthiness, which is a segment of morality. A corollary of this is that Mill unwittingly identifies justice with almost the whole sphere of duty. This is clearly mistaken. Finally, it is worth pointing out that Mill's sanction theory must be interpreted as having primary application to kinds of acts rather than individual acts, and that the reason for the sanction in the event of nonperformance, is only a prima facie reason. For there are clearly many excuses and indeed justifications for not doing one's duty upon some specific occasions.

VI. HART'S MODIFIED SANCTION THEORY

The most elaborate and sophisticated theory of duty expounded in recent times is Hart's.[54] It is a modified sanction

[54] Hart's most detailed discussion is in *The Concept of Law*. The following sum-

theory, for although duties are essentially and necessarily connected with sanctions, it is also the case that duties are essentially acts the performance of which is required by a social rule. The theory is therefore a normative one. It is also positivist in the sense that it provides a social-fact analysis of duty-imposing rules.

The gist of Hart's theory can be captured by the following schema: A duty is an act the performance of which is required by a social rule of a certain kind, and the non-performance of which is generally held to justify the critical reactions with which it is normally met. The schema must be filled in by specifying the nature of the social rule and the nature of the critical reactions. Hart specified four conditions which must be met by the duty-imposing rule:

1. It must require members of a specified class of persons to do or abstain from a given act upon specified occasions. 2. The rule is thought, by most members of the social group, to be important because it is believed necessary to the maintenance of social life or some valued feature of it. 3. The conduct required by the rule may conflict with the wishes of those subject to it. 4. Compliance with the rule is general. Hart specifies four further conditions which must be met in the event of deviations from the rule: 5. Such deviations are usually met with serious critical reactions, demands for conformity, sanctions etc. The nature of the critical reactions varies from one social type of rule to another. 6. Deviation is generally accepted as a good reason for the ensuing critical reactions. 7. Such critical reactions are themselves regarded as legitimate, i.e. they are not themselves normally met with counter critical reactions. 8. Normative language is extensively used in the expression of such critical responses.[55] Where these eight conditions are satisfied then duties may be said to exist.

I suggested above that Hart's theory is a *modified* sanction theory. The important modification which Hart has introduced relative to the previous two sanction theories is the explicit insistence that duties are imposed by rules, that fulfilment of

---

mary rests exclusively upon the theory propounded in that book. Subsequent references to it are abbreviated to *C.L.*

[55] *C.L.*, p. 56.

duty constitutes compliance with a rule and failure to fulfil one's duty is equivalent to deviation from a rule. Mill hinted at but never developed this important feature. Bentham captured an element of it in his imperative theory of legal duty, but the substitution of a normative account of law instead of an imperative one is clearly a great gain. An equal advantage is gained by the corresponding analysis of moral duty. I shall return to this feature and its important ramifications below. For all that, however, Hart's primary emphasis in his analysis of duty is upon the sanctions for non-performance rather than upon the rule imposing the duty. 'What is important', he writes,[56] 'is that the insistence on importance or seriousness of social pressure behind the rules is the primary factor determining whether they are thought of as giving rise to obligations.' Similarly he emphasizes the employment of normative language in response to deviation from duty rather than in the context of practical reasoning, advice, and exhortation.

Like Mill, Hart conceives the non-performance of duty to be a reason for a sanction. Unlike Mill, however, the account given of this nexus between duty and sanction is in terms of social facts. Deviation normally meets with critical reactions, and these are thought of as justified, i.e. the deviation is considered a sufficient reason for the critical responses, and they are not themselves met with further critical attitudes. This conforms with the general social fact account Hart gives of rules, as well as with his account of duty-imposing rules.

Hart's analysis constitutes a great advance on those of his predecessors. It affords valuable insight into the structure of normative concepts and hence into the nature of the phenomena we describe by this means. The generic account is constructed with the general notion of social standards of conduct in view. With some modifications specific accounts of legal, moral, and other social types of duty are readily generated. Legal duties are imposed by legal rules and their non-performance normally is a condition which provides legal grounds for the application of a legal sanction by a legal organ. Because of the systematic nature of a legal system and the organized application of relatively determinate legal sanctions

[56] *C.L.*, p. 84.

many of the features characteristic of the general concept of obligation must be modified. The rule imposing a duty need not be eminently general[57]—it need not be thought to be important *per se* but only *qua* authoritative law; compliance need not be general, but the law must then be a valid law of a system compliance with most laws of which is general. Some legal duties are not backed up by sanction stipulating laws; nevertheless critical reactions to non-performance of such mandatory legal acts are normally forthcoming from law applying organs, and are normally held to be legitimate.[58] Hart characterizes moral rules of a social group by reference to the eight features[59] specified above in conjunction with the specification of the nature of the social pressure for conformity. Where the social pressure is heavily dependent upon the operation of feelings of shame, remorse, and guilt, Hart remarks 'we may be inclined to classify the rules as part of the morality of the social group and the obligation under the rules as moral obligation.'[60] The ultimate sanction of morality is, it seems, the internal 'sanction' of conscience. For Hart this is an analytic truth. Other social types of duty, e.g. the duties of occupants of certain social roles (e.g. of a host, of a committee chairman), may also be accommodated within this analysis.

Hart's theory is, I think, defective at two points. The first concerns Hart's emphasis upon the stringency of social pressure for conformity to a rule requiring one to do or abstain from some act as determining whether the act in question is rightly thought of as a duty. As I have already indicated, this emphasis seems to me to treat what is of secondary significance as if it were of primary importance. To identify a moral duty by reference to the nature of the critical response assumes that the affective reactions of shame, guilt, and remorse, as opposed to loss of face, embarrassment, and regret, are readily identifiable independently of the prior identification of the offensive act which occasions the reaction as non-performance of a moral

---

[57] For the notion of 'eminently general' norms, see G. H. von Wright, *Norm and Action*, pp. 79 ff.

[58] See J. Raz, *The Concept of a Legal System* (1970), pp. 149–54.

[59] One should point out that eminent generality is not necessary in the case of content-independent moral duties, e.g. duties created by norm-creating acts such as promising.

[60] *C.L.*, p. 84.

duty.[61] It assumes that the identification of other-regarding criticisms as reflecting upon one's moral standing and character is possible independently of the conception of moral virtues (or vices) as including one's will to satisfy (or not to satisfy) moral standards of conduct which are conceived of as imposing obligations. It is not clear that this is possible, or, if possible, illuminating. Similarly this inversion of the order of significance suggests that the relevant act of omission is a violation of moral duty because it standardly occasions such critical responses. It is arguable that such acts of omission occasion the relevant critical responses because they constitute violations of stringent moral requirements. As in Mill's theory, the reasons or grounds for censure must be considered as only prima facie reasons.[62] It is significant that many acts are duties even though their non-performance is, due to exceptional circumstances, excusable or justifiable, and their performance, in these dangerous and demanding circumstances, is praiseworthy. Nevertheless, such acts are not supererogatory but obligatory. If attention is shifted away from the fact that non-performance is a ground for the sanction to the rule requiring performance, this feature can be readily explained.

In Hart's account the primary emphasis is upon the pressure for conformity to the duty-imposing rule, consequently attention is diverted from the rule and the primary reasons for doing the duty which it imposes, and directed to a secondary feature, namely the sanctions the reason for which is violation of the duty. The rule is thus viewed primarily as a standard for evaluation of conduct, and that largely in the breach rather than in the performance. This is especially marked in Hart's stress upon the employment of characteristic normative language in critical responses rather than in advice, guidance, and deliberation. Hence attention is diverted from the rule as a guide to action which constitutes in itself a reason for action. How is this feature of a rule to be explained? That an action is a duty entails, according to Hart, that its performance is required by a rule. However, if one is to grasp the guiding function of duties the introduction of a further 'fictitious entity', a rule, provides

---

[61] Or, more accurately, identification of the remorseful agent's belief as the belief that he has failed to do his moral duty.

[62] *C.L.*, p. 167.

insufficient explanation. Eliminating this fictitious entity may shed further light upon the structure of the concepts in question. That one ought to do an action entails that there is a reason for doing it, but tells us nothing about the nature of the reason. That an action is a duty, however, is in itself a reason for doing it. It entails that there are further reasons which justify doing it and reasons which justify its being a duty. I may be ignorant of what these further reasons are, but my ignorance does not entail that I have no reason for doing the action. The fact that it is a duty provides me with one. By contrast if I am ignorant of the reasons for doing an act which ought to be done, then I have no reason for doing it. If I know only that I ought to do it, then I have only the weakest of reasons for doing it, namely that there is a reason (of which I am ignorant) for doing it. But I am in no position to weigh the force of this un- known reason. Even if I know that I ought morally to do the act I cannot weigh this consideration against my inclinations, desires, interests, which speak against it. For there are many morally good actions, i.e. actions for which there are moral reasons of a certain kind, which need not outweigh inclinations, desires, and self-interest on particular occasions. But that an act is a duty is in itself a powerful exclusionary reason.[63] It entails, negatively, that not doing the act on whim or inclination is unjustifiable. It entails that not doing the act because one does not want to is no excuse. It entails that the fact that the act is not in one's interest, or even that it is contrary to one's interests,[64] will not constitute an acceptable reason for not doing it. This much at any rate is necessary, though perhaps insufficient, to capture the exclusionary force of the fact that an act is a moral duty. The exclusionary force of the fact that an

[63] The ingenious notion of an exclusionary reason as a key to the understanding of a mandatory norm has been developed by Joseph Raz in 'Reasons for Action, Decisions and Norms' (forthcoming). An exclusionary reason is explained as a reason which, in every situation in which it applies it is not only a reason for (or against) doing the action in question, but also a reason for not considering at all the force of certain other reasons and desires. It is contrasted with strong reasons which are those which in the situations in which they apply *normally* outweigh the standard reasons and desires likely to be present in those normal circumstances. Much of the ensuing discussion is indebted to Dr. Raz's illuminating paper.

[64] There are clearly limitations upon the extent to which self-interest is required to be sacrificed for certain duties. Morality does not require one to ruin one's life to keep a trivial promise.

act is a legal duty seems to encompass not only this but all extra-legal considerations, limited perhaps *in extremis* by fundamental principles of justice and morality.[65] Whether the subjects of the legal system accept the law as possessing such a status is another matter. Normally the law provides sanctions as motivation additional to respect for the law. The law-applying organs are themselves required to treat legal duties as possessing such status, and to apply sanctions to offenders on the grounds of deviation in those cases in which there are sanction-stipulating laws.

Thus far the implications of the negative, exclusionary force of duty. Positively, however, the notion of moral duty, as Hart indicates, entails that in general performance of acts of the kind in question is necessary to the maintenance of social life or some indispensable, highly valued feature of it.[66] Such reasons justifying the duty-imposing rule are strong or weighty reasons. They are not arbitrary as are many of the reasons justifying rules of etiquette. Nor are they justified by the amusing, interesting, or skilful consequences that acting on them has, as are most rules of games. They are justified by reference to fundamental moral values.[67] Hence the importance we attribute to moral duties. But that an act is a moral duty implies not merely weighty moral reasons for doing acts of that kind, it also implies the exclusion of certain kinds of countervailing reasons. Why? The exclusionary force of moral duty is justified, crudely speaking, by reference to such features as the need for predictability, mutual reliability, the multiplicity of temptations to disregard moral reasons, the importance of training and acquisition of habitual patterns of conduct and the like.

The exclusionary force of the fact that an act is a legal duty has already been mentioned. Positively, however, the notion of legal duty entails a justification of a very different kind from that underlying moral duties. While the justification of

[65] See, e.g. the discussion of the revival of Natural Law doctrines in post-war Germany in H. L. A. Hart, 'Positivism and the Separation of Law and Morals' (1958), 71 Harvard Law Review and *C.L.*, pp. 254 f.

[66] Hart specifies this condition in terms of what is, in a social group, *thought* to be important and valuable. This accords with his social fact analysis.

[67] Or, in the case of content-independent obligations (e.g. those created by promising) by reference to obligation-imposing acts, the status of which is justified by reference to such values.

moral duties is, for the most part, by reference to weighty, content-dependent, reasons, the justification of legal duties is, in the first instance, by reference to authority. As such it is content-independent. Legal duties are created by duty-imposing acts, or some other legally recognized way of establishing standards of conduct. To be sure, the duty-creating status of such facts does itself require justification. But the nature of such justification takes one beyond the confines of analytical legal philosophy. Moreover it is debatable whether this ultimate justification, in contrast with the content-independent justification, is part of the meaning of 'legal duty'.

Though the reasons which justify a certain kind of moral duty are necessarily strong or weighty reasons, it is of course not the case that in every instance of a moral duty there are strong reasons for performing the particular act in question. Some particular acts which instantiate a kind of moral duty are trivial and might, were other things equal, be outweighed by other considerations. However the exclusionary force of the duty is not eliminated by the triviality of the act and its consequences upon specific occasions. Conversely, where a duty is instantiated in circumstances in which its performance is of great consequence but exceptional self-sacrifice is necessary, the exclusionary force of the duty may not apply, for not *all* countervailing reasons are excluded by the fact that an act is a duty. Hence omission, in such extreme circumstances, does not constitute a ground for censure. But the act may nevertheless be conceived of as a duty, even though doing it may, unlike the normal case, be praiseworthy.

The fact that non-performance of a duty is normally a ground for censure or sanction must, I suggest, be seen as a consequential feature of the weight of the reasons for acts of the kind in question, and the nature and extent of the exclusionary reasons for every instance of it.

The second point of strain in Hart's account lies in its excessively positivist nature. This is of no importance for the analysis of duties of positive law. But it is of great importance for the account of moral duty. Hart's analysis may be useful for anthropological or sociological descriptions of the *mores* of a social group. However, much discourse about moral duties is not concerned with *mores* but with morals, not with mere description but with rational justification. A moralist frequently declares an act to be morally obligatory, and will not withdraw his claim upon being told that its omission is not viewed by most members of his social group in the critical reflective way which, on Hart's account, is analytically involved in the notion of obligation. Bentham, as we have seen, drove a wedge between 'duty' and 'ought', reserving the former for discourse about positive law, and the latter for his own critical morality. Hart, in his modified sanction theory, follows Bentham in restricting the concept of moral duty to positive morality. He provides a social-fact analysis of 'duty' in terms of reactive attitudes, critical responses, demands for certain patterns of conduct, and the like. Hence, in the absence of these social facts it must be illegitimate for a moral reformer or critic to declare an act to be a duty in the primary sense of the term 'moral duty'.

To be sure there are various ways in which the Hartian analysis might accommodate this difficulty. Bentham argued that an assertion that there is a moral right is to be understood as a recommendation that there ought to be a legal right. Hart might claim analogously that an assertion that an act is a moral duty, though not recognized as such and not part of positive morality, is to be understood as a recommendation that it ought to be a moral duty even though it is not. But this is inadequate. It is one thing to claim that a certain kind of act ought to be accepted as a duty, that people ought to recognize its obligatoriness. It is another thing to claim that it is morally obligatory. The latter statement does not entail that it is recognized as such by members of a social group. What can be meant by saying that it ought to be a duty?—that there are reasons for making it a duty? Moral duties (barring certain kinds of content-independent duties and duties of co-operative practices) are not made. That there are reasons why it is a duty? To be sure there are, but then it *is*, not *ought to be*, a duty. That there are reasons why it should be recognized as a duty? To be sure there are. Members of the relevant social group may not recognize it as such, through insensitivity, hypocrisy, stupidity, or through distinctive empirical or non-empirical beliefs reflected in their order of values. But lack of recognition does not obviously imply absence of duty.

How important these considerations are for the preferred

analysis or moral duty turns largely upon the general conception a philosopher has of morality. The suggestions made above
imply that the notion of moral justification cannot be wholly
accounted for in terms of social facts, of what people take to be
justified. The notion of moral duty cannot be prized off the
concept of what ought to be done. Hence the notion of moral
duty cannot be completely detached from that of rational
justification of action. These contentions verge upon the
fundamental problems of moral philosophy, upon the problems
of whether there is, and to what extent there is, a rational
foundation for ethics. This is not the place to go any further.

VII. CONCLUSION

If the foregoing critical remarks about the various theories
of duty are plausible then the possibility of a general theory
of duty in which the various social types of duty are displayed
as species of a uniform genus recedes into the distance. Such an
attractive explication of the concept cannot do justice to usage,
nor can it meet the different needs which our untidy and ram-
shackle concept of duty meets in the domains of law, morality,
religion, etc. The phenomena of law, morality, social practices,
and religious ethics differ profoundly despite the numerous similarities, interconnections, and analogies. The needs for certain
kinds of conceptual distinctions vary from one domain to
another. It should not therefore be surprising that the concept
of duty, prominent in each of these domains, should reflect
the structural similarities as well as the differences. This much
is evident from the Hartian analysis, and further supported by
the above critical remarks and modifications.

I have suggested that a pure sanction theory of duty is
unsatisfactory. But it has not been disputed that the sanction
theorists focused correctly upon one important constituent of
the general concept of duty. Though predictive and imperative
analyses of the nexus between non-performance of a duty act
and the consequent sanction are inadequate, the suggestion that
the omission must be seen as a ground for sanction or censure
is illuminating. The main general defect of sanction theories is,
I have suggested, to place excessive emphasis upon the sanction
and too little upon the duty-imposing standard of conduct. For
duty is a guide to action while the threat of a sanction is a

'goad', and the former function should be seen as prior to the latter. The concept of a duty-imposing norm can be further analysed in terms of justifying reasons, thus laying greater emphasis upon the guiding function of duty. The combination of weighty justifying reasons and exclusionary reasons goes some way to elucidating the concept of a mandatory norm, and serves to bring out further distinctive features of duty-imposing norms. However, even given this explanatory apparatus, the differences between legal duty and moral duty are far-reaching. For even though it has been suggested that a straightforward social-fact analysis of a duty-imposing norm obscures the roles of justifying and exclusionary reasons, the extension of the analysis of a legal duty to the content-independent justification characteristic of law and to the exclusionary force of legal duty does not imply that a positivist analysis is inappropriate. Nor does it imply that a modified sanction theory is incorrect, even though it may be necessary to relax the classical requirement of a legal sanction for every legal duty. By contrast the notion of a sanction in the strict sense plays an insignificant part in our notion of a moral duty, and although the more flexible notion of censure is involved, it is, not surprisingly, less significant than the distinctive justificative characteristics of moral duty. Equally, a positivist analysis of moral duty fails to capture some of the salient features of the concept. In particular it fails to illuminate what has, to many moralists and philosophers, appeared an essential element in morality in general and moral duty in particular, namely their reasonableness.

VII

Bentham on Legal Rights[1]

H. L. A. HART

I. INTRODUCTORY

Most English students of jurisprudence learn to take the first steps towards the analysis of the notion of a legal right from Hohfeld's *Fundamental Legal Conceptions*.[2] In my view Bentham is a more thought-provoking guide than Hohfeld, and indeed than any other writer on the subject, though unfortunately his doctrine has to be collected from observations scattered through his voluminous and not always very readable works. Bentham certainly anticipated much of Hohfeld's work and he has moreover much to say about important aspects of the subject on which Hohfeld did not touch. But his account of legal rights is by no means free from objections; for at some important points his utilitarianism gets in the way of his analytical vision. Bentham's doctrine has however the supreme merit of confronting problems ignored by other theories, even where as in the case of 'interest-theories' of rights, they are similar to or even derived from his own.

The notion of a legal right has proved in the history of jurisprudence to be very elusive: how elusive may be judged not only from the well-known division of theories into 'Will theories' and 'Interest theories' but also from some of the

---

[1] The present account of Bentham's doctrine of rights is collected from his *An Introduction to the Principles of Morals and Legislation* (referred to here as *P.M.L.*), *Of Laws in General* (referred to here as *O.L.G.*) and passages in *Bentham's Works* (Bowring ed. 1843), vol. III (referred to here as Bowring, vol. III). All references here to *P.M.L.* and *O.L.G.* are to the 1970 edition of these works in the *Collected Works of Jeremy Bentham* (University of London: Athlone Press). A brief exposition and criticism of part of Bentham's doctrine, based mainly on Bowring, vol. III, was given in my lecture on 'Bentham': *British Academy Proceedings*, 48 (1962), 313–17. This was criticized by David Lyons in 'Rights, Claimants and Beneficiaries', (1969) 6 *American Philosophical Quarterly*, 173, and the present fuller and, I hope, more precise account and criticism of Bentham owes much to the stimulus of his article.

[2] 1919 (3rd reprint 1964).

interesting though also strange things that jurists and others have said about rights. They have on the whole hammered rights with sceptical doubts much harder than obligations or duties. Duguit, for example, held that there were legal duties but no legal rights;[3] Austin,[4] Bentham,[5] and in our own day, Ross,[6] while apparently admitting that there may be non-legal obligations or duties insist that 'strictly' the only rights are legal rights. It has moreover often been observed that the concept of a right, legal or moral, is not to be found in the work of the Greek philosophers, and certainly there is no noun or noun phrase in Plato or Aristotle which is the equivalent of our expression 'a right', as distinct from the 'right action' or 'the right thing to do'. Jurists of stature[7] have even held that lawyers of some sophisticated systems of law, including Roman Law, never achieved a clear concept of a legal right. Thus Maine wrote: 'singular as the fact may appear to those unacquainted with it, the Romans had not attained, or had not fully attained, to the conception of a legal Right, which seems to us elementary'[8] and 'The clear conception of a legal right . . . belongs distinctively to the modern world.'[9] He added that 'unquestionably a clear and consistent meaning was for the first time given to the expression "a right" by the searching analysis of Bentham and Austin.'[10]

Maine's reference to Bentham not as discovering or revealing the meaning of the expression 'a right', but as *giving* a clear meaning to it is accurate; and raises a methodological issue of some importance. When we ask for the analysis of such notions as that of a legal right, what precisely is it that we are seeking and by what criteria should success or failure be judged? Bentham's views on these matters are astonishingly modern and are still worth attention. He thought that the expression 'a right' was one of a fairly short list of terms including the

---

[3] *Traité de droit constitutionel* (1911), 1: 64, 130–45, discussed by Allen *Legal Duties* (1931), p. 158, and Ross, *On Law and Justice* (1958), p. 186.

[4] *Lectures on Jurisprudence* (5th ed.), ch. XII, p. 344.

[5] Bowring II. 501; III. 221.

[6] Ross, op. cit., pp. 248, 365.

[7] Besides Maine (see n. 8) Buckland, *Text Book of Roman Law*, 2nd ed. (1950) 58 and Villey, *Leçons d'histoire de la philosophie de droit* (1957), chs. XI and XIV.

[8] *Early Law and Custom* (1891), p. 365; cf. p. 366.

[9] Op. cit., p. 390.   [10] Op. cit., p. 366.

term 'law' which were the subject matter of 'universal expository jurisprudence',[11] and its task was to expound the
ideas annexed to these terms. But he did not think that in
discharging this task he was strictly bound by common usage,
or that definitions, if they were to be useful in jurisprudence,
should merely follow or reflect that usage, which at points he
found to be confused, arbitrary, and vague and in various
other ways unsatisfactory. Quite frequently and explicitly, he
departed from usage in order to construct a meaning for a term
which, while generally coinciding with usage and furnishing
an explanation of its main trends, would not only be clear,
but would pick out and collect clusters of features frequently
recurrent in the life of a legal system, to which it was important
to attend for some statable theoretical or practical purpose.
Hence Bentham spoke of himself as expounding the meaning
of terms by 'fixing' rather than 'teaching' their import;[12] and
when he came in *Of Laws in General* to elaborate his definition
of a law he spoke of 'rather a meaning which I wish to see
annexed to the term law than one which it has any settled and
exclusive possession of already'.[13] In modern terminology,
Bentham's conception of analysis is that of 'rational recon-
struction' or refinement of concepts in use: his general standpoint is critical and corrective, and in the sequel I shall appeal
to it in criticism of part of Bentham's own doctrine concerning
legal rights.

II. SURVEY OF BENTHAM'S DOCTRINE

Bentham distinguishes three principal kinds of right which
correspond roughly to Hohfeld's 'claim-right', 'liberty' or
'privilege', and 'power', though he does not include an element
corresponding to Hohfeld's 'immunity'. In spite of this rough
correspondence there are many differences of which perhaps
the most important is that unlike Bentham, Hohfeld considers
that the very common use of the expression of a right to cover
all the four cases which he distinguishes to be a 'loose'[14] and
even 'nebulous'[15] usage: the 'proper meaning'[16] of the term
according to Hohfeld is to designate the element which he

[11] *P.M.L.*, pp. 6, 295.   [12] Bowring III. 217.   [13] *O.L.G.*, p. 11.
[14] Hohfeld, op. cit., pp. 42, 51.   [15] Op. cit., p. 54.
[16] Op. cit., pp. 38, 39.

terms a claim-right, and the broad or loose use is described as 'unfortunate'[17] because it leads to confusion of thought. Notwithstanding these strictures Hohfeld recognizes that the use of the term to cover claim-right, liberty, power, and immunity is a use of the term in a 'generic'[18] sense and hints that the characteristic common to the genus is 'any sort of legal advantage'[19] though he does not explain this idea further. Bentham does not express any similar misgivings concerning the wide extension of the term in ordinary usage, and though in the cases of other terms he is prepared to distinguish what is 'strictly and properly so called' from what is not, he does not do so in the case of rights.

Bentham starts by making what he says is a fundamental distinction between two sorts of rights distinguished by different relationships to the idea of obligation or duty.[20] The first sort of rights owe their existence to (or as he says 'result from') the absence of legal obligation:[21] the second sort result from obligations imposed by law.[22] Rights of the first sort are rights to do or abstain from some action, and rights of the second sort are rights to what Bentham calls the 'services',[23] i.e. the actions or forbearance, of others. Corresponding to these two different sorts of rights are two different sorts of law or states of the law. Rights resulting from obligation are conferred by (or as Bentham puts it, 'have as their base') coercive laws; rights resulting from the absence of obligation have as their base discoercive or permissive laws.[24] In this last phrase Bentham includes three different cases. These are (i) *active* permission[25] or countermand: where the law permits some action, previously legally prohibited or obligatory, to be done or not done; (ii) *inactive* or original permission:[26] where the law simply declares that some action not previously prohibited or obligatory may be done or not done; (iii) the case where the law is silent.[27] Such permissive laws or legal silence leave the individual who

[17] Op. cit., p. 51.   [18] Op. cit., p. 42.   [19] Op. cit., p. 71.
[20] Obligation and duty are treated as synonymous terms by Bentham: see *O.L.G.*, p. 294.
[21] Bowring III. 181, 217–18; *P.M.L.*, p. 212.
[22] Bowring III, loc. cit., *O.L.G.*, pp. 57–8, 294.
[23] Bowring III. 159, *O.L.G.*, pp. 57–8.
[24] Bowring III. 181, *P.M.L.*, p. 302.   [25] *O.L.G.*, pp. 57–8.
[26] Ibid.   [27] *O.L.G.*, pp. 98–9, Bowring III. 159.

is the right-holder free or at liberty to do or not to do some action; I shall use the expression 'liberty-right' instead of Bentham's more explicit though clumsy circumlocution for this sort of right, and I shall use instead of Bentham's expression 'right resulting from obligation' the more familiar 'right correlative to obligation' for his second sort of right, which arises when the law imposes a duty not on the right-holder, but on another and thus restricts the other's freedom to act as he chooses.

A. LIBERTY-RIGHTS

Bentham in my view was certainly justified in regarding liberty-rights as of very great importance. Some later theorists have thought that so negative an idea could be of little significance for jurisprudence and could not represent 'a legal relation'.[28] This I am sure is a great mistake. Without attention to this negative and apparently insignificant element there cannot be any clear understanding of such important ideas as that of ownership, or of the legal character of the sphere left open by the law to economic competition, or any clear formulation of many legal problems to which that has given rise.[29] Indeed in the sequel I shall claim that this element of a liberty-right is involved in all the most important kinds of legal right at least in the civil law. But the notion of a liberty-right needs some further characterization beyond that given to it by Bentham's phrase, 'right resulting from the absence of obligation'. The following points in particular deserve attention.

The bilateral character of liberty-rights

In England and in most other countries a man has a right to look over his garden fence at his neighbour; he is under no obligation not to look at him and under no obligation to look at him. In this example the liberty is therefore bilateral; both the obligation not to look and the obligation to look are in Bentham's phrase 'absent'. Most of Bentham's examples of a liberty-right and his general account of them represents them as bilateral; they are, he says, such rights as men have in the state of nature where there are no obligations. But he occasionally speaks as if a unilateral liberty, that is the absence of

---

[28] e.g. Pollock, *Jurisprudence* (2nd ed., 1902), p. 62, but see Hohfeld op. cit., p. 48 n.   [29] See below, p. 181 n. 53

either an obligation not to do something *or* an obligation to do it were enough to constitute a right of this kind.[30] On that footing a right to do an action would merely exclude an obligation not to do it, and men always have a right to do what they have an obligation to do. Hohfeld's 'liberty' or 'privilege' is by his definition a unilateral liberty,[31] and, in some special contexts, to treat unilateral liberties as rights accords with a common and intelligible usage for which I offer an explanation below.[32] But I shall treat Bentham as committed to regarding bilateral liberties as the standard type of liberty-right.

Liberty-rights and correlative obligations not to interfere

The fact that a man has a right to look at his neighbour over the garden fence does not entail that the neighbour has a correlative obligation to let himself be looked at or not to interfere with the exercise of this specific liberty-right. So he could, for example, erect a screen on his side of the fence to block the view. But though a neighbour may do this if he wishes, and so has himself a liberty-right or bilateral liberty to erect or not to erect such a fence, there are other things that, in most countries, he cannot legally do to prevent his tormentor looking at him. For he has certain legal obligations or duties, civil or criminal, or both, which preclude some, though not all forms of interference, and these in practice more or less adequately protect the exercise of the liberty-right. Thus he cannot enter the next-door garden and beat up his tormentor, for this would be a breach of certain duties not indeed correlative to his tormentor's liberty-right to look at him, but correlative at least in the case of civil duties to certain other rights, which his tormentor has and which are not mere liberties. These are the tormentor's rights not to be assaulted and his right that others should not enter on his land without his consent. These are rights correlative to obligations and to Bentham's account of these I now turn.

B. RIGHTS CORRELATIVE TO OBLIGATIONS

The right not to be assaulted and the right of an owner or occupier of land that others should not enter on it without

---

[30] e.g. Bowring III. 218 but cf. III. 159.
[31] Hohfeld, op. cit., p. 39.   [32] Below, pp. 182–3, 196 n. 93.

his consent are rights to what Bentham terms a negative service,[33] that is to the abstention from 'hurtful action';[34] in other cases of rights correlative to obligations, where the obligation is to *do* something rather than abstain from action the right is to an 'affirmative' or 'positive' service,[35] or, as Bentham paraphrases it, to 'a useful action'.[36] All rights correlative to obligations are rights to services which consist in the performance of their correlative obligation and with two exceptions all legal obligations or duties have correlative rights. One exception is the case of 'self-regarding duties'[37] where the duty is imposed by law solely for the benefit of the agent on whom they are imposed. Bentham's examples of self-regarding duties include duties to abstain from suicide, from 'indecency not in public', incest, idleness, gaming, and 'other species of prodigality'.[38] The other more important exception to the principle that all legal obligations have correlative rights is where the legislator has disregarded entirely the dictates of utility and created obligations by which no one at all benefits. Such obligation Bentham terms 'ascetic', 'pure', or 'barren', or 'useful to no one'[39] and he thought they had been all too numerous in the history of human law. But apart from these two cases, whenever the law creates civil or criminal obligations, it always thereby creates what Bentham terms 'an enforced service' negative or positive, for the benefit of others; and to have a right correlative to an obligation is to be the person or persons intended to benefit from the performance of the obligation.[40] But not only individuals have rights; the public and also distinct classes included in it have, according to Bentham, rights in those cases where the persons intended to benefit are what he terms 'unassignable individuals'.[41]

Accordingly, with the two exceptions mentioned, every offence, crime or civil wrong, is a violation of some right and a case of 'wrongful withholding of services'[42] so that 'there is no law whatsoever that does not confer on some person or

[33] Bowring III. 159; *O.L.G.*, pp. 58–9.   [34] Bowring III. 159.
[35] *O.L.G.*, pp. 58–9; Bowring III. 159.   [36] Bowring III. 159.
[37] *O.L.G.*, pp. 58, 294; *P.M.L.*, p. 206.
[38] *P.M.L.*, pp. 225 n., 296 n., 232 n.
[39] Bowring III. 181, 221.   [40] *P.M.L.*, p. 206; *O.L.G.*, p. 58.
[41] See below, pp. 186–8.   [42] *P.M.L.*, p. 228 n.

other a right'.[43] I shall call this identification of a right-holder by reference to the person or persons intended to benefit by the performance of an obligation 'the benefit theory' of rights; and when I come to criticize it I shall try to make precise the sense not only of benefit but of a person intended to benefit and to clarify the distinction which Bentham makes between assignable and unassignable individuals.

C. POWERS

Legal powers are for Bentham a species of right[44] and his works contain a most elaborate taxonomy of the different kinds of legal powers together with a sophisticated analysis of the idea of a legal power and of the legal provisions by which powers are conferred on individuals.[45] The simplest kind of power is that which a man has when he is allowed by law to interfere with or physically control things or the bodies of persons or animals. Bentham subsumes such interference (which of course may take a great variety of forms such as touching, holding, moving, confining) under the general notion of handling and he calls such powers 'powers of contrectation': examples are an owner's power to make physical use of his property or a policeman's power of arrest. Such powers are in fact liberty-rights differing from other liberty-rights in two respects: first the action which, in such cases, there is liberty to do is re-stricted to actions physically affecting things or bodies; secondly in such cases the liberty is exclusive or exceptional[46] in the sense that it is a liberty to do something that others are generally under an obligation not to do. Such powers are conferred by permissive laws,[47] but like other liberty-rights they may be protected or 'corroborated'[48] by duties imposed on others not to obstruct, or even requiring them to assist, their exercise. If they are not so corroborated, they exist as 'bare' liberties: and then like other liberty-rights their existence does not entail the existence of any correlative obligations.

[43] *O.L.G.*, p. 220.   [44] *O.L.G.*, pp. 84, 220.

[45] See *O.L.G.*, *passim*, and esp. ch. IX and my 'Bentham on Legal Powers', Yale Law Review, (forthcoming).

[46] For an examination of Bentham's notion of powers of contrectation as ex-clusive or exceptional liberties see my 'Bentham on Legal Powers', loc. cit.

[47] *O.L.G.*, pp. 81, 86–7, 137 n.

[48] *P.M.L.*, p. 302; *O.L.G.*, p. 260 (48); *O.L.G.*, p. 261.

More important for our present purpose is the kind of power which Bentham calls 'investitive' and 'divestitive'.[49] These are the powers which a man has when he is enabled by law to change the legal position of others, or of himself and others as he does for example when he alienates property or makes a will or contract. In entering into such legal transactions he does an act (usually the writing or saying of certain words according to more or less strictly prescribed forms) which manifest certain intentions as to future rights and duties of himself and others. Such acts, or acts in the law, are not only *permitted* by the law but are *recognized* by the law as having certain legal consequences: given certain circumstances, a duly executed conveyance of land is 'valid', i.e. legally effective in divesting the transferor of certain rights and duties and in investing the transferee with similar ones. Bentham's elaborate account of the legal provisions by which such investitive and divestitive powers are conferred is designed to reconcile their existence with his general 'imperative' theory of law according to which all laws either impose duties or grant permissions.[50] There is not according to Bentham a further special kind of laws which confer powers; but powers are conferred when laws imposing duties or granting permissions are 'imperfect mandates',[51] i.e. incomplete in some respects and so contain 'blanks'[52] left to 'power-holders' to 'fill up', and when they do this they thereby determine or vary the incidence of existing 'imperfect' laws.

III. CRITICISM OF BENTHAM'S DOCTRINE

A. LIBERTY-RIGHTS

Liberty-rights and their protective perimeter

Those who have doubted the importance of liberties or mere absence of obligation for the analysis of legal rights have felt that so negative a notion without some positive correlate is not worth a lawyer's attention. This is a mistaken way of presenting the important fact that where a man is left free by the law to do or not to do some particular action, the exercise of this liberty will always be protected by the law to some

---

[49] *O.L.G.*, pp. 82–4; cf. *P.M.L.*, p. 217 n., Bowring III. 186–90 on 'collative and ablative events'.

[50] *O.L.G.*, pp. 95–9 and *passim*. *P.M.L.*, p. 302.

[51] *O.L.G.*, pp. 26, 80–91.   [52] Bowring III. 222; cf. III. 197.

extent, even if there is no strictly correlative obligation upon others not to interfere with it. This is so because at least the cruder forms of interference, such as those involving physical assault or trespass, will be criminal or civil offences or both, and the duties or obligations not to engage in such modes of interference constitute a protective perimeter behind which liberties exist and may be exercised. Thus, to take a trivial example, my right to scratch my head is protected, not by a correlative obligation upon others not to interfere with my doing that specific kind of act, but by the fact that obligations to refrain from assault or trespass to my person will generally preclude effective interference to it. In most cases the protection of my liberty afforded by this perimeter of obligations will be adequate but it may not be complete: if others could stop me scratching my head without any breach of these obligations e.g. by hypnotizing me, they may do so. This makes clear the difference between a liberty-right to do some kind of act protected by a strictly correlative obligation upon others not to interfere with it, and a liberty-right protected only by a normally adequate perimeter of general obligations.

It may be that jurists who have doubted the importance of the negative notion of absence of obligation or liberty have done so because the protective perimeter has obscured their view of it; but it is in fact important not to lose sight of either the liberty or the perimeter. Both are required in the analysis of many legal phenomena including that of economic competition. Two people walking in an empty street see a purse lying on the pavement: each has a liberty so far as the law is concerned to pick it up and each may prevent the other doing so if he can race him to the spot. But though each has this liberty there are also several specific things which each has a right that the other should not do; these are rights with correlative obligations and these correlative obligations together with the duties of the criminal law protect (and also restrict) each party's liberty. Thus neither of the competitors may hit or trip up the other, or threaten him with violence in order to get the prize. The perimeter of obligations to abstain from such actions constitutes the ring within which the competitors compete in the exercise of their liberties. Of course where competition is not in question, as in the case of 'fundamental' human rights or liberties, great importance may be attached to their unimpeded exercise and in such cases the law may protect the liberty by a strictly correlative obligation not to interfere by any means with a specific form of activity. But most liberties are not so protected.[53]

Bentham appreciated the importance of this combination of a liberty with a protective perimeter of obligations, but his formulations on the point are casual and somewhat ambiguous. He distinguishes between a 'naked' right and a 'vested' or 'established' one.[54] A naked light is a liberty unprotected by any obligation and are the rights which men have in the state of nature; a man has a vested or established right when he has a right that others should abstain from interfering with a liberty which he has. This language suggests that Bentham thought of rights as vested only where there was a strictly correlative obligation not to interfere, but in other passages in discussing liberty-rights he envisages their protection by a perimeter of general obligations not strictly correlative to the liberty.

> I may stand or sit down—I may go in or out—I may eat or not eat etc.: the law says nothing upon the matter. Still, the right which I exercise I derive from the law because it is the law which erects into an offence every species of violence by which one may seek to prevent me from doing what I like.[55]

Notwithstanding his appreciation of the importance of the combination of liberties with a perimeter of protective though not correlative obligation, Bentham, like Hobbes in describing the state of nature, treats liberties even when 'naked' as rights. But it is not at all clear that lawyers or anyone else would speak of a completely naked or unprotected liberty as a right, or that any useful purpose would be served if they did. The

---

[53] Thus the famous cases *Allen* v. *Flood* (1898) A.C. 1, *Mogul Steamship* v. *Macgregor & Others* (1892) A.C. 25, *Quinn* v. *Leathern* (1901) A.C. 495 and (in part) *Rookes* v. *Barnard* (1964) A.C. 1129, are best understood as raising the question whether an individual's liberty-rights to trade or employ labour or sell his labour are protected by a perimeter consisting only of duties corresponding to the specific torts of conspiracy, intimidation, and inducement of breach of contract, or by a perimeter consisting also of a duty corresponding to a more general tort of interfering with the trade, business, or employment of a person without lawful justification or excuse.

[54] Bowring III. 218.   [55] Bowring III. 159–60.

state of nature, if worth describing at all, can be described adequately in other terms. So far as organized society is concerned there would be something not only strange but misleading in describing naked liberties as rights: if we said, for example, that a class of helots whom free citizens were allowed to treat as they wished or interfere with at will, yet had rights to do those acts which they were not forbidden by the law to do. All the very important points in Bentham's doctrine distinguishing between liberty-rights and rights correlative to obligations can be preserved by treating bilateral liberty as an essential *element* in the analysis of liberty-rights but only constituting a liberty-right in conjunction with a perimeter of some protecting obligations or duties. It is not necessary, nor I think useful for any purpose, to treat liberties without any such protection as a distinct kind of legal right.

Unilateral liberty-rights

Bentham, as I have said, occasionally speaks as if a unilateral liberty were sufficient to constitute a liberty-right. On this footing a liberty-right to do an act would be compatible with, and indeed entailed by, an obligation to do it. The right-holder would not, as in the case of bilateral liberty, be free to choose whether to do an act or not; he would be at liberty to do an act only in the sense that he was not under an obligation not to do it. Bentham does not discuss the appropriateness or otherwise of extending the notion of rights to include unilateral liberty; but it seems clear that a general extension to include all unilateral liberties would neither accord with usage nor be useful. In the ordinary case, where the law imposes general obligations, e.g. to pay taxes, or to abstain from assault or trespass, it would be pointless or even confusing to describe those who had these obligations as having rights to pay taxes or to abstain from assault. Yet there undoubtedly are certain specific contexts where unilateral liberties are intelligibly spoken of as rights to do actions even where there is also an obligation to do the same action. Among these are cases where individuals by way of exception to a general rule are not merely permitted but also legally required to do some act generally prohibited.

Thus a policeman ordered to arrest a man might be asked

'What right have you to arrest him?' and might well produce his orders as showing that he had a right to arrest. In general the query 'What right have you to do that?' invites the person addressed to show that some act of his which is prima facie wrongful because generally prohibited is one which in the particular case he is at liberty to do. The questioner is not concerned to know whether the liberty is unilateral, i.e. accompanied by an obligation, or bilateral; so the form of his question covers both.[56]

B. THE BENEFIT THEORY OF RIGHTS CORRELATIVE TO OBLIGATION

The most striking feature of Bentham's analysis of legal rights is his benefit theory of rights correlative to obligation: the view that with the exception of 'barren' and 'self regarding' obligation *all* obligations, civil or criminal, have correlative rights held by those intended to benefit by their performance. In considering this doctrine certain features of Bentham's elaborate classification of offences[57] must be kept in mind, since, according to him, every offence, i.e. every breach of obligation with the two exceptions mentioned, violates a right. Bentham distinguishes between offences which are primarily or in the first instance detrimental to 'assignable persons' (which he terms 'offences against individuals' or 'private offences')[58] and offences detrimental only to unassignable individuals.[59] Of the latter there are two kinds, viz. public offences against a whole community or state, or semi-public offences against classes of persons within the community distinguished either by some class characteristic or by residence in a particular area. Offences of the first kind violate individual rights: examples of them are murder, assault, theft, and breach of contract:[60] offences of the second kind violate the rights of the public or a class, and examples of them are failure to pay

[56] Further examples of unilateral liberties spoken of as rights are afforded by cases where duties in Bentham's phrase, are 'superadded' to liberty-rights (*O.L.G.*, pp. 270–1, 296). Thus a trustee who has equitable duties to put the trust property to a certain use may be said to have a right to do this since the equitable duty is for historical reasons conceived as something distinct grafted on to his still persistent legal bilateral liberty-rights, though its actual effect is to render the liberty-right unilateral.

[57] *P.M.L.*, ch. XVI, pp. 187 ff.   [58] *P.M.L.*, p. 188.
[59] Op. cit., p. 189.   [60] Op. cit., pp. 223–4, 228 n.

taxes or desertion from the army (public offences)[61] and violation of health regulations imposed for the protection of a particular neighbourhood (semi-public offences).[62]

Intended benefits to assignable versus unassignable individuals

Before attempting any general criticism of Bentham's benefit theory, it is necessary to explore the ambiguities of the central ideas involved in it. These ambiguities are, I think, involved in all theories which attempt to define the notion of an individual's right in terms of benefits or interests, and they concern (a) the ideas of benefit and detriment, (b) the distinction between assignable and unassignable persons, and (c) the idea of a person intended by the law to benefit. These are difficult notions requiring fuller investigation than is attempted here, but the following may suffice for the present purposes.

(a) *Benefit and detriment.* Bentham, though committed to the doctrine that pleasure and pain are the only things good and bad in themselves,[63] does not in his account of rights and offences simply identify benefit with pleasure or avoidance of pain or detriment with pain or loss of pleasure. Hence, for him, as for others, theft of £1 from a millionaire indifferent to the loss constitutes a detriment to him and an offence against him; while forbearance from such theft constitutes a negative service and a benefit to which he has a legal right. So, too, security of the person or of reputation are benefits, even if in some cases the particular individual concerned would have welcomed an attack or found it pleasurable or otherwise desirable. So in general the idea of benefit or services, positive or negative, includes the provision or maintenance of conditions or treatment which are regarded by human beings generally, or in a particular society, as desirable or 'in their interest' and so to be sought from others. Correspondingly the idea of a detriment or harm includes the loss of such benefits and conditions and treatment generally regarded as undesirable and to be avoided. No doubt Bentham thought also that what makes anything a benefit or desirable is its general tendency to produce pleasure or to avoid pain,[64] and if, in a particular society, the notion

---

[61] Op. cit., p. 262.   [62] Op. cit., pp. 194 n., 225 n.

[63] *P.M.L.*, pp. 88–9, 100.   [64] *P.M.L.*, pp. 191–3. Bowring III. 214.

of benefits or detriments had no such connection with pleasure and pain, this was an aberration to be deplored.

Given this conception of benefits and detriments, it follows that in the case of those offences which Bentham calls offences against individuals and regards as violating the rights of assignable individuals, the breach of the law necessarily, and not merely contingently, constitutes a detriment to individuals, and compliance with the law in such cases necessarily, and not merely contingently, constitutes a benefit to individuals. This feature is secured simply by the definition of the offence in terms of actions which constitute in themselves detriments to individuals even if they do not always cause pain. For killing or wounding or slandering an individual or thieving from him or false imprisonment or 'wife-stealing' (abduction), given the above account of detriments, necessarily constitute detriments and do not merely contingently cause them or make them more likely. Since it is perfectly reasonable, without further investigation of 'legislative intent', to ascribe to laws prohibiting offences which thus necessarily constitute a detriment to individuals, an intention to benefit them, it is by reference to this feature that Bentham's central conception of assignable individuals intended to benefit from the law is mainly to be explained.

In such cases we may call the benefit or detriment 'direct' and it is to be observed that in the case of Bentham's public and semi-public offences benefits and detriments are not involved in the same direct way. As Bentham points out[65] compliance with laws requiring payment of taxes will make funds available to a government, but whether or not benefits as above defined will result for any individuals is a contingent matter, depending on what Bentham terms 'a various and remote concatenation of causes and effects',[66] including the nature of the government's policies for use of the funds and their skill or even luck in implementing them. The same is true of laws requiring military service or prohibiting treason. General compliance with such laws will constitute certain conditions without which it would be impossible or less likely that various benefits will be ultimately received by individuals, and in that sense these conditions may be said to make their receipt more likely than

[65] *O.L.G.*, pp. 62–3; *P.M.L.*, pp. 149–51.   [66] *O.L.G.*, p. 62.

would otherwise be the case. Such contingently beneficial laws may be said to provide indirect benefits.[67]

(*b*) *Assignable and unassignable individuals.* This distinction appears in many places in Bentham's works[68] and he uses it to explain what is meant by saying that certain offences are against the public or against a class, and that the public or a class are intended to benefit by a law and so have rights resulting from the obligations which it imposes. Bentham does not conceive of the public or of a class as an entity distinct from its members, and for him to speak of the public or class of persons as having rights is still to speak only of individuals, but of individuals who cannot be 'individually assigned' included in the community or class.[69] What then is it for an individual to be 'assignable'? Bentham's most explicit statement on this subject is in a footnote which merely tells us that an individual may be assignable 'by name or at least by description in such manner as to be sufficiently distinguished from all others'.[70] This leaves the notion of a law intended to benefit assignable individuals still obscure; because the various laws, such as the laws forbidding murder or assault which he does in fact regard as intended to benefit assignable individuals (and so as conferring rights upon them), do not refer to individuals either by name or by some uniquely applicable description, nor on any

---

[67] Of course the distinction between direct and indirect benefits will present disputable borderline cases, since whether anything is to be counted as in itself a benefit or only making the receipt of benefits more likely will often depend on degrees of likelihood, numbers of contingencies and also on analogies with standard direct individual benefits. Thus compliance by an employer with a duty to provide each of his workmen working in dangerous conditions with protective clothing might, like a law requiring him to pay each of them a sum of money, be considered as constituting a direct benefit, and its breach as constituting a direct detriment; whereas a law requiring him to fit a fence or guard on dangerous machinery while men are at work, might be considered not as constituting a direct benefit for them but only as making the avoidance of harm more likely, and so constituting an indirect benefit. It is also to be noted that if provision of such a fence or guard is treated as constituting a direct benefit it would be a *common* benefit, in contrast with the *separate* or *individual* benefits constituted by the provision of each workman with protective clothing. It seems likely that Bentham would regard all laws providing such common benefits as intended to benefit classes not 'assignable individuals'. (See below, p. 188, with regard to statutory duties.)

[68] e.g. *P.M.L.*, pp. 143, 188–9; *O.L.G.*, p. 37. It also appears in John Stuart Mill's account of rights in *Utilitarianism*, ch. V.

[69] *P.M.L.*, p. 189.   [70] *P.M.L.*, p. 188 n.

account of legislative intent does it seem that they are intended only to benefit individuals so identified,[71] if that means identified at the time when the law comes into existence.

None the less Bentham's brief explanation of his distinction can be used indirectly to determine whether or not the individuals intended to be benefited by a law are assignable, since the corresponding question whether or not an *offence*[72] is against assignable individuals can be answered by direct reference to it. Thus the laws which Bentham regards as creating offences against assignable individuals and so as conferring rights upon them are such that to establish that the offence has been committed it must be shown that an individual who *is* 'assignable' in Bentham's sense, i.e. distinguished from others in some way and so uniquely identified, has suffered some individual detriment from the commission of the offence. It seems therefore that we may interpret the statement that a law is intended to benefit assignable individuals (and so confers rights upon them) as meaning no more than that to establish its breach an assignable individual must be shown to have suffered an individual detriment.[73] This seems to give the required contrast with those laws creating offences which Bentham classes as against unassignable individuals, such as failure to pay taxes or military desertion; for in such cases it is not necessary to show that any individual has suffered any detriment and it may often be the case that no individual has suffered or will suffer thereby. On this footing, an offence may be said to be against unassignable

[71] Of course they may be said to be intended to benefit 'each individual' in the community but this does not make the individuals 'assignable' in Bentham's sense.

[72] Bentham observes that rights may best be 'expounded' by considering the corresponding offences: *P.M.L.*, p. 206 and see *O.L.G.*, p. 58.

[73] This interpretation is not I think inconsistent with Bentham's remark (*P.M.L.*, p. 189 n.) that the divisions between private, semi-public, and public offences are liable to be 'confounded'. He points out that 'the fewer the individuals of which a class is composed . . . the more likely are the persons to whom an offence is detrimental to *become* assignable.' This seems merely to point out that though an offence (e.g. breach of health regulations imposed for the benefit of a particular area) is correctly regarded as one against a class in accordance with the interpretation offered above, it will in the case of small *closed* classes be possible to determine which individuals ultimately suffer from a given offence even though proof of their suffering is not, as in the case of offences against individuals, necessary to establish that the offence has been committed. But Bentham's point here is certainly not clear.

individuals, and so one which violates the rights not of individuals but of the public or a class, if (a) it is not an offence against assignable individuals, and (b) general compliance with the law creating an offence is intended to constitute an indirect benefit for any one or more individuals who are or may be included in the community or in a class within it but who are not otherwise identified.[74]

(c) *Intended by the law to benefit.* If the statement that a law intends to benefit an individual and so confers a right upon him is interpreted as meaning no more than that its breach constitutes a direct individual detriment, then we have a criterion for determining when laws confer individual rights which avoids difficult inquiries into 'actual' legislative intent. More-

---

[74] It should be observed that Bentham's distinction between laws which confer rights on individuals and those which confer them on the public or classes, based as it is on assignability as interpreted above, is *not* the same as the apparently similar distinction which has sometimes been invoked by English courts in their attempts to formulate tests for determining whether breach of a statutory duty, such as the duty to fence dangerous machinery or provide specified forms of fire-escape, gives rise to an action for damages on the part of individuals for injuries caused by the breach. Breach of most such statutory duties would, according to Bentham's assignability test, not be offences against individuals and so would not confer a right upon them to performance of the statutory duty; since to establish their breach it would not be necessary to show that any individual had suffered any individual detriment, but only that e.g. the machinery had not been fenced as required: such an offence, for Bentham, would either be against a class (e.g. of workmen) or against the public. It is on the other hand true that in determining whether the legislature in creating such statutory duties also by implication created a statutory tort, courts have flirted with the idea that this depended on whether the statutory duty was 'owed to' individuals or imposed in their interests and not merely imposed for the general welfare of the public (see *Solomons* v. *R. Gertzenstein* [1954] 2 Q.B. 243). This test has been rejected by some judges (see per Atkin L.J. in *Phillips* v. *Britannia Hygienic Laundry* [1923] 2 K.B. 832) and indeed the finding that a statutory duty was owed to or for the benefit of individuals seems rather to be a conclusion from a finding, made on other grounds, that the statute conferred a right of action upon individuals, than a reason for such a finding. But whatever this distinction is it does not, for the reasons stated above, turn, as Bentham's does, upon assignability. It appears rather to be a distinction (which the Courts have found very difficult to apply in practice) between the cases where, on the construction of the statute, it can be said that its main purpose was to secure to each individual of a specific class some specific benefit or protection from some specific harm and those cases where either there was no such discernible purpose, or, if there was, this was merely ancillary to a dominant purpose to create or maintain conditions (e.g. the conservation of manpower or resources) whereby all or any unspecified members of the public might benefit in various unspecified ways.

over this criterion will give a decisive and at least an intelligible answer to some questions which have confronted theorists who, within the general framework of an interest- or benefit-theory of rights, have wished to limit, in some reasonable way, the class of intended beneficiaries who should count as having rights. Thus, to take an example, famous from Ihering's[75] discussion of it, in a similar context, should a law, forbidding in general terms the importation of manufactured goods, which was in fact enacted solely in order to benefit a particular domestic manufacturer be taken to confer a right upon him? Ihering was anxious to distinguish such a case as a mere '*Reflexwirkung* (reflex operation) of a duty and not as a right, and he sought for, but never clearly formulated, some criterion which would distinguish a right violated by a demonstrable 'individual breach of the law' (*Individuelle Rechtsverletzung*) from a mere reflex operation of duty.[76] Kelsen believed that no such distinction could be drawn; but Bentham's conception of a direct detriment to an assignable individual, interpreted as above, might well have served this purpose and the test later suggested by Ross[77] in discussing Ihering's case is in substance identical with it.

For the purpose of criticism of the benefit theory I shall assume that the above interpretation of Bentham is correct.[78] I do so because this is the strongest form of the benefit theory and if it is vulnerable to criticism it is not likely that a theory depending on a more extended sense of 'intended by the law to benefit' is likely to be successful. For the same reason I shall

[75] *Geist des römischen Rechts* (1924 ed.), III. 351–3, discussed by Kelsen in *Haupt probleme des Staatrechts* (1960 ed.), pp. 578–81, and Ross in *Towards a Realistic Jurisprudence* (1946), pp. 167–8, 179 ff.

[76] Ihering's earlier account of rights (op. cit., 2nd ed., III. 339) had avoided this problem since it restricted rights to cases where the enforcement by legal proceedings of duties protecting interests was left to the individual concerned. ('Selbstschutz des Interesses.')

[77] Op. cit., pp. 179 ff. Lyons's account of the 'qualified beneficiary theory' which he favours and considers may be attributable to Bentham (op. cit., pp. 173–4, 176–80) is very close to the above interpretation of Bentham.

[78] There are certainly passages in Bentham (e.g. *O.L.G.*, pp. 55–6) where he seems to contemplate that if the legislator intended an 'assignable' individual to benefit even very indirectly from the performance of an obligation this would confer a right to its performance on him. On this view the favoured manufacturer in Ihering's case would have a right that the goods should not be imported.

not consider further Bentham's account of rights of the public or a class.[79]

Absolute and relative duties

The principal advocates of benefit or 'interest' theories of rights correlative to obligations have shown themselves sensitive to the criticism that, if to say that an individual has such a right means no more than that he is the intended beneficiary of a duty, then 'a right' in this sense may be an unnecessary, and perhaps confusing, term in the description of the law; since all that can be said in a terminology of such rights can be and indeed is best said in the indispensable terminology of duty. So the benefit theory appears to make nothing more of rights than an alternative formulation of duties: yet nothing seems to be gained in significance or clarity by translating, e.g. the statement that men are under a legal duty not to murder, assault, or steal from others into the statement that individuals have a right not to be murdered, assaulted, or stolen from, or by saying, when a man has been murdered, that his right not to be killed has been violated.[80]

Ihering as I have said was visited by just such doubts. Bentham confronted them in his codification proposals in the form of an inquiry whether the law should be expounded at length in a list of rights or a list of obligations. The test which he proposed was 'Present the entire law to that one of the parties that has most need to be instructed'[81] and he thought that the law should generally be expounded at length in terms of obligations but need 'only be mentioned' in a list of rights; his principal reason for this was that because of the penalties imposed the party on whom the law imposed the obligation had most need for instruction.[82]

---

[79] In fact Bentham seems to have made very little use of his idea that in the sense explained the public or a class within it have legal rights. Nearly all of his examples of rights are rights of individuals. Austin expressly confines legal rights to the rights of 'determinate persons' (op. cit., Lecture XVII, p. 401).

[80] Under the American Civil Rights Act 1964 suits were brought against white men who had murdered negroes alleging 'that they had deprived their victims of their civil rights'. This desperate expedient was necessary because murder is a state crime and prosecutions in such cases were not likely to succeed in Southern state courts. I owe this point to Mrs. Carolyn Irish.

[81] Bowring III. 195.

[82] Ibid.

(*a*) *Criminal* versus *civil law*. The most cogent criticisms of the benefit theory are those that on the one hand press home the charge of redundancy or uselessness to a lawyer of the concept of right correlative to obligation defined simply in terms of the intended beneficiary of the obligation, and on the other hand constructively presents an alternative selective account of those obligations which are for legal purposes illuminatingly regarded as having correlative rights. This latter task amounts to a re-drawing of the lines between 'absolute'[83] and relative duties which for Bentham merely separated 'barren' and self-regarding duties from duties 'useful to others'. This has been done sometimes in too sweeping a fashion as a distinction precisely coinciding with that between the criminal and civil law, and on the assumption, which seems dogmatic, if not plainly mistaken, that the purpose of the criminal law is not to secure the separate interests of individuals but 'security and order', and that all its duties are really duties not to behave in certain ways which are prejudicial to the 'general interests of society'.[84]

None the less a line may be drawn between most duties of the criminal law and those of the civil law which does not depend on this assumption, but would, on principles quite distinct from those of the benefit theory, reserve the notion of relative duties and correlative rights mainly for the obligations of the civil law, such as those which arise under contracts or under the law of tort, and other civil wrongs. For what is distinctive about these obligations is not their content which sometimes overlaps with the criminal law, since there are some actions, e.g. assault, which are both a crime and a civil wrong; nor is the only distinction of importance the familiar one that crime has as its characteristic consequence liability to punishment, and civil wrong liability to pay compensation for harm done. The crucial distinction, according to this view of relative duties, is the special manner in which the civil law as distinct from the criminal law provides for individuals: it recognizes or gives them a place or *locus standi* in relation to the law quite different from that given by the criminal law. Instead of utilitarian notions of benefit or intended benefit we need, if we are to reproduce this distinctive concern for the individual, a different

---

[83] So Austin (op. cit., Lecture XVII, 401–2).
[84] Allen, *Legal Duties*, pp. 184–6.

idea. The idea is that of one individual being given by the law exclusive control, more or less extensive, over another person's duty so that in the area of conduct covered by that duty the individual who has the right is a small-scale sovereign to whom the duty is owed. The fullest measure[85] of control comprises three distinguishable elements: (i) the right holder may waive or extinguish the duty or leave it in existence; (ii) after breach or threatened breach of a duty he may leave it 'unenforced' or may 'enforce' it by suing for compensation or, in certain cases, for an injunction or mandatory order to restrain the continued or further breach of duty; and (iii) he may waive or extinguish the obligation to pay compensation to which the breach gives rise. It is obvious that not all who benefit or are intended to benefit by another's legal obligation are in this unique sovereign position in relation to the duty. A person protected only by the criminal law has no power to release anyone from its duties, and though, as in England, he may in theory be entitled to prosecute along with any other member of the public he has no unique power to determine whether the duties of the criminal law should be enforced or not.

These legal powers (for such they are) over a correlative obligation are of great importance to lawyers: both laymen and lawyers will need, in Bentham's phrase, 'to be instructed' about them; and their exercise calls for the specific skills of the lawyer. They are therefore a natural focus of legal attention, and there are I think many signs of the centrality of those powers to the conception of a legal right. Thus it is hard to think of rights except as capable of *exercise* and this conception of rights correlative to obligations as containing legal powers accommodates this feature.[86] Moreover, we speak of a breach of duty in the

---

[85] The right holder will have less than the full measure of control if, as in the case of statutory duties, he is unable to release or extinguish the duty or if principles of public policy prevent him, even after breach of the duty, making a binding agreement not to sue for injury caused by its breach (see e.g. *Bowmaker Ltd.* v. *Tabor* (1942) 2 K.B. 1). In such cases the choice left to him is only to sue or not to sue. There are suggestions, never fully developed, that such a choice is a necessary element in a legal system in Bentham's *A Fragment on Government* Ch. V para. 6 n. 1 s. 2.

[86] Where infants or other persons not *sui juris* have rights, such powers and the correlative obligations are exercised on their behalf by appointed representatives and their exercise may be subject to approval by a court. But since (a) what such representatives can and cannot do by way of exercise of such power is determined

civil law, whether arising in contract or in tort, not only as wrong, or detrimental to the person who has the correlative right, but as *a wrong to* him and a breach of an obligation *owed to* him;[87] we also speak of the person who has the correlative right as *possessing* it or even *owning* it. The conception suggested by these phrases is that duties with correlative rights are a species of normative property belonging to the right holder, and this figure becomes intelligible by reference to the special form of control over a correlative duty which a person with such a right is given by the law. Whenever an individual has this special control, as he has in most cases in the civil law but not over the duties of the criminal law, there is a contrast of importance to be marked and many jurists have done so by distinguishing the duties of the criminal law as 'absolute duties' from the 'relative' duties of the civil law.[88]

It is an incidental, though substantial merit of this approach that it provides an intelligible explanation of the fact that animals, even though directly protected by the duties of the criminal law prohibiting cruelty to them, are not spoken or thought of as having rights. However it is to be observed that if the distinction between absolute and relative duties is drawn as above suggested, this does not entail that only duties of the civil law have correlative rights. For there are cases made prominent by the extension of the welfare functions of the

---

by what those whom they represent could have done if *sui juris* and (b) when the latter become *sui juris* they can exercise these powers without any transfer or fresh assignment; the powers are regarded as belonging throughout to them and not to their representatives, though they are only exercisable by the latter during the period of disability.

[87] Lyons (loc. cit., p. 178) assumes that 'rights under the civil law' arise only from 'special relations or transactions between the parties' (e.g. contracts) and that only in such cases are the right holders 'claimants' to whom duties are 'owed'. But individuals have rights corresponding to the primary duties in tort which do not arise from such special relations or transactions and such duties are 'owed' to them.

[88] It is sometimes argued that in the case of persons not *sui juris* e.g. infants, it is only the fact that they are direct beneficiaries of the correlative duties which explains the ascription of rights to them, rather than to their representatives who alone can exercise the powers over the correlative duties. But the explanation offered above (p. 192, n. 86) seems adequate; even if it is not, this would only show that being the direct beneficiary of a duty was a *necessary* condition of a person not *sui juris* having a right. Hence it would still be possible so far as this argument goes, to distinguish the duties of the criminal law (over which there are no such powers of control exercisable by the beneficiaries' representatives) as not having correlative rights.

state where officials of public bodies are under a legal duty to provide individuals if they satisfy certain conditions, with benefits which may take the form of money payments (e.g. public assistance, unemployment relief, farming subsidies) or supply of goods or services, e.g. medical care. In such cases it is perfectly common and natural to speak of individuals who have satisfied the prescribed conditions as being legally entitled to and having a right to such benefits. Yet it is commonly not the case that they have the kind of control over the official's duties which, according to the view suggested above, is a defining feature of legal rights correlative to obligations. For though such obligations are not always supported by criminal sanctions they cannot be extinguished or waived by beneficiaries, nor does their breach necessarily give rise to any secondary obligation to make compensation which the beneficiaries can enforce, leave unenforced or extinguish. None the less there are in most of such cases two features which link them to the paradigm cases of rights correlative to obligations as these appear in the civil law. In most cases where such public duties are thought of as having correlative rights, the duty to supply the benefits are conditional upon their being demanded and the beneficiary of the duty is free to demand it or not. Hence, though he has no power to waive or extinguish the duty he has a power by presenting a demand to substitute for a conditional duty not requiring present performance an unconditional duty which does, and so has a choice. Secondly, though breach of such duties may not give rise to any secondary duties of compensation, there are in many such cases steps which the beneficiary if he has suffered some peculiar damage may take to secure its performance, and in regard to which he has a special *locus standi* so that on his application a court may make a peremptory or mandatory order or injunction directing the official body to carry out the duty or restraining its breach.[89] These two features of the case differentiate the beneficiary of such public duties from that of the ordinary duties of the criminal law. This explains why, though it is generally enough to describe the criminal law only in terms of duties, so to

---

[89] Difficult questions may arise concerning the nature of the interest which a successful applicant for such relief must possess. See *R.* v. *Manchester Corp.* [1911] 1 K.B. 560.

describe the law creating these public welfare duties would obscure important features. For the necessity that such beneficiaries if they wish the duty to be performed must present demands, and the availability to them of means of enforcement, make their position under the law a focus for legal attention needing separate description from that of the duties beneficial to them.[90]

(*b*) *Contracts and third parties.* The identification of a right-holder with the person who is merely benefited by the performance of a duty not only obscures a very important general dividing line between criminal and civil law, but is ill adapted to the law relating to contract. Whereas in the last paragraph it was urged that to be an intended beneficiary of an obligation is not a satisfactory *sufficient* condition of having a right, the present criticism is that it is not satisfactory as a *necessary* condition. For where there is a contract between two people, not all those who benefit and are intended to benefit by the performance of its obligations have a legal right correlative to them. In many jurisdictions contracts expressly made for the benefit of third parties, e.g. a contract between two people to pay a third party a sum of money, is not enforceable by the third party and he cannot waive or release the obligation. In such a case although the third party is a direct beneficiary since breach of the contracts constitutes a direct detriment to him, he has no legal control over the duty and so no legal right. On the other hand the contracting party having the appropriate control has the legal right, though he is not the person intended to benefit by the performance of the contract.[91] Where, however, the law is modified as it is in some jurisdictions so as to give the third party power to enforce the contract then he is consistently with the view presented here spoken of as having legal right.[92]

[90] But so far as such public welfare duties are thought of as providing for essential human needs they may on that ground alone be regarded as constituting legal rights. See below, pp. 197–200.

[91] It is sometimes argued that the fact that in some jurisdictions a third-party beneficiary may sue shows this point against the beneficiary theory of rights to be mistaken. But of course a third party entitled to sue or not to sue would on *that* account be recognized as having a legal right and this does nothing to confirm the beneficiary theory.

[92] Lyons, loc. cit., pp. 183–4, argues that 'one of the conditions of a valid and binding promise and thus a condition of a right accruing to a promisee is that he really wants what is promised' (even if this is true of 'promises' it scarcely seems applicable to legal contracts). He then suggests that performance of a contract

The analysis of a right correlative to obligation which is suggested by the foregoing criticisms of the benefit theory is that for such a right to exist it is neither sufficient nor necessary for the person who had the right to be the beneficiary of the obligation; what is sufficient and necessary is that he should have at least some measure of the control, described above, over the correlative obligation.

IV. THE LIMITS OF A GENERAL THEORY

If the arguments of the last section are accepted and if we substitute for the utilitarian idea of benefit, as a defining feature of a right correlative to obligation, the individual's legal powers of control, full or partial, over that obligation, a generalization may be made concerning all three kinds of right distinguished by Bentham. This is attractive because it imposes a pattern of order on a wide range of apparently disparate legal phenomena. Thus in all three kinds of right the idea of a bilateral liberty is present and the difference between the kinds of right lies only in the kind of act which there is liberty to do. In the case of liberty-rights such as a man's right to look at his neighbour, his act may be called a natural act in the sense that it is not endowed by the law with a special legal significance or legal effect. On the other hand in the case of rights which are powers, such as the right to alienate property, the act which there is a bilateral liberty[93] to do is an act-in-the-law, just in the sense that it is specifically recognized by the law as having legal effects in varying the legal position of various parties. The case

---

for the benefit of a third party must 'assure a good' to the promisee, since this satisfies his want to have what is promised done, and that it is this, not his control over the promisors obligation, which accounts for the ascription of a right to him. But if the performance of the obligation beneficial to the third party is not sufficient to lead lawyers to recognize the third party as having a legal right, surely the secondary benefit to the promisee consisting in gratification of his wish to benefit the third party is not sufficient to account for his right.

[93] As in the case of liberty-rights, duties may be superimposed on rights which are powers and such duties will render the liberty to exercise the power unilateral (a simple example from property law is where an owner of property binds himself by contract either to sell it or not to sell it). In general where there is a duty to exercise a power the resultant unilateral liberty is not described as a right nor is there usually any point in so describing it. Exceptions to this are again cases such as that of a trustee whose legal rights are theoretically distinguishable from his equitable duties (see above, p. 183, n. 56) and are thought of as coexisting even where they in fact conflict.

of a right correlative to obligation then emerges as only a special case of legal power in which the right-holder is at liberty to waive or extinguish or to enforce or leave unenforced another's obligation. It would follow from these considerations that in each of these three types of case one who has a right has a choice respected by the law. On this view there would be only one sense of legal right—a legally respected choice—though it would be one with different exemplifications, depending on the kind of act or act-in-the-law which there is liberty to do.

The merits of this analysis are therefore threefold. First, it coincides with a very wide area of common and legal usage. Secondly it explains why liberty-rights, powers, and rights correlative to obligations are all described as rights and does so by identifying as common to three superficially diverse types of case, an element which, on any theory of law or morals, is of great importance; namely an individual choice respected by the law. Thirdly, the concept which it defines is well adapted to a lawyer's purpose; for it will lead him to talk in terms of rights only where there is something of importance to the lawyer to talk about which cannot be equally well said in terms of obligation or duty, and this is pre-eminently so in the case of the civil law.[94]

However, in spite of its attractions, this theory, centred on the notion of a legally respected individual choice, cannot be taken as exhausting the notion of a legal right: the notion of individual benefit must be brought in, though *not* as the benefit theory brings it in, to supplement the notion of individual choice. Unless this is done no adequate account can be given of the deployment of the language of rights, in two main contexts, when certain freedoms and benefits are regarded as essential for the maintenance of the life, the security, the development, and the dignity of the individual. Such freedoms and benefits are recognized as rights in the constitutional law of many countries by Bills of Rights, which afford to the individual protection even against the processes of legislation. In countries such as our own, where the doctrine of legislative sovereignty is held to preclude limiting the powers of the legislature by Bills of Rights, they are, though given only the lesser

[94] But not exclusively, see pp. 194–5 above.

measure of legal protection in the form of duties of the criminal law, thought and spoken of as legal rights by social theorists or critics of the law who are accustomed to view the law in a wider perspective than the lawyer concerned only with its day-to-day working.

IMMUNITY RIGHTS

Both the benefit theory of rights and the alternative theory of a right as a legally respected choice are designed primarily as accounts of the rights of citizen against citizen; that is of rights under the 'ordinary' law. From that point of view the benefit theory was criticized above (*inter alia*) for offering no more than a redundant translation of duties of the criminal law into a terminology of rights, e.g. not be murdered or assaulted. But this accusation of redundancy is no longer pertinent when what is to be considered are not rights under the ordinary law, but fundamental rights which may be said to be against the legislature, limiting its powers to make (or unmake) the ordinary law, where so to do would deny to individuals certain freedoms and benefits now regarded as essentials of human well-being, such as freedom of speech and of association, freedom from arbitrary arrest, security of life and person, education, and equality of treatment in certain respects.

The various elements which the benefit theory uses to analyse rights correlative to obligations and those which the rival 'choice' theory uses to analyse these and other kinds of right (that is: duty, absence of duty, benefit, act, and act-in-the-law) are not sufficient to provide an analysis of such constitutionally guaranteed individual rights. These require for their analysis the notion of an immunity. Bentham, unlike Hohfeld, did not isolate this notion in distinguishing different kinds or meanings of legal right, and indeed his attention was never seriously given to the analysis of fundamental legal rights. This was, no doubt, because, although, unlike Austin, he did not think that there were logical or conceptual objections to the notion of legal limitations of a sovereign legislature[95] he viewed with extreme suspicion any legal arrangements which would prevent

---

[95] See for his discussion of such limitations, *O.L.G.*, pp. 18, 64–71, 306, and *A Fragment of Government*, ch. IV, paras. 23–36, and my 'Bentham on Sovereignty' (1967) Irish Jurist 327.

the legislature enacting whatever measures appeared from time to time to be required by the dictates of general utility; and suspicion became contempt at the suggestion that such arrangements should be used to give legal form to doctrines of natural or fundamental individual rights. Hohfeld, who identified among the various 'loose' uses of the expression 'a right' its use to refer to an immunity, defined an immunity as the correlative of 'disability' or 'no power';[96] so that to say that a man, *X*, had a certain immunity meant that someone else lacked legal power to alter *X*'s legal position in some respect. But, plainly, even in the loosest usage, the expression 'a right' is not used to refer to the fact that a man is thus immune from an *advantageous* change; the facts that the City Council cannot legally, i.e. has 'no power', to award me a pension, and my neighbour has no power to exempt me from my duty to pay my income-tax, do not constitute any legal rights for me. An individual's immunity from legal change at the hands of others is spoken and thought of as a right only when the change in question is *adverse*, that is, would deprive him of legal rights of other kinds (liberty-rights, powers, rights correlative to obligations) or benefits secured to him by law.

The chief, though not the only employment[97] of this notion of an immunity from adverse legal change which we may call an 'immunity right' is to characterize distinctively the position of individuals protected from such adverse change by constitutional limitations or, as Hohfeld would say, by disabilities of the legislature. Such immunity rights are obviously of extreme importance to individuals and may usually be asserted in the form of justiciable claims that some purported enactment is invalid because it infringes them. There is here an illuminating contrast with the redundancy of rights as defined by the beneficiary theory; for whereas, as I have urged above, nothing is to be gained for the lawyer, either in clarity or the focusing of legal attention, by expounding, say, the law of murder or assault in terms of rights, the case is altered if a constitutional Bill of Rights precludes the legislature from depriving individuals

---

[96] Hohfeld, op. cit., p. 60.

[97] Immunities against divestment of various kinds of rights are involved in the notion of ownership. See A. M. Honoré, 'Ownership' in *Oxford Essays on Jurisprudence*, First Series (1961), p. 119.

of the protections of the criminal law. For then there is every reason why lawyers and others should have picked out for them, as rights to life or security of the person, legal immunities the assertion of which on behalf of the individual calls for their advice and skill. That is why I said above that though certain legally secured individual benefits would have to be brought in to any adequate account of legal rights, they would not be brought in as the benefit theory brings them in.

WIDER PERSPECTIVES

Law is however too important a thing to leave to lawyers— even to constitutional lawyers; and the ways of thinking about rights common among serious critics of the law and social theorists must be accommodated even though they are different from and may not serve any of the specific purposes of the lawyer. Here also a concept of legal rights limited to those cases where the law, in the ways described above, respects the choice of individuals would be too narrow. For there is a distinct form of the moral criticism of law which, like the constitutional immunity rights already described, is inspired by regard for the needs of the individual for certain fundamental freedoms and protections or benefits. Criticism of the law for its failure to provide for such individual needs is distinct from, and sometimes at war with, the criticism with which Bentham was perhaps too exclusively concerned, that the law often fails to maximize aggregate utility. A critic of the former, individualistic, kind will of course not address himself only to those legal systems in which there are immunity rights guaranteed by Bills of Rights; but in scrutinizing systems like our own, where the maximum form of provision for such individual needs must fall short of constitutional immunity rights, he will count the measure of protection afforded by the ordinary criminal law as a provision for those needs, together with the duties to provide for them which fall on public bodies or officials. Viewed in this light the law against murder and assault will be considered and described quite properly as securing rights to life and security of the person; though if it were a question simply of expounding the criminal law this would be redundant and even confusing.

Hence in cases where the criminal law provides for such

essential human needs the individualistic critic of the law would agree with the benefit-theorist in speaking of rights corresponding to certain duties of the criminal law. They would however differ in two ways: first the critic need entertain no *general* theory that every direct beneficiary of a legal obligation had a corresponding legal right and he could therefore consistently subscribe to all the criticisms of the beneficiary theory made above; secondly the individualistic critic implicitly draws a distinction quite foreign to the letter and the spirit of the beneficiary theory between the legal provision of benefits simply as a contribution to general utility and as a contribution to the satisfaction of individual needs. It is the latter which leads him to talk of rights secured by the duties of the criminal law.

The upshot of these considerations is that instead of a general analytical and explanatory theory covering the whole field of legal rights I have provided a general theory in terms of the notion of a legally respected individual choice which is satisfactory only at one level—the level of the lawyer concerned with the working of the 'ordinary' law. This requires supplementation in order to accommodate the important deployment of the language of rights by the constitutional lawyer and the individualistic critic of the law, for whom the core of the notion of rights is neither individual choice nor individual benefit but basic or fundamental individual needs. This result may be felt as distressingly untidy by some, and they may be tempted to combine the perspectives which I have distinguished of the ordinary lawyer, the constitutional lawyer, and the individualistic critic of the law in some general formula embracing all three. Such a general formula is suggested by Hohfeld's statement that the generic sense of a right means 'any legal advantage'.[98] But I fear that, behind the comfortable appearance of generality, we would have only an unilluminating combination or mere juxtaposition of the choice theory together with the benefit theory; and this would fail to be sensitive to the important reasons for describing only some legally secured benefits, only in some contexts, as legal rights.

[98] Op. cit., pp. 42, 71. Cf. also Bentham's discussion in *O.L.G.*, pp. 55–9 of the inclusion in the idea of a 'party favoured by the law' of two kinds of favour: favour in 'point of interest' and 'in point of agency'. A party is 'favoured in point of agency' when he has an *exceptional* liberty, i.e. a liberty to do some act generally prohibited.

VIII

Taking Rights Seriously[1]

RONALD DWORKIN

1. THE RIGHTS OF CITIZENS

THE language of rights now dominates political debate in the United States. Does the Government respect the moral and political rights of its citizens? Or does the Government's war policy, or its race policy, fly in the face of these rights? Do the minorities whose rights have been violated have the right to violate the law in return? Or does the silent majority itself have rights, including the right that those who break the law be punished? It is not surprising that these questions are now prominent. The concept of rights, and particularly the concept of rights against the Government, has its most natural use when a political society is divided, and appeals to co-operation or a common goal are pointless.

The debate does not include the issue of whether citizens have *some* moral rights against their Government. It seems accepted on all sides that they do. Conventional lawyers and politicians take it as a point of pride that our legal system recognizes, for example, individual rights of free speech, equality, and due process. They base their claim that our law deserves respect, at least in part, on that fact, for they would not claim that totalitarian systems deserve the same loyalty.

Some philosophers, of course, reject the idea that citizens have rights apart from what the law happens to give them. Bentham thought that the idea of moral rights was 'nonsense on stilts'. But that view has never been part of our orthodox political theory, and politicians of both parties appeal to the rights of the people to justify a great part of what they want to do. I shall not be concerned, in this essay, to defend the thesis that citizens have moral rights against their governments; I want instead to explore the implications of that thesis for those,

[1] First published in the *New York Review of Books*, 18 December 1970.

including the present United States Government, who profess to accept it.

It is much in dispute, of course, what *particular* rights citizens have. Does the acknowledged right to free speech, for example, include the right to participate in nuisance demonstrations? In practice the Government will have the last word on what an individual's rights are, because its police will do what its officials and courts say. But that does not mean that the Government's view is necessarily the correct view; anyone who thinks it does must believe that men and women have only such moral rights as Government chooses to grant, which means that they have no moral rights at all.

All this is sometimes obscured in the United States by the constitutional system. The American Constitution provides a set of individual *legal* rights in the First Amendment, and in the due process, equal protection, and similar clauses. Under present legal practice the Supreme Court has the power to declare an act of Congress or of a state legislature void if the Court finds that the act offends these provisions. This practice has led some commentators to suppose that individual moral rights are fully protected by this system, but that is hardly so, nor could it be so.

The Constitition fuses legal and moral issues, by making the validity of a law depend on the answer to complex moral problems, like the problem of whether a particular statute respects the inherent equality of all men. This fusion has important consequences for the debates about civil disobedience; I have described these elsewhere[2] and I shall refer to them later. But it leaves open two prominent questions. It does not tell us whether the Constitution, even properly interpreted, recognizes all the moral rights that citizens have, and it does not tell us whether, as many suppose, citizens would have a duty to obey the law even if it did invade their moral rights.

Both questions become crucial when some minority claims moral rights which the law denies, like the right to run its local school system, and which lawyers agree are not protected by the Constitution. The second question becomes crucial when, as now, the majority is sufficiently aroused so that Constitutional amendments to eliminate rights, like the right against

[2] 'On Not Prosecuting Civil Disobedience', *NYR*, 6 June 1968.

self-incrimination, are seriously proposed. It is also crucial in nations, like the United Kingdom, that have no constitution of a comparable nature.

Even if the Constitution were perfect, of course, and the majority left it alone, it would not follow that the Supreme Court could guarantee the individual rights of citizens. A Supreme Court decision is still a legal decision, and it must take into account precedent and institutional considerations like relations between the Court and Congress, as well as morality. And no judicial decision is necessariiy the right decision. Judges stand for different positions on controversial issues of law and morals and, as the fights over Nixon's Supreme Court nominations showed, a President is entitled to appoint judges of his own persuasion, provided that they are honest and capable.

So, though the constitutional system adds something to the protection of moral rights against the Government, it falls far short of guaranteeing these rights, or even establishing what they are. It means that, on some occasions, a department other than the legislature has the last word on these issues, which can hardly satisfy someone who thinks such a department profoundly wrong.

It is of course inevitable that some department of government will have the final say on what law will be enforced. When men disagree about moral rights, there will be no way for either side to prove its case, and some decision must stand if there is not to be anarchy. But that piece of orthodox wisdom must be the beginning and not the end of a philosophy of legislation and enforcement. If we cannot insist that the Government reach the right answers about the rights of its citizens, we can insist at least that it try. We can insist that it take rights seriously, follow a coherent theory of what these rights are, and act consistently with its own professions. I shall try to show what that means, and now it bears on the present political debates.

II. RIGHTS AND THE RIGHT TO BREAK THE LAW

I shall start with the most violently argued issue. Does an American ever have the moral right to break a law? Suppose someone admits a law is valid; does he therefore have a duty to obey it? Those who try to give an answer seem to fall into two camps. The conservatives, as I shall call them, seem to disapprove of any act of disobedience; they appear satisfied when such acts are prosecuted, and disappointed when convictions are reversed. The other group, the liberals, are much more sympathetic to at least some cases of disobedience; they sometimes disapprove of prosecutions and celebrate acquittals. If we look beyond these emotional reactions, however, and pay attention to the arguments the two parties use, we discover an astounding fact. Both groups give essentially the same answer to the question of principle that supposedly divides them.

The answer that both parties give is this. In a democracy, or at least a democracy that in principle respects individual rights, each citizen has a general moral duty to obey all the laws, even though he would like some of them changed. He owes that duty to his fellow citizens, who obey laws that they do not like, to his benefit. But this general duty cannot be an absolute duty, because even a society that is in principle just may produce unjust laws and policies, and a man has duties other than his duties to the State. A man must honour his duties to his God and to his conscience, and if these conflict with his duty to the State, then he is entitled, in the end, to do what he judges to be right. If he decides that he must break the law, however, then he must submit to the judgment and punishment that the State imposes, in recognition of the fact that his duty to his fellow citizens was overwhelmed but not extinguished by his religious or moral obligation.

Of course this common answer can be elaborated in very different ways. Some would describe the duty to the State as fundamental, and picture the dissenter as a religious or moral fanatic. Others would describe the duty to the State in grudging terms, and picture those who oppose it as moral heroes. But these are differences in tone, and the position I described represents, I think, the view of most of those who find themselves arguing either for or against civil disobedience in particular cases.

I do not claim that it is everyone's view. There must be some who put the duty to the State so high that they do not grant that it can ever be overcome. There are certainly some who would deny that a man ever has a moral duty to obey the law, at least in the United States today. But these two extreme positions are the slender tails of a bell curve, and all those who fall in between hold the orthodox position I described—that men have a duty to obey the law but have the right to follow their consciences when it conflicts with that duty.

But if that is so, then we have a paradox in the fact that men who give the same answer to a question of principle should seem to disagree so much, and to divide so fiercely, in particular cases. The paradox goes even deeper, for each party, in at least some cases, takes a position that seems flatly inconsistent with the theoretical position they both accept. This position is tested, for example, when someone evades the draft on grounds of conscience, or encourages others to commit this crime. Conservatives argue that such men must be prosecuted, even though they are sincere. Why must they be prosecuted? Because society cannot tolerate the decline in respect for the law that their act constitutes and encourages. They must be prosecuted, in short, to discourage them and others like them from doing what they have done.

But there seems to be a monstrous contradiction here. If a man has a right to do what his conscience tells him he must, then how can the State be justified in discouraging him from doing it? Is it not wicked for a state to forbid and punish what it acknowledges that men have a right to do?

Moreover, it is not just conservatives who argue that those who break the law out of moral conviction should be prosecuted. The liberal is notoriously opposed to allowing Southern school officials to go slow on segregation, even though he acknowledges that these school officials think they have a moral right to do what the law forbids. The liberal does not often argue, it is true, that the desegregation laws must be enforced to encourage general respect for law. He argues instead that the desegregation laws must be enforced because they are right. But his position also seems inconsistent: can it be right to prosecute men for doing what their conscience requires, when we acknowledge their right to follow their conscience?

We are therefore left with two puzzles. How can two parties to an issue of principle, each of which thinks it is in profound disagreement with the other, embrace the same position on that issue? How can it be that each side urges solutions to particular problems which seem flatly to contradict the position of principle that both accept? One possible answer is that some or all of those who accept the common position are hypocrites, paying lip service to rights of conscience which in fact they do not grant.

There is some plausibility in this charge. A sort of hypocrisy must be involved when public officials who claim to respect conscience deny Muhammad Ali the right to box in their states. If Ali, in spite of his religious scruples, had joined the Army, he would have been allowed to box even though, on the principles these officials say they honour, he would have been a worse human being for having done so. But there are few cases that seem so straightforward as this one, and even here the officials do not seem to recognize the contradiction between their acts and their principles. So we must search for some explanation beyond the truth that men often do not mean what they say.

The deeper explanation lies in a set of confusions that often embarrass arguments about rights. These confusions have clouded all the issues I mentioned at the outset and have crippled attempts to develop a coherent theory of how a government that respects rights must behave.

In order to explain this, I must call attention to the fact, familiar to philosophers but often ignored in political debate, that the word 'right' has different force in different contexts. In most cases when we say that someone has a 'right' to do something, we imply that it would be wrong to interfere with his doing it, or at least that some special grounds are needed for justifying any interference. I use this strong sense of right when I say that you have the right to spend your money gambling, if you wish, though you ought to spend it in a more worthwhile way. I mean that it would be wrong for anyone to interfere with you even though you propose to spend your money in a way that I think is wrong.

There is a clear difference between saying that someone has a right to do something in this sense and saying that it is the 'right' thing for him to do, or that he does no 'wrong' in doing it. Someone may have the right to do something that is the wrong thing for him to do, as might be the case with gambling. Conversely, something may be the right thing for him to do and yet he may have no right to do it, in the sense that it would not be wrong for someone to interfere with his trying. If our army captures an enemy soldier, we might say that the right thing for him to do is to try to escape, but it would not follow that it is wrong of us to try to stop him. We might admire him for trying to escape, and perhaps even think less of him if he did not. But there is no suggestion here that it is wrong of us to stand in his way; on the contrary, if we think our cause is just, we think it right for us to do all we can to stop him.

Ordinarily this distinction, between the issues of whether a man has a right to do something and whether it is the right thing for him to do, causes no trouble. But sometimes it does, because sometimes we say that a man has a right to do something when we mean only to deny that it is the wrong thing for him to do. Thus we say that the captured soldier has a 'right' to try to escape when we mean, not that we do wrong to stop him, but that he has no duty not to make the attempt. We use 'right' this way when we speak of someone having the 'right' to act on his own principles, or the 'right' to follow his own conscience. We mean that he does no wrong to proceed on his honest convictions, even though we disagree with these convictions, and even though, for policy or other reasons, we must force him to act contrary to them.

Suppose a man believes that welfare payments to the poor are profoundly wrong, because they sap enterprise, and so declares his full income-tax each year but declines to pay half of it. We might say that he has a right to refuse to pay, if he wishes, but that the Government has a right to proceed against him for the full tax, and to fine or jail him for late payment if that is necessary to keep the collection system working efficiently. We do not take this line in most cases; we do not say that the ordinary thief has a right to steal, if he wishes, so long as he pays the penalty. We say a man has the right to break the law, even though the State has a right to punish him, only when we think that, because of his convictions, he does no wrong in doing so.[3]

These distinctions enable us to see an ambiguity in the ortho-

---

[3] It is not surprising that we sometimes use the concept of having a right to say that others must not interfere with an act and sometimes to say that the act is not the wrong thing to do. Often, when someone has *no* right to do something, like attacking another man physically, it is true *both* that it is the wrong thing to do and that others are entitled to stop it, by demand, if not by force. It is therefore natural to say that someone has a right when we mean to deny *either* of these consequences, as well as when we mean to deny both.

dox question: Does a man ever have a right to break the law? Does that question mean to ask whether he ever has a right to break the law in the strong sense, so that the Government would do wrong to stop him, by arresting and prosecuting him? Or does it mean to ask whether he ever does the right thing to break the law, so that we should all respect him even though the Government should jail him?

If we take the orthodox position to be an answer to the first—and most important—question, then the paradoxes I described arise. But if we take it as an answer to the second, they do not. Conservatives and liberals do agree that sometimes a man does not do the wrong thing to break a law, when his conscience so requires. They disagree, when they do, over the different issue of what the State's response should be. Both parties do think that sometimes the State should prosecute. But this is not inconsistent with the proposition that the man prosecuted did the right thing in breaking the law.

The paradoxes seem genuine because the two questions are not usually distinguished, and the orthodox position is presented as a general solution to the problem of civil disobedience. But once the distinction is made, it is apparent that the position has been so widely accepted only because, when it is applied, it is treated as an answer to the second question but not the first. The crucial distinction is obscured by the troublesome idea of a right to conscience; this idea has been at the centre of most recent discussions of political obligation, but it is a red herring drawing us away from the crucial political questions. The state of a man's conscience may be decisive, or central, when the issue is whether he does something morally wrong in breaking the law; but it need not be decisive or even central when the issue is whether he has a right, in the strong sense of that term, to do so. A man does not have the right, in that sense, to do whatever his conscience demands, but he may have the right, in that sense, to do something even though his conscience does not demand it.

If that is true, then there has been almost no serious attempt to answer the questions that almost everyone means to ask. We can make a fresh start by stating these questions more clearly. Does an American ever have the right, in a strong sense, to do something which is against the law? If so, when? In order to answer these questions put in that way, we must try to become clearer about the implications of the idea, mentioned earlier, that citizens have at least some rights against their government.

I said that in the United States citizens are supposed to have certain fundamental rights against their Government, certain moral rights made into legal rights by the Constitution. If this idea is significant, and worth bragging about, then these rights must be rights in the strong sense I just described. The claim that citizens have a right to free speech must imply that it would be wrong for the Government to stop them from speaking, even when the Government believes that what they will say will cause more harm than good. The claim cannot mean, on the prisoner-of-war analogy, only that citizens do no wrong in speaking their minds, though the Government reserves the right to prevent them from doing so.

This is a crucial point, and I want to labour it. Of course a responsible government must be ready to justify anything it does, particularly when it limits the liberty of its citizens. But normally it is a sufficient justification, even for an act that limits liberty, that the act is calculated to increase what the philosophers call general utility—that it is calculated to produce more over-all benefit than harm. So, though the New York City government needs a justification for forbidding motorists to drive up Lexington Avenue, it is sufficient justification if the proper officials believe, on sound evidence, that the gain to the many will outweigh the inconvenience to the few. When individual citizens are said to have rights against the Government, however, like the right of free speech, that must mean that this sort of justification is not enough. Otherwise the claim would not argue that individuals have special protection against the law when their rights are in play, and that is just the point of the claim.

Not all legal rights, or even Constitutional rights, represent moral rights against the Government. I now have the legal right to drive either way on Fifty-seventh Street, but the Government would do no wrong to make that street one-way if it thought it in the general interest to do so. I have a Constitutional right to vote for a congressman every two years, but the national and state governments would do no wrong if, following the amendment procedure, they made a congressman's term four years instead of two, again on the basis of a judgment that this would be for the general good.

But those Constitutional rights that we call fundamental, like the right of free speech, are supposed to represent rights against the Government in the strong sense; that is the point of the boast that our legal system respects the fundamental rights of the citizen. If citizens have a moral right of free speech, then governments would do wrong to repeal the First Amendment that guarantees it, even if they were persuaded that the majority would be better off if speech were curtailed.

I must not overstate the point. Someone who claims that citizens have a right against the Government need not go so far as to say that the State is *never* justified in overriding that right. He might say, for example, that although citizens have a right to free speech, the Government may override that right when necessary to protect the rights of others, or to prevent a catastrophe, or even to obtain a clear and major public benefit (though if he acknowledged this last as a possible justification he would be treating the right in question as not among the most important or fundamental). What he cannot do is to say that the Government is justified in overriding a right on the minimal grounds that would be sufficient if no such right existed. He cannot say that the Government is entitled to act on no more than a judgment that its act is likely to produce, overall, a benefit to the community. That admission would make his claim of a right pointless, and would show him to be using some sense of 'right' other than the strong sense necessary to give his claim the political importance it is normally taken to have.

But then the answers to our two questions about disobedience seem plain, if unorthodox. In our society a man does sometimes have the right, in the strong sense, to disobey a law. He has that right whenever that law wrongly invades his rights against the Government. If he has a moral right to free speech, that is, then he has a moral right to break any law that the Government, by virtue of his right, had no right to adopt. The right to disobey the law is not a separate right, having something to do with conscience, additional to other rights against the Government. It is simply a feature of these rights against the Government, and it cannot be denied in principle without denying that any such rights exist.

These answers seem obvious once we take rights against the Government to be rights in the strong sense I described. If I have a right to speak my mind on political issues, then the Government does wrong to make it illegal for me to do so, even if it thinks this is in the general interest. If, nevertheless, the Government does make my act illegal, then it does a further wrong to enforce that law against me. My right against the Government means that it is wrong for the Government to stop me from speaking; the Government cannot make it right to stop me just by taking the first step.

This does not, of course, tell us exactly what rights men do have against the Government. It does not tell us whether the right of free speech includes the right of demonstration. But it does mean that passing a law cannot affect such rights as men do have, and that is of crucial importance, because it dictates the attitude that an individual is entitled to take toward his personal decision when civil disobedience is in question.

Both conservatives and liberals suppose that in a society which is generally decent everyone has a duty to obey the law, whatever it is. That is the source of the 'general duty' clause in the orthodox position, and though liberals believe that this duty can sometimes be 'overridden', even they suppose, as the orthodox position maintains, that the duty of obedience remains in some submerged form, so that a man does well to accept punishment in recognition of that duty. But this general duty is almost incoherent in a society that recognizes rights. If a man believes he has a right to demonstrate, then he must believe that it would be wrong for the Government to stop him, with or without benefit of a law. If he is entitled to believe that, then it is silly to speak of a duty to obey the law as such, or of a duty to accept the punishment that the State has no right to give.

Conservatives will object to the short work I have made of their point. They will argue that even if the Government was wrong to adopt some law, like a law limiting speech, there are independent reasons why the Government is justified in enforcing the law once adopted. When the law forbids demonstration, then, so they argue, some principle more important than the individual's right to speak is brought into play, namely the principle of respect for law. If a law, even a bad law, is left unenforced, then respect for law is weakened, and society as a whole suffers. So an individual loses his moral right to speak when speech is made criminal, and the Government must, for the common good and for the general benefit, enforce the law against him.

But this argument, though popular, is plausible only if we forget what it means to say that an individual has a right against the State. It is far from plain that civil disobedience lowers respect for law, but even if we suppose that it does, this fact is irrelevant. The prospect of utilitarian gains cannot justify preventing a man from doing what he has a right to do, and the supposed gains in respect for law are simply utilitarian gains. There would be no point in the boast that we respect individual rights unless that involved some sacrifice, and the sacrifice in question must be that we give up whatever marginal benefits our country would receive from overriding these rights when they prove inconvenient. So the general benefit cannot be a good ground for abridging rights, even when the benefit in question is a heightened respect for law.

But perhaps I do wrong to assume that the argument about respect for law is only an appeal to general utility. I said that a state may be justified in overriding or limiting rights on other grounds, and we must ask, before rejecting the conservative position, whether any of these apply. The most important—and least well understood—of these other grounds invokes the notion of *competing rights* that would be jeopardized if the right in question were not limited. Citizens have personal rights to the State's protection as well as personal rights to be free from the State's interference, and it may be necessary for the Government to choose between these two sorts of rights. The law of defamation, for example, limits the personal right of any man to say what he thinks, because it requires him to have good grounds for what he says. But this law is justified, even for those who think that it does invade a personal right, by the fact that it protects the right of others not to have their reputations ruined by a careless statement.

The individual rights that our society acknowledges often conflict in this way, and when they do it is the job of government to discriminate. If the Government makes the right choice, and protects the more important at the cost of the less, then it has not weakened or cheapened the notion of a right; on the contrary it would have done so had it failed to protect the more important of the two. So we must acknowledge that the Government has a reason for limiting rights if it plausibly believes that a competing right is more important.

May the conservative seize on this fact? He might argue that I **did** wrong to characterize his argument as one that appeals to the general benefit, because it appeals instead to competing rights, namely the moral right of the majority to have its laws enforced, or the right of society to maintain the degree of order and security it wishes. These are the rights, he would say, that must be weighed against the individual's right to do what the wrongful law prohibits.

But this new argument is confused, because it depends on yet another ambiguity in the language of rights. It is true that we speak of the 'right' of society to do what it wants, but this cannot be a 'competing right' of the sort that may justify the invasion of a right against the Government. The existence of rights against the Government would be jeopardized if the Government were able to defeat such a right by appealing to the right of a democratic majority to work its will. A right against the Government must be a right to do something even when the majority thinks it would be wrong to do it, and even when the majority would be worse off for having it done. If we now say that society has a right to do whatever is in the general benefit, or the right to preserve whatever sort of environment the majority wishes to live in, and we mean that these are the sort of rights that provide justification for overruling any rights against the Government that may conflict, then we have annihilated the latter rights.

In order to save them, we must recognize as competing rights only the rights of other members of the society as individuals. We must distinguish the 'rights' of the majority as such, which cannot count as a justification for overruling individual rights, and the personal rights of members of a majority, which might well count. The test we must use is this. Someone has a competing right to protection, which must be weighed against an individual right to act, if that person would be entitled to demand that protection from his government on his own title, as an individual, without regard to whether a majority of his fellow citizens joined in the demand.

It cannot be true, on this test, that anyone has a right to have all the laws of the nation enforced. He has a right to have enforced only those criminal laws, for example, that he would have a right to have enacted if they were not already law. The laws against personal assault may well fall into that class. If the physically vulnerable members of the community—those who need police protection against personal violence—were only a small minority, it would still seem plausible to say that they were entitled to that protection. But the laws that provide a certain level of quiet in public places, or that authorize and finance a foreign war, cannot be thought to rest on individual rights. The timid lady on the streets of Chicago is not entitled to just the degree of quiet that now obtains, nor is she entitled to have boys drafted to fight in wars she approves. There are laws—perhaps desirable laws—that provide these advantages for her, but the justification for these laws, if they can be justified at all, is the common desire of a large majority, not her personal right. If, therefore, these laws do abridge someone else's moral right to protest, or his right to personal security, she cannot urge a competing right to justify the abridgement. She has no personal right to have such laws passed, and she has no competing right to have them enforced either.

So the conservative cannot advance his argument much on the ground of competing rights, but he may want to use another ground. A government, he may argue, may be justified in abridging the personal rights of its citizens in an emergency, or when a very great loss may be prevented, or, perhaps, when some major benefit can clearly be secured. If the nation is at war, a policy of censorship may be justified even though it invades the right to say what one thinks on matters of political controversy. But the emergency must be genuine. There must be what Oliver Wendell Holmes described as a clear and pr sent danger, and the danger must be one of magnitude.

Can the conservative argue that when any law is passed, even a wrongful law, this sort of justification is available for enforcing it? His argument might be something of this sort. If the Government once acknowledges that it may be wrong— that the legislature might have adopted, the executive approved, and the courts left standing, a law that in fact abridges important rights—then this admission will lead not simply to a marginal decline in respect for law, but to a crisis of order. Citizens may decide to obey only those laws they personally approve, and that is anarchy. So the Government must insist that whatever a citizen's rights may be before a law is passed and upheld by the courts, his rights thereafter are determined by that law.

But this argument ignores the primitive distinction between what may happen and what will happen. If we allow speculation to support the justification of emergency or decisive benefit, then, again, we have annihilated rights. We must, as Learned Hand said, discount the gravity of the evil threatened by the likelihood of reaching that evil. I know of no genuine evidence to the effect that tolerating some civil disobedience, out of respect for the moral position of its authors, will increase such disobedience, let alone crime in general. The case that it will must be based on vague assumptions about the contagion of ordinary crimes, assumptions that are themselves unproved, and that are in any event largely irrelevant. It seems at least as plausible to argue that tolerance will increase respect for officials and for the bulk of the laws they promulgate, or at least retard the rate of growing disrespect.

If the issue were simply the question whether the community would be marginally better off under strict law enforcement, then the Government would have to decide on the evidence we have, and it might not be unreasonable to decide, on balance, that it would. But since rights are at stake, the issue is the very different one of whether tolerance would destroy the community or threaten it with great harm, and it seems to me simply mindless to suppose that the evidence makes that probable or even conceivable.

The argument from emergency is confused in another way as well. It assumes that the Government must take the position either that a man never has the right to break the law, or that he always does. I said that any society that claims to recognize rights at all must abandon the notion of a general duty to obey the law that holds in all cases. This is important, because it shows that there are no short cuts to meeting a citizen's claim of right. If a citizen argues that he has a moral right not to serve in the Army, or to protest in a way he finds effective, then an official who wants to answer him, and not simply bludgeon him into obedience, must respond to the particular point he makes, and cannot point to the draft law or a Supreme Court decision as having even special, let alone decisive, weight. Sometimes an official who considers the citizen's moral arguments in good faith will be persuaded that the citizen's claim is plausible, or even right. It does not follow, however, that he will always be persuaded or that he always should be.

I must emphasize that all these propositions concern the strong sense of right, and they therefore leave open important questions about the right thing to do. If a man believes he has the right to break the law, he must then ask whether he does the right thing to exercise that right. He must remember that reasonable men can differ about whether he has a right against the Government, and therefore the right to break the law, that he thinks he has; and therefore that reasonable men can oppose him in good faith. He must take into account the various consequences his acts will have, whether they involve violence, and such other considerations as the context makes relevant; he must not go beyond the rights he can in good faith claim, to acts that violate the rights of others.

On the other hand, if some official, like a prosecutor, believes that the citizen does *not* have the right to break the law, then *he* must ask whether he does the right thing to enforce it. In the article I mentioned earlier I argued that certain features of our legal system, and in particular the fusion of legal and moral issues in our Constitution, mean that citizens often do the right thing in exercising what they take to be moral rights to break the law, and that prosecutors often do the right thing in failing to prosecute them for it. I will not repeat those arguments here; instead I want to ask whether the requirement that Government take its citizens' rights seriously has anything to do with the crucial question of what these rights are.

III. CONTROVERSIAL RIGHTS

The argument so far has been hypothetical: if a man has a particular moral right against the Government, that right survives contrary legislation or adjudication. But this does not tell us what rights he has, and it is notorious that reasonable men disagree about that. There is wide agreement on certain clear-cut cases; almost everyone who believes in rights at all would admit, for example, that a man has a moral right to speak his mind in a non-provocative way on matters of political concern, and that this is an important right that the State must go to great pains to protect. But there is great controversy as to the limits of such paradigm rights, and the so-called 'anti-riot' law involved in the Chicago Seven trial is a case in point.

The defendants were accused of conspiring to cross state lines with the intention of causing a riot. This charge is vague—perhaps unconstitutionally vague—but the law apparently defines as criminal emotional speeches which argue that violence is justified in order to secure political equality. Does the right of free speech protect this sort of speech? That, of course, is a legal issue, because it invokes the free-speech clause of the First Amendment of the Constitution. But it is also a moral issue, because, as I said, we must treat the First Amendment as an attempt to protect a moral right. It is part of the job of governing to 'define' moral rights through statutes and judicial decisions, that is, to declare officially the extent that moral rights will be taken to have in law. Congress faced this task in voting on the anti-riot bill, and the Supreme Court will face it if the Chicago Seven case goes that far. How should the different departments of government go about defining moral rights?

They should begin with a sense that whatever they decide might be wrong. History and their descendants may judge that they acted unjustly when they thought they were right. If they take their duty seriously, they must try to limit their mistakes, and they must therefore try to discover where the dangers of mistake lie.

They might choose one of two very different models for this purpose. The first model recommends striking a balance between the rights of the individual and the demands of society at large. If the Government *infringes* on a moral right (for example, by defining the right of free speech more narrowly than justice requires), then it has done the individual a wrong. On the other hand, if the Government *inflates* a right (by defining it more broadly than justice requires) then it cheats society of some general benefit, like safe streets, that it is perfectly entitled to have. So a mistake on one side is as serious as a mistake on the other. The course of government is to steer to the middle, to balance the general good and personal rights, giving to each its due.

When the Government, or any of its branches, defines a right, it must bear in mind, according to the first model, the social cost of different proposals and make the necessary adjustments. It must not grant the same freedom to noisy demonstrations as it grants to calm political discussion, for example, because the former causes much more trouble than the latter. Once it decides how much of a right to recognize, it must enforce its decision to the full. That means permitting an individual to act within his rights, as the Government has defined them, but not beyond, so that if anyone breaks the law, even on grounds of conscience, he must be punished. No doubt any government will make mistakes, and will regret decisions once taken. That is inevitable. But this middle policy will ensure that errors on one side will balance out errors on the other over the long run.

The first model, described in this way, has great plausibility, and most laymen and lawyers, I think, would respond to it warmly. The metaphor of balancing the public interest against personal claims is established in our political and judicial rhetoric, and this metaphor gives the model both familiarity and appeal. Nevertheless, the first model is a false one, certainly in the case of rights generally regarded as important, and the metaphor is the heart of its error.

The institution of rights against the Government is not a gift of God, or an ancient ritual, or a national sport. It is a complex and troublesome practice that makes the Government's job of securing the general benefit more difficult and more expensive, and it would be a frivolous and wrongful practice unless it served some point. Anyone who professes to take rights seriously, and who praises our Government for respecting them, must have some sense of what that point is. He must accept, at the minimum, one or both of two important ideas. The first is the vague but powerful idea of human dignity. This idea, associated with Kant, but defended by philosophers of different schools, supposes that there are ways of treating a man that are inconsistent with recognizing him as a full member of the human community, and holds that such treatment is profoundly unjust.

The second is the more familiar idea of political equality. This supposes that the weaker members of a political community are entitled to the same concern and respect of their government as the more powerful members have secured for themselves, so that if some men have freedom of decision whatever the effect on the general good, then all men must have the same freedom. I do not want to defend or elaborate these ideas here, but only to insist that anyone who claims that citizens have rights must accept ideas very close to these.[4]

It makes sense to say that a man has a fundamental right against the Government, in the strong sense, like free speech, if that right is necessary to protect his dignity, or his standing as equally entitled to concern and respect, or some other personal value of like consequence. It does not make sense otherwise.

So if rights make sense at all, then the invasion of a relatively important right must be a very serious matter. It means treating a man as less than a man, or as less worthy of concern than other men. The institution of rights rests on the conviction that this is a grave injustice, and that it is worth paying the incremental cost in social policy or efficiency that is necessary to prevent it. But then it must be wrong to say that inflating rights is as serious as invading them. If the Government errs on the side of the individual, then it simply pays a little more in social efficiency than it has to pay; it pays a little more, that is, of the same coin that it has already decided must be spent. But if it errs against the individual it inflicts an insult upon him that, on its own reckoning, it is worth a great deal of that coin to avoid.

---

[4] He need not consider these ideas to be axiomatic. He may, that is, have reasons for insisting that dignity or equality are important values, and these reasons may be utilitarian. He may believe, for example, that the general good will be advanced, *in the long run*, only if we treat indignity or inequality as very great injustices, and never allow our *opinions* about the general good to justify them. I do not know of any good arguments for or against this sort of 'institutional' utilitarianism, but it is consistent with my point, because it argues that we must treat violations of dignity and equality as special moral crimes, beyond the reach of ordinary utilitarian justification.

So the first model is indefensible. It rests, in fact, on a mistake I discussed earlier, namely the confusion of society's rights with the rights of members of society. 'Balancing' is appropriate when the Government must choose between competing claims of right—between the Southerner's claim to freedom of association, for example, and the black man's claim to an equal education. Then the Government can do nothing but estimate the merits of the competing claims, and act on its estimate. The first model assumes that the 'right' of the majority is a competing right that must be balanced in this way; but that, as I argued before, is a confusion that threatens to destroy the concept of individual rights. It is worth noticing that the community rejects the first model in that area where the stakes for the individual are highest, the criminal process. We say that it is better that a great many guilty men go free than that one innocent man be punished, and that homily rests on the choice of the second model for government.

The second model treats abridging a right as much more serious than inflating one, and its recommendations follow from that judgment. It stipulates that once a right is recognized in clear-cut cases, then the Government should act to cut off that right only when some compelling reason is presented, some reason that is consistent with the suppositions on which the original right must be based. It cannot be an argument for curtailing a right, once granted, simply that society would pay a further price in extending it. There must be something special about that further cost, or there must be some other feature of the case, that makes it sensible to say that although great social cost is warranted to protect the original right, this particular cost is not necessary. Otherwise, the Government's failure to extend the right will show that its recognition of the right in the original case is a sham, a promise that it intends to keep only until that becomes inconvenient.

How can we show that a particular cost is not worth paying without taking back the initial recognition of a right? I can think of only three sorts of grounds that can consistently be used to limit the definition of a particular right. First, the Government might show that the values protected by the original right are not really at stake in the marginal case, or are at stake only in some attenuated form. Second, it might show that if the right is defined to include the marginal case, then some competing right, in the strong sense I described earlier, would be abridged. Third, it might show that if the right were so defined, then the cost to society would not be simply incremental, but would be of a degree far beyond the cost paid to grant the original right, a degree great enough to justify whatever assault on dignity or equality might be involved.

It is fairly easy to apply these grounds to one problem the Supreme Court has recently faced, and must face soon again. The draft law provides an exemption for conscientious objectors, but this exemption, as interpreted by the draft boards, has been limited to those who object to *all* wars on *religious* grounds. If we suppose that the exemption is justified on the ground that an individual has a moral right not to kill in violation of his own principles, then the question is raised whether it is proper to exclude those whose morality is not based on religion, or whose morality is sufficiently complex to distinguish among wars. The Court has just held that the draft boards are wrong to exclude the former, and it will soon be asked to decide whether they are wrong to exclude the latter as well.

None of the three grounds I listed can justify either of these exclusions. The invasion of personality in forcing men to kill when they believe killing immoral is just as great when these beliefs are based on secular grounds, or take account of the fact that wars differ in morally relevant ways, and there is no pertinent difference in competing rights or in national emergency. There are differences among the cases, of course, but they are insufficient to justify the distinction. A government that is secular on principle cannot prefer a religious to a non-religious morality as such. There are utilitarian arguments in favour of limiting the exception to religious or universal grounds—an exemption so limited may be less expensive to administer, and may allow easier discrimination between sincere and insincere applicants. But these utilitarian reasons are irrelevant, because they cannot count as grounds for limiting a right.

What about the anti-riot law, as applied in the Chicago trial? Does that law represent an improper limitation of the right to free speech, supposedly protected by the First Amendment? If we were to apply the first model for government to this issue, the argument for the anti-riot law would look strong. But if we set aside talk of balancing as inappropriate, and turn to the proper grounds for limiting a right, then the argument becomes a great deal weaker. The original right of free speech must suppose that it is an assault on human personality to stop a man from expressing what he honestly believes, particularly on issues affecting how he is governed. Surely the assault is greater, and not less, when he is stopped from expressing those principles of political morality that he holds most passionately, in the face of what he takes to be outrageous violations of these principles.

It may be said that the anti-riot law leaves him free to express these principles in a non-provocative way. But that misses the point of the connection between expression and dignity. A man cannot express himself freely when he cannot match his rhetoric to his outrage, or when he must trim his sails to protect values he counts as nothing next to those he is trying to vindicate. It is true that some political dissenters speak in ways that shock the majority, but it is arrogant for the majority to suppose that the orthodox methods of expression are the proper ways to speak, for this is a denial of equal concern and respect. If the point of the right is to protect the dignity of dissenters, then we must make judgments about appropriate speech with the personalities of the dissenters in mind, not the personality of the 'silent' majority for whom the anti-riot law is no restraint at all.

So the argument fails, that the personal values protected by the original right are less at stake in this marginal case. We must consider whether competing rights, or some grave threat to society, nevertheless justify the anti-riot law. We can consider these two grounds together, because the only plausible competing rights are rights to be free from violence, and violence is the only plausible threat to society that the context provides.

I have no right to burn your house, or stone you or your car, or swing a bicycle chain against your skull, even if I find these to be natural means of expression. But the defendants in the Chicago trial were not accused of direct violence; the argument runs that the acts of speech they planned made it likely that others would do acts of violence, either in support of or out of hostility to what they said. Does this provide a justification?

The question would be different if we could say with any confidence how much and what sort of violence the anti-riot law might be expected to prevent. Will it save two lives a year, or two hundred, or two thousand? Two thousand dollars of property, or two hundred thousand, or two million? No one can say, not simply because prediction is next to impossible, but because we have no firm understanding of the process by which demonstration disintegrates into riot, and in particular of the part played by inflammatory speech, as distinct from poverty, police brutality, blood lust, and all the rest of human and economic failure. The Government must try, of course, to reduce the violent waste of lives and property, but it must recognize that any attempt to locate and remove a cause of riot, short of a reorganization of society, must be an exercise in speculation, trial, and error. It must make its decisions under conditions of high uncertainty, and the institution of rights, taken seriously, limits its freedom to experiment under such conditions.

It forces the Government to bear in mind that preventing a man from speaking or demonstrating offers him a certain and profound insult, in return for a speculative benefit that may in any event be achieved in other if more expensive ways. When lawyers say that rights may be limited to protect other rights, or to prevent catastrophe, they have in mind cases in which cause and effect are relatively clear, like the familiar example of a man falsely crying 'Fire!' in a crowded theatre.

But the Chicago story shows how obscure the causal connections can become. Were the speeches of Hoffman or Rubin necessary conditions of the riot? Or had thousands of people come to Chicago for the purposes of rioting anyway, as the Government also argues? Were they in any case sufficient conditions? Or could the police have contained the violence if they had not been so busy contributing to it, as the staff of the President's Commission on Violence said they were?

These are not easy questions, but if rights mean anything, then the Government cannot simply assume answers that justify its conduct. If a man has a right to speak, if the reasons that support that right extend to provocative political speech, and if the effects of such speech on violence are unclear, then the Government is not entitled to make its first attack on that problem by denying that right. It may be that abridging the right to speak is the least expensive course, or the least damaging to police morale, or the most popular politically. But these are utilitarian arguments in favour of starting one place rather than another, and such arguments are ruled out by the concept of rights.

This point may be obscured by the popular belief that political activists look forward to violence and 'ask for trouble' in what they say. They can hardly complain, in the general view, if they are taken to be the authors of the violence they expect, and treated accordingly. But this repeats the confusion I tried to explain earlier between having a right and doing the right thing. The speaker's motives may be relevant in deciding whether he does the right thing in speaking passionately about issues that may inflame or enrage the audience. But if he has a right to speak, because the danger in allowing him to speak is speculative, his motives cannot count as independent evidence in the argument that justifies stopping him.

But what of the individual rights of those who will be destroyed by a riot, of the passer-by who will be killed by a sniper's bullet or the shopkeeper who will be ruined by looting? To put the issue in this way, as a question of competing rights, suggests a principle that would undercut the effect of uncertainty. Shall we say that some rights to protection are so important that the Government is justified in doing all it can to maintain them? Shall we therefore say that the Government may abridge the rights of others to act when their acts might simply increase the risk, by however slight or speculative a margin, that some person's right to life or property will be violated?

Some such principle is relied on by those who oppose the Supreme Court's recent liberal rulings on police procedure. These rulings increase the chance that a guilty man will go free, and therefore marginally increase the risk that any particular member of the community will be murdered, raped, or robbed. Some critics believe that the Court's decisions must therefore be wrong.

But no society that purports to recognize a variety of rights, on the ground that a man's dignity or equality may be invaded in a variety of ways, can accept such a principle. If forcing a man to testify against himself, or forbidding him to speak, does the damage that the rights against self-incrimination and the right of free speech assume, then it would be contemptuous for the State to tell a man that he must suffer this damage against the possibility that other men's risk of loss may be marginally reduced. If rights make sense, then the degrees of their importance cannot be so different that some count not at all when others are mentioned.

Of course the Government may discriminate and may stop a man from exercising his right to speak when there is a clear and substantial risk that his speech will do great damage to the person or property of others, and no other means of preventing this are at hand, as in the case of the man shouting 'Fire!' in a theatre. But we must reject the suggested principle that the Government can simply ignore rights to speak when life and property are in question. So long as the impact of speech on these other rights remains speculative and marginal, it must look elsewhere for levers to pull.

IV. WHY TAKE RIGHTS SERIOUSLY?

I said at the beginning of this essay that I wanted to show what a government must do that professes to recognize individual rights. It must dispense with the claim that citizens never have a right to break its law, and it must not define citizens' rights so that these are cut off for supposed reasons of the general good. The present Government's policy towards civil disobedience, and its campaign against vocal protest, may therefore be thought to count against its sincerity.

One might well ask, however, whether it is wise to take rights all that seriously after all. America's genius, at least in her own legend, lies in not taking any abstract doctrine to its logical extreme. It may be time to ignore abstractions, and concentrate instead on giving the majority of our citizens a new sense of their Government's concern for their welfare, and of their title to rule.

That, in any event, is what Vice-President Agnew seems to believe. In a recent policy statement on the issue of 'weirdos' and social misfits, he said that the liberals' concern for individual rights was a headwind blowing in the face of the ship of state. That is a poor metaphor, but the philosophical point it expresses is very well taken. He recognizes, as many liberals do not, that the majority cannot travel as fast or as far as it would like if it recognizes the rights of individuals to do what, in the majority's terms, is the wrong thing to do.

The Vice-President supposes that rights are divisive, and that national unity and a new respect for law may be developed by taking them more sceptically. But he is wrong. America will continue to be divided by its social and foreign policy, and if the economy grows weaker the divisions will become more bitter. If we want our laws and our legal institutions to provide the ground rules within which these issues will be contested, then these ground rules must not be the conqueror's law that the dominant class imposes on the weaker, as Marx supposed the law of a capitalist society must be. The bulk of the law—that part which defines and implements social, economic, and foreign policy—cannot be neutral. It must state, in its greatest part, the majority's view of the common good. The institution of rights is therefore crucial, because it represents the majority's promise to the minorities that their dignity and equality will be respected. When the divisions among the groups are most violent, then this gesture, if law is to work, must be most sincere.

The institution requires an act of faith on the part of the minorities, because the scope of their rights will be controversial whenever they are important, and because the officers of the majority will act on their own notions of what these rights really are. Of course these officials will disagree with many of the claims that a minority makes. That makes it all the more important that they take their decisions gravely. They must show that they understand what rights are, and they must not cheat on the full implications of the doctrine. The Government will not re-establish respect for law without giving the law some claim to respect. It cannot do that if it neglects the one feature that distinguishes law from ordered brutality. If the Government does not take rights seriously, then it does not take law seriously either.

IX

Rights, Options, and Entitlements

GEOFFREY MARSHALL

MOST general concepts in legal and political theory can be used without absurdity in broader or narrower senses and this is true of the notion of a right. On the one hand a right may be thought of as a rather special sort of proprietary article. In 'the strict usage of most modern English jurists following Austin' a person who has a right is not simply the beneficiary of a duty. He is a person 'who may at his option demand the execution of the duty or waive it'.[1] On the other hand, it may be that this 'choice' or 'option' theory, does not entirely fit the sense of the terms 'rights' and 'immunities' as these are frequently used in many political and constitutional arguments. Perhaps we might ask whether a wider use than that of the modern English jurist has any merit and how it should be specified. A right, it would be safe to say, is obviously a form of entitlement arising out of moral, social, political, or legal rules. But this formulation conceals notorious difficulties about the relationship of entitlements to duties, obligations, and duty-imposing rules.

'ENTITLEMENT'

The term 'entitlement' seems broad enough to cover all of Hohfeld's categories—'claim-right', 'privilege', 'power', and 'immunity'. It obviously cannot be used so as to settle any of the disputed questions at issue about the meaning or ambit of the term 'right'. But one thing to be said in its favour is that it avoids criticisms commonly levelled at the term 'power' as it occurs in Holmes's definition of a right—'a permission to exercise certain natural powers and upon certain conditions to obtain protection, restitution or compensation by the aid of the

---

[1] H. L. A. Hart, 'Bentham', 48 *Proc. Brit. Acad.*, 297, 315. See also, 'Are there any Natural Rights', reprinted in *Political Philosophy*, ed. A. M. Quinton (1968).

public force'.[2] Many institutional arrangements create entitlements that do not seem to be compensatory or protective or restitutory. Nor does the phrase 'natural powers' always seem apt. If all citizens were allotted by law the right or entitlement to one free airline ticket each year, it is difficult to see what exercise of their natural powers would be involved in the use of the facility.

Some also have spoken of rights in terms of 'claims' to particular benefits or treatment. Presumably, to constitute rights, claims would at least have to be justifiable or defensible claims, rather than anything that happened to be claimed. But though rights may certainly be justifiably claimed, it seems conceivable that they may never be claimed at all by those who have them or by anyone else.

'Entitlement' also suggests conveniently that a right is something that is not only due to, but also considered beneficial to, the agent, and not everything that it is proper for him to have as the result of other people's obligations or duties. We need not think of mental patients or convicted criminals, whom officials have the duty to confine or punish, as being in possession of an entitlement or right to everything that they rightly undergo.

'ARISING UNDER A RULE'

The phrase 'arising under a rule' is also a vague one that leaves room for various answers to questions of *locus standi* that arise when somebody is under a duty to follow a rule. An acute form of this problem arises when the duties result from special transactions such as promises or contracts whose implementation will confer benefits or disadvantages on persons other than the promising or contracting parties. On one view it may be insisted that such beneficiaries enjoy no rights and can make no legitimate demands to have the undertakings implemented. Such a view may or may not be reflected in the legal arrangements of a particular society, and it is arguably an open issue both of legal policy and of morality whether the breach of an undertaking by A to B, which if carried out would have benefited C, ought to give C a legitimate ground to complain[3] of

---

[2] *The Common Law* (ed. Mark de Wolfe Howe, 1968), p. 169.

[3] Someone might, of course, have good reasons to lament, bewail, or grumble without grounds to complain in this sense. For a discussion of 'moral right holders'

its breach and in that sense a right to have the undertaking implemented. To assert such a right is of course to assert that there *is* a duty of some kind towards such a benefiting third party. Perhaps the existence of such a duty might be more strongly intuited in some circumstances than in others, according to the characters of the parties, their consciousness of the arrangements made, the reliance known to be placed upon them, and the relationship of the parties to each other outside the particular transaction in question. This last point may be particularly relevant if it is felt that, in relation to the keeping of undertakings, everybody is related to every other person by some kind of implicit social bond. When Thomas Hobbes's men agreed not with their ruler but each with every other to obey the Sovereign Leviathan, did the ruler Leviathan himself merely benefit without acquiring a *right* to the obedience of his subjects? He was no party to the compact, but could it be argued on that ground that only the citizens who were parties to it could have any right to the peace and order specified in the social contract and they only because they were entitled to the performance of each other's obligations? The citizens were certainly under an obligation to each other to do what they had covenanted to do. They were obliged not simply because they had so covenanted but because of that fact in conjunction with the maxim or law of nature that covenants should be kept, once made. Everyone, ruler and ruled, could be said to have had some sort of entitlement not to be damaged by a breach of this rule. Contracts and promises always take place against the background of a general acknowledgement that undertakings should in general be kept. This might well be allotted as a ground for the feeling that at least in some cases the making of agreements or promises gives rise to rights in persons other than the promising or contracting parties. It may, of course, be characteristic of, or implied by, or specifically written into particular transactions that one party has a special right to release the other party from his obligation. But that may be a different matter from the belief that it is always

and 'mere beneficiaries' see Daniel Lyons, 'Entitled to Complain' (1966) *Analysis* 119; and Marvin Schiller 'Complaints about Entitled to Complain' (1967–8) *Analysis* 27. Also David Lyons, 'Rights, Claimants and Beneficiaries' (1969) *American Philosophical Quarterly* 173.

necessarily true that only he can be said to be wronged by a breach of the other party's obligation.

RIGHTS AS FREEDOMS FROM OBLIGATION

Suppose that we were to insist upon tying the notion of a right consistently to the notion of an entitlement to benefit from the performance of obligations. We should have to begin by meeting the criticism that there is a traditional sense of right, notoriously emphasized by Hobbes, which turns upon the absence of law or obligation and which some have labelled 'freedom', 'privilege', or 'liberty'. Natural right, Hobbes held, is 'the liberty each man hath, to use his own power, as he will himself, for the preservation of his own nature'. In his natural condition 'every man has a right to every thing.'[4] This so-called right or liberty is the equal liberty men have in the pre-social condition to pursue their own safety and salvation. But here one might say just as appropriately that the only sense in which men have rights or equal rights is that nobody has any rule-governed rights or liberties. The question of rights does not arise and the freedom all enjoy is not freedom under a rule but freedom from or absence of rules. This is the only sense in which Hobbes's sovereign has the right to put his subjects to death, whilst they, if their lives are in danger from him, have a 'right' to resist. Perhaps the best way to put this is not in terms of rights at all but simply to say that sovereign and subject are, for this purpose, each in a state of nature in relation to each other and there is no established rule to arbitrate between them. No normative framework exists, therefore, from which any obligation can be derived to refrain from acting in a hostile manner towards each other. Why should one see in this absence of rule any kind of right or liberty? Might one not say that the respective obligations of subject and sovereign cannot here be discussed in terms of rights or rules at all. For if any coherent rule governs their relationship one could ask in any given set of circumstances in which the sovereign exercises his 'liberty'—when, for example, the citizen is dispatched to lose his life in the wars—whether the sovereign was *rightly* free from obligations towards him. Even if we dub the sovereign's title to act a 'liberty' we cannot (since we are not of

[4] *Leviathan*, ch. 14, pp. 84–5 (ed. Oakeshott).

course merely considering his physical freedom or liberty to get his way) avoid the question whether the liberty was rightly his and if it was rightly exercised. Any rule which answers this question must tell us who is in the right when their objects or activities conflict in this crucial way.[5] If according to the rule governing their relationships the sovereign's conscription or execution of his subject is rightful, legitimate, or justified, it cannot be legitimate or rightful for the subject to frustrate it. He must be under some obligation not to resist the execution of what is rightfully done to him and the sovereign's consequent entitlement is a right.

DIFFICULTIES ABOUT 'OBLIGATION' AND 'DUTY'

In asserting that rights always arise where rules create obligations we should not of course assume that the notions of obligation and duty themselves create no difficulty. Not everybody, for example, would agree with Mill that 'It is a part of the notion of Duty in all its forms that a person may rightfully be compelled to fulfil it. Duty is a thing which may be exacted from a person as one exacts a debt.'[6] This is a notion of duty clearly modelled on legal duties and impositions. Mill adds that reasons of prudence or the interests of other people may militate against actually exacting the performance of a duty, though any person under a duty would not be entitled to complain if its performance were exacted from him.

Someone might, however, deny this and say that the question of the propriety of *compelling* people to do their duty or fulfil their obligations is a separate issue and not a part of what is meant by duty or obligation. Are there not, he might say, duties that ought not to be exacted and that on grounds of principle not of expediency? The sphere of morally obligatory actions which it would be wrong not to perform is surely wider than the sphere of actions which can properly be made the objects of compulsion. The legalism in Mill's approach can be seen in his insistence that the idea of penal sanction which is the essence of law enters not only into the idea of injustice but

[5] There are of course some contexts (of which games and other competitions are typical) in which objects or purposes conflict and each party may have an equal right to try to achieve success at the expense of the other. Though competitors may oppose each other's legitimate efforts they are not without duties to each other.

[6] *Utilitarianism* (Everyman ed.), p. 45.

into that of every kind of wrong. 'We do not call anything wrong unless we mean to imply that a person ought to be punished in some way or other for doing it; if not by law then by the opinion of his fellow creatures; if not by opinion, by the reproaches of his own conscience.'[7] Without accepting this equation of the culpable with the punishable, some people may nevertheless feel obligation and duty to be relatively confined notions so that not all the things we ought to do are obligatory or can be classed as obligations. This conclusion is sometimes supported by the following kind of example.[8] Suppose that a stranger makes a polite request for a match, and Jones, who is in a sour mood and does not like strangers, brusquely refuses him. When reproached for his incivility he says:

... surely I was under no obligation ... He had no claim on me; he has no authority to command any performance from me; I don't owe him anything ... a favour by definition is nothing that we are legally or morally required to do ... I did not fail to honour a commitment; neither did I fail to discharge an obligation, moral or legal ... You have therefore no right to reproach me.[9]

Nevertheless someone might reproach him. They might say that he did not behave as he should have done. He really ought to have given the stranger a match. If this is the case it sounds as if there must be actions that a man ought to do, that he nevertheless has no obligation to do. It is perhaps unfortunate that there is no easy way of turning the statement that a man ought to do something into the passive tense without using some such construction as that he is morally required, or morally obliged, or under an obligation, and the language of requirement and obligatoriness sounds somewhat heavy and final. It may be that the reluctance to talk about obligation in this type of case stems from giving insufficient weight to the fact that obligations and requirements have to be qualified, that they are not all of equal seriousness, and that there are different types of obligations stemming from different rules. There can be greater and lesser obligations, more and less serious obligations, and obligations that conflict with other

[7] Ibid.

[8] Taken from Joel Feinberg 'Supererogation and Rules' (reprinted in *Ethics*, ed. J. J. Thomson and G. Dworkin, p. 391).

[9] Ibid., p. 393.

obligations. Could we not say to the selfish match-refuser that there is, when it is properly formulated, an obligation that he is under. If the stranger needs the match and if Jones has a plentiful supply, and the offer costs him nothing and there are no other countervailing requirements, then he *is* under a moral obligation to offer the match. Of course it is not a very weighty requirement or obligation and there are many other requirements and obligations to which it might easily have had to yield. Mill said that no one has a right to generosity or beneficence. This may be generally true because there are generally good reasons why most people, given their circumstances and obligations, are not obliged to behave beneficently. But some people in some circumstances could be said to be entitled to generous treatment. When they are and when we ought to be generous their right or entitlement, it could be argued, create for us an obligation.

RIGHTS AND THE RELATIONSHIP WITH DUTIES

A number of reasons has been advanced for saying that rights do not always arise where there are obligations or duties from whose performance persons are capable of benefiting. 'This view would have as its consequence', it has been urged, 'that all laws including criminal laws, which imposed duties that were capable of benefiting anyone would confer correlative rights.'[10] But 'only the rules of civil law, such as torts, trusts, or contracts confer rights'.[11] They do this because they provide in a distinctively distributive way for individuals by placing in their hands a mechanism for demanding the execution of or waiving the performance of a duty. It is this, it is argued, that constitutes the essential feature of a right rather than the fact that its bearer may benefit from the performance of the duty.

Benefits also arise from the carrying out of obligations towards animals and children and possibly from the existence of duties to ourselves in so far as these are acted upon. But in each case, it is argued, it would be a mistake to think of rights arising. What is the force of these arguments?

Both duties to, and rights against, oneself are of course dubious articles and 'I owe it to myself' is a palpably meta-

[10] Hart, 'Bentham', p. 314.   [11] Ibid., p. 315.

phorical remark. But if we are willing in imagination to split ourselves into two, a right against ourselves is as sensible and as senseless (though non-idiomatic) as a duty to ourselves.

As to children and animals, it must be conceded that common usage does ascribe rights to them. But 'if common usage sanctions talk of the rights of animals or babies' perhaps it 'makes an idle use of the expression "a right".'[12] We may, it is admitted, properly say that we ought not to batter babies, that it is wrong to batter them—possibly, though less certainly—that we are doing them a wrong by battering them. But to suggest that they have a right not to be battered will, it is urged, only confuse the situation with other moral situations where the expression 'a right' has a specific force which cannot be replaced by any other expression. This will of course be the case only if it *is* desirable—and this is precisely the question in issue—to give the notion of a right this specific force and to confine it to being a kind of personally owned facility or option invoked or able to be invoked by a specific individual. The obligations that arise in a large number of rule-governed situations, including relationships with children and animals and duties arising under criminal and constitutional laws will not then be thought of as giving rise to rights, since the benefits properly or legitimately enjoyed under such rules are not things possessed by individuals who can invoke them, or not, at their pleasure. On this view the appropriate image conjured up by the term 'right' is that of a bond or chain which restrains some person or persons but leaves 'the other end of the chain lying in the hands of another to use if he chooses'.[13] Rights are the chains or perhaps the handles on the chains. They are 'typically perceived of as possessed or owned by or belonging to individuals.' They reflect 'the conception of moral rules as not only prescribing conduct but as forming a kind of moral property of individuals to which they are as individuals entitled' and 'only when rules are conceived in this way can we speak of *rights* and *wrongs* as well as right and wrong actions.'[14]

To say that rights are typically perceived in this fashion may be going too far. Indeed it might perhaps be more plausible to say that it takes a good deal of juristic determination to perceive

---

[12] Hart, 'Are there any Natural Rights?', p. 58.
[13] Ibid., p. 59.   [14] Ibid., p. 59.

of them in this way. Moreover, some odd consequences follow, particularly as to what can properly be said about different sorts of rules and codes of behaviour. A moral or legal code prescribing what is to be done need not on this view create any rights. It may define what is wrong but we cannot allow ourselves to say that it creates 'wrongs'. Disobedience to the injunctions of a moral code such as the Decalogue may be wrong and harmful to others—'but it would be a surprising interpretation of them that treated them as conferring rights.' [15] The seventh commandment is an obligation-imposing rule but we must not say, except in an idle moment, that it gives spouses a right not to have adulterous actions performed. Adultery— or killing—we have to say—is harmful and wrong, but not really 'a wrong'. There could only be wrong and rights if the commandments were conceived as duties owed not to God but to individuals. Like penal statutes such prohibitions are designed to rule out certain types of behaviour; they are not rules placed at the disposal of individuals and regulating the extent to which *they* may demand certain behaviour from others.

PROHIBITIONS, OPTIONS, AND ENTITLEMENTS

Two queries may be raised here. One is about the person or persons to whom duties are owed by those who obey rules. The other is about the difficulty of sorting out rules according to whether they are designed to prescribe or prohibit conduct, or intended to create facilities or entitlements for individuals. Take, for example, a simple prohibition that occurs in the rules of a number of sporting activities, namely a rule against tripping or fouling opponents. To whom is the duty not to trip owed, and is the rule designed to prohibit conduct or to create an entitlement? The answers to these questions will determine whether we can rightly say that players in the game have a right not to be tripped. Most games players would undoubtedly say that they had and that the rule was designed and intended to give them that right. They could not mean by this that they were benefiting from a rule placed at their disposal allowing them as individuals to demand non-tripping behaviour or not, as the mood took them. The rule, they might feel, both prescribes conduct and creates entitlements. An Aus-

[15] Ibid., p. 59.

tinian sportsman would have to deny this. Any participant injured by a breach of the prohibitory rule, he might say, is like the beneficiary of a promise or contract. There is an undertaking between games players and those who make the rules not to trip or foul him. The duty to refrain is owed to the Governing Body, not to him, and he cannot have a right to complain of its breach. This last conclusion at least is not one commonly drawn by the typical injured sportsman when subjected to foul play by an opponent.

The question 'To whom is the duty owed?' is not entirely clear. Two sorts of duty may be in question. The duty not to trip might seem to be owed to, or at least defined by reference to, the individual opponent. On the other hand a duty to obey the rule about tripping might well be thought of as being owed also to the rule-making body and perhaps to every other participant in that particular sporting activity. Equally, the duty to avoid adultery and to pay taxes could be said to be owed to spouses and tax-collectors, whilst duties to obey the rules about marital propriety and taxation are possibly also owed to God, the Queen in Parliament, and perhaps the whole community.

If we consider the variety of different types of rule that occur in codes and games there seems little inclination to think of them as embodying rights or entitlements only to the extent that they create options or facilities that can be invoked or not as the agent pleases. The Association Football code provides for example that if Team *A* kicks the ball out of play, Team *B* has (colloquially) the right to throw it in, in the sense that they are entitled to insist that they throw it and not their opponents. But there is nothing else Team *A* can do and they cannot decline to do it if the game is to continue according to the rules. It seems better to say that some rights embody options than that all rights are essentially options. Options may indeed be embodied in various forms. If, for example, Team *A* loses the toss, Team *B* has the right or option to choose either to kick off or to nominate the direction of play. Some rights can simply be exercised or the relevant entitlement waived. In a game of squash an invalid first service gives an opponent an option to ignore the breach of rule and play the ball if he wishes. But this sort of right is rather rare.

Whether there should be options to waive what are frequently thought of as rights seems, in fact, an independent question of some importance. Some things to which human beings are entitled we often feel should not be the subject of options. Obvious examples are the right to life and the right to protection from criminal offences that do serious damage. It is precisely in describing as rights the protections given in civilized countries to life, liberty, and property that general usage and that of political theorists may depart from the juristic notion that rights can only exist where those who benefit from the performance of a duty towards them can themselves demand or waive the execution of the duty.

Possible concessions may be offered by proponents of the 'proprietary' view of rights. One justification for extending the term 'right' to include the securities, immunities, and protections guaranteed by criminal and constitutional law is that assignable individuals may be thought of as being the beneficiaries of duties imposed by such laws. Thus the distributive character of the idea of a right can be preserved in these cases, unlike those which involve the creation of duties such as military service or tax-paying, whose beneficiaries are the community or unassignable individuals.

About this concession two comments might be made. In the first place it seems inconsistent to allow these cases to count when, however much they may be thought of as designed to protect or benefit assignable individuals, they lack the element so much insisted on of leaving the individual both the option of taking or not taking what is due to him. Secondly, the notion of assignable beneficiaries is far from clear. The community or supposedly indiscriminate class of persons who are benefited by the payment of taxes, or made secure by the armed forces, or protected by the constitution, consists of particular individuals and each of them may speak and think of his right. So equally the Government or the Crown are assignable persons who may be thought of as having rights to payment or service from citizens.

For proponents of the wider view of rights, particularly those who are willing to talk about human rights, the notion of a right as a facility placed at the disposal of individuals may be subsidiary to the feeling that certain rules protecting and benefiting individuals—whether considered individually or as members of groups—are fitting or necessary rules. When these rules touch on important areas of human experience we may be inclined to speak of the resulting benefits or entitlements as natural or inalienable rights. If such expressions make any sense, the sense they make is that certain benefits and protections are such that all men ought to have them and that men in general cannot properly alienate or deprive themselves of these rights or deem themselves to have no rights. Thus the ability to waive one's rights is seen as one common feature of some—possibly not the most important—rights, rather than as a necessary characteristic of the concept of a right.

COMPETITION AND QUALIFICATION OF RIGHTS

There is an obvious characteristic of a right which can be seen most clearly in the case of the typical constitutional or 'human' right, but which may have been partially obscured when 'claim rights' have been contrasted with 'liberties'. This is that a right is always subject to competition from other rights and entitlements. If we believe that citizens have rights we see also that rights have to be shared and that they potentially collide with other legitimate interests. This point is sometimes made by saying that rights cannot be 'absolute'. This term is not free from ambiguity. We might simply mean by asserting a right to be absolute that some principle is to be regarded as of fundamental or absolute importance. Even if we meant by this that it must never be made to yield to any other principle it would not follow that any particular person could claim it in a simple unqualified form, since at least the necessity for others to share in its benefits will imply that a single individual's title to it may have to be regulated. At least this will be true of some principles. One man's entitlement to, and pursuit of, happiness may not impinge on anyone else's but his pursuit of, for example, freedom almost certainly will. In fact most people would also concede that no one principle can be given an absolute and unvarying priority and that freedom may have to be limited by the claims of other principles also deserving respect, such as equality, and security.

There is, in view of this, something odd in the tendency (though it may be lessening) for declarations of human and constitutional rights to be couched in unqualified terms. Rights to equal treatment or to freedoms of speech, movement, or assembly are often promulgated in quite absolute or unrestricted terms. Perhaps the word 'absolute' itself is not much used, but it does occur. The Australian constitution, for example, provides that trade, commerce, and intercourse among the states shall be 'absolutely free'.[16] That means, as Sir Ivor Jennings once noted,[17] that trade, commerce, and intercourse shall be 'relatively free'. Wherever Bills of Rights fall to be applied the process of balancing, modification, and qualification can be seen. A statement of a simply enunciated right to freedom of movement comes into conflict with a legislative enactment regulating immigration. A guaranteed right to freedom of expression comes into competition with the equally guaranteed right to a fair trial. The right to use property competes with the demands of equal treatment. The right of free association collides with the need to maintain law and order. By contrast, the sort of right that is often exemplified when juristic rights are contrasted with 'liberties' or 'privileges' (the Hohfeldian 'claim-right' or 'right of recipience')[18] tends to be illustrated by such examples as a debt or engagement between two parties. The obligation to pay has as its direct correlative the right to payment. The right here is simply defined and unqualified and the suggested need to distinguish it from other forms of entitlement by dubbing them 'liberties' is illuminating. What characterizes these other forms of entitlement is that they have no such exact correlative obligation as has the 'claim-right'. The use of the term 'liberty' seems in part a way of acknowledging that rights are frequently only qualified rights. The 'right' for example to carry on a trade is clearly not an unqualified one. It has to be adjusted to, and balanced against, the right to be protected from unfair competition. *A*'s 'right' or 'liberty' to park on an unrestricted highway is obviously a shared right. It is not (unlike a right to payment) an unqualified right. It is a right to park in a

---

[16] Commonwealth of Australia Constitution Act (1900), s. 92.

[17] *Some Characteristics of the Indian Constitution* (1953), p. 74.

[18] A term used by D. D. Raphael in *Political Theory and the Rights of Man* (1967), p. 56, where it is contrasted with a 'right of action' ('a right to do something—an absence of obligation').

place of his choice provided that *B* or *C* or *D* do not park there first; and the rights of *B*, *C*, and *D* are similarly qualified. But since most rights are of this kind it is perhaps odd to choose the rather special case of an unqualified right to set the pattern for rights properly so called. A debt and a right to payment constitute one of the few unqualified right situations. Trade unionists and employers for example have rights that impinge on each other. But only if all rights were unqualified would it be the case that the employer's right to carry on his business would imply that his employees had no right to strike. Since, however, 'right' does not mean 'unqualified right', and since even English judges in the nineteenth century cannot have imagined that it did, it may have been unnecessary to cavil at their usage; or to suppose that any faults in their decisions stemmed from it. It may be that the substitution of the term 'liberty' for right is not the best way of making the point that the competing 'rights' of trade unionists and employers react upon and modify each other.

To sum up: rights in a wide sense may properly be seen as universally related to, and always derivable from, obligations, though the obligations must be carefully specified and are not usually of the unqualified kind associated with the simpler type of 'claim-right'. Some rights or entitlements can be waived or invoked at the instance of those who have them; but it is not a necessary feature of a right or entitlement that this should be so, and it is a common feature of many important rights that it is felt not to be so.

X
Powers and Secondary Rules of Change

C. F. H. TAPPER

IT is often convenient for teachers and commentators to think of their subjects as a chain of self-contained units, whether these are lectures or chapters, or both. It is most convenient of all to adopt a traditional scheme of classification and arrangement from one's predecessors. In law, a combination of the conservatism of the profession, the nature of the subject, the rules of procedure, and the economics of publishing has created a plethora of new editions of old books, with the consequential sclerosis of thought patterns. Even in a subject like Jurisprudence, where there is least justification for it, the disease is present. It is especially rife among the single-volume and second-hand surveys with which this subject is plagued. It is thus a pleasant surprise to find Professor Fuller writing of Professor Hart's distinction between primary and secondary rules, that: 'The distinction is a familiar one, especially in this country where it has served as the keystone of the Hohfeldian analysis.'[1] This identification is more fully elaborated in his footnote to this sentence, in which he says:

The Hohfeldian analysis concerns four basic legal relations: right–duty, no-right–privilege, power–liability, and disability–immunity. Of these, however, the second and fourth are simply the negations of the first and third. Accordingly the basic distinction on which the whole system is built is that between right–duty and power–liability; this distinction coincides exactly with that taken by Hart.[2]

It is true that in isolation these distinctions are familiar, if not always well understood. But they are usually regarded as examples of two quite separate approaches to jurisprudence subsumed under the distinct rubrics of 'Legal Theory' and 'Juristic Concepts'. Perhaps an incidental merit of Professor Hart's book *The Concept of Law*, and this criticism of it by Professor

---

[1] *The Morality of Law* (1964), p. 134.   [2] Ibid., n. 50.

Fuller, will be the wider realization that these aspects should no longer be insulated from each other.

Hohfeld's distinctions have been much misunderstood. Even Fuller's point that there is really only one basic distinction has not always been grasped, and its nature is still not so clear that further explanation is unnecessary. Hohfeld himself must accept some of the blame for this. His diagrammatic presentation can lead one to imagine that all eight terms should be considered, and the most appropriate one for characterizing the position of one party to a legal situation selected. Thus one might be tempted to ask whether a diplomat, say, enjoys a privilege or an immunity. This is quite wrong, and if pursued can lead only to impenetrable confusion. As Fuller, in the quoted passage, and the logic of the analysis makes clear, the only alternatives offered by the analysis for the characterization of the legal situation of a given party are those between a given pair of opposites. Thus one can only meaningfully consider whether one party has a right or a no-right, a duty or a privilege, a power or a disability, an immunity or a liability, as against the other. The situation of the other can then be characterized by reference to the table of correlatives. It must be stressed at the outset that all of Hohfeld's legal relations are considered by him to exist between two specifically designated human beings, and for this reason his examples tend to be chosen from the area of private law, where this condition is most plausibly fulfilled, rather than from that of public law, whether constitutional or criminal, where such an insistence can at best lead only to unwieldy and unfamiliar analysis. Thus if in considering the legal relationships between A and B in relation to a given subject, it is decided that A has a duty and not a privilege against B, it follows that B has a right and not a no-right against A. If it is decided that X has a power and not a disability as against Y, it follows that Y has a liability and not an immunity as against X. Once it is appreciated that Hohfeld's concepts fall into two discrete groups, it is apparent that questions demanding a choice between terms taken from different groups, like privilege and immunity in the case of the diplomat, can only meaningfully be asked if the groups are themselves alternative. Fuller distinguishes these groups as the right–duty group and the power–liability group. It is felt to be clearer to refer to them by reference to pairs of opposites, since in any application of the analysis the very first question must involve a choice from a pair of opposites. For the same reason the pairs chosen are duty–privilege and power–disability which are by far the clearest and most common starting-points within each group. When these groups are compared it becomes apparent that the relationship between them is not the same as that between the terms characterized as opposites within a group. Within a group the relationship is best described as one of limiting negatives. The two terms are exclusive and exhaustive. *A* must have either a duty or a privilege as against *B*. He cannot have neither or both in relation to a given situation. This does not hold true of the groups themselves. It does not follow that because *A* has, say, a duty as against *B*, that he cannot therefore have a power or a disability against him. In fact, because the two groups have internally an identical logical structure, the converse is true. If *A* has a duty as against *B*, he must *also* have a power or a disability against him. This follows because it is implicit in the decision that *A* has a duty against *B* that a legal relationship exists between them. Since both the duty–privilege and power–disability pairs exhaustively cover the universe of legal relationships from the point of view of a potential actor, it follows that one term from each pair must be applicable. In other words the two groups are looking at the same legal situation from different points of view. They seek to answer quite different questions which might be asked about it. The duty–privilege group is concerned with whether or not there is a rule in existence which either forbids or compels a given course of action. The power–disability group is concerned with whether or not that course of action will effect a change in legal relationships. It is quite clear that both questions can be asked of any given situation, and that the answer to one is not decisive of the answer to the other. Thus while in most cases if *A* has a duty not to sell *B*'s property, he will have a disability as against *B* to alienate it; yet if the sale is made in market overt he may have a power to alienate despite still being under a duty not to do so. Conversely while it is usual for one who is under a duty to sell another's property

to have a power to alienate it, it may occur, in forward transactions on the Stock Exchange for example, that *A* is under a
contractual duty to sell *B*'s property, but at that time has no
power to do so. Before going on to consider whether Hart's
distinction between primary and secondary rules is of an identical nature, it is first necessary to examine Hohfeld's power a
little more closely.

<h3 style="text-align:center">HOHFELD'S CONCEPT OF POWER</h3>

Hohfeld defined power as 'one's affirmative "control" over
a given legal relation as against another.'[3] Control seems to
mean the ability to bring about a change in legal relations.
There are, however, a number of unresolved ambiguities in
this definition. The first relates to the mode of control. Thus
if *A* contemplates striking *B*, he might be thought to have a
power since by striking he would probably alter their legal
relationship to the extent of investing *B* with a right to damages,
and himself with a duty to pay them. Yet it seems odd to say
that *A* has a legal power to strike *B*. One way of resolving the
difficulty is to say that Hohfeld's classification is of *legal* relations, and that since striking another is manifestly illegal it
cannot give rise to a legal power. But this resolution is un-
acceptable since it confuses Hohfeld's two groups in just the
way illustrated earlier. This argument really amounts to saying
that because *A* has a duty not to strike *B*, he can have no power
to do so. It also ignores the consequence which would follow
from this in Hohfeld's scheme that *A* must, therefore, have a
disability which is just as much a *legal* relation as a power, and
follows in just the same way from an illegal act. In fact all that
can be inferred from the fact that *A* has a duty not to strike *B*,
is that *B* has a right not to be struck and *A* has no privilege to
strike. A much more convincing solution to the problem is to
say that *A* has no power as against *B*, because by striking him
he induces no relevant change in their legal relations. It may
be said that *A* always had a duty not to strike *B*, and that *B*
always had a right not to be struck. None of this is changed by
A's act of striking. This analysis depends upon a further distinction between substantive or primary rights, and adjectival

---

[3] 'Some Fundamental Legal Conceptions as Applied in Judicial Reasoning'
(1913), 23 Yale L.J. 55.

or remedial rights. In Hohfeld's analysis the existence of the latter is the test for the existence of the former. It is only if an infraction of a rule gives rise to a remedy in the courts that the rule can be said to impose a duty. Thus the mere fact that *B* secures a remedy against *A* in respect of being struck by him cannot be equated with a change in rights and duties. Indeed it is just because he has a remedy that one can validly say that he always had a right. This situation may be contrasted with one in which primary rights and duties are changed, say by the acceptance of a contractual offer. Before acceptance the parties were under no duties to carry out the provisions of the contract, after acceptance they are. The first qualification then of Hohfeld's definition is that to induce changes in remedial rights and duties does not count as control over the legal relations of another. It may be said that this is implicit in the exclusion of remedial rights and duties from the table of legal relations, and that Hohfeld intended the term 'legal relations' to refer to the terms included in his table. If so, did he intend it to refer to all of them? Is the power–disability group itself to be included? Hohfeld's definition and text are unhelpful on this. So are his examples. In none of them is the *only* change induced a change in powers and disabilities though in a number such changes are combined with changes in duties and privileges. The problem is conveniently illustrated by considering a simple contract. Hohfeld himself speaks of the offer as creating in the offeree a power, and in the offeror a liability, in that the offeree can, by accepting the offer, bring into existence new primary rights and duties. Thus the offeree has a power in relation to his acceptance. It may be noted as an illustration of the earlier argument that he also has a privilege, since he is free either to accept or not as he chooses. The problem arises in respect of the characterization of the position of the potential offeror. By making an offer he will leave primary rights and duties unchanged, but his offer will change the powers and liabilities of the parties. Is this a sufficient change for him to be said to have a power? Hohfeld gives no answer. But whatever the answer, the question reveals an important ambiguity in his analysis. There are two terms to characterize three situations. The effect of an action may be to vary the duty–privilege group of relations, or to vary the power–disability group alone, or to vary neither. It therefore follows that a power must include both the ability to vary the duty–privilege group *and* the power–disability group, or his disability must include the ability to vary the power–disability group *and* the disability to change the duty–privilege group. There can be no more simple solution without adding new terms. The ambiguity is important in any assessment of Hohfeld's work in relation to that of Hart, because it is only on one of these interpretations that he can be regarded as permitting the creation of chains of powers.

Before going on to examine the relationship between Hohfeld's analysis and Hart's distinction between primary and secondary rules, it must be noted that there is a significant divergence of emphasis. As stated above Hohfeld dealt almost exclusively with the relationship between two specific human beings under rules of private law. The reason for this, no doubt, being that the treatment of criminal and constitutional law in terms of relations between two specific human beings at a time would be impossibly unwieldy. Hart is quite free of any similar theoretical encumbrance, and does indeed deal with both private and public law. This is most obvious in his list of the features which an educated man would expect a legal system to exhibit, where he distinguishes as separate features rules of public and private law at both primary and secondary level.[4] But at the primary level rules of criminal law soon become the main example despite the over-simplification which Hart recognizes that this entails.[5] At the secondary level there is an illuminating investigation of the nature of private rules,[6] but their importance is undermined by a much greater stress on the role of public secondary rules. It sometimes seems to be only the latter which can transmute a set of rules into a system. Thus Hart asserts that the addition of such *public* secondary rules 'may fairly be considered as *the*[7] step from the pre-legal into the legal world'.[8] In further discussion of this transition it is true that the point is blunted since there no explicit distinction is drawn between private and public secondary rules of change, and it is said that the introduction as a remedy for the static

[4] H. L. A. Hart, *The Concept of Law* (1961), p. 3.
[5] Hart, p. 237, note to p. 27.   [6] Hart, especially in ch. 5.
[7] Italics supplied.   [8] Hart, p. 41.

character of a regime of primary rules of such undifferentiated secondary rules of change might be considered '*a*[9] step from the pre-legal into the legal world'.[10] Finally there appears a reversion to the earlier view. In the discussion of international law, the analogue of private secondary rules, that is the rules providing for the binding force of treaties, are lumped together with primary rules pending the introduction of a public rule of recognition which is needed to transform them into an international legal system.[11] Despite this difference of emphasis it is still instructive to pursue Fuller's suggestion that there is no difference between these two approaches.

HART'S DISTINCTION BETWEEN PRIMARY AND SECONDARY RULES

This distinction is recognized by Hart to be similar to that made by Ross between norms of competence and norms of obligation. But it had not previously been developed so fully, nor given so central a place in any scheme of analysis. Hart himself describes the introduction of secondary rules as 'a step forward as important to society as the invention of the wheel'.[12] It would seem to follow that its recognition is equally important for the analysis of society. Hart himself draws this inference in describing the union of these two types of legal rule as 'a most powerful tool for the analysis of much that has puzzled both the jurist and the political theorist'.[13] At the same time he recognizes that it is 'only a beginning'. He also admits that it is blurred by rules of a hybrid character. It is necessary to have a clear understanding of this key distinction. This is rendered somewhat more difficult than might have been expected by its being formulated in a variety of ways even within 'The Concept of Law'. A number of different facets of the main distinction are emphasized in different places. Their precise number is unimportant since further sub-division or conflation is always possible. Here it has been thought convenient to draw attention to eight different points of distinction which are made between primary and secondary rules:

(a) whether the rule imposes duties or confers powers;
(b) whether the rule governs actions or rules;

---

[9] Italics supplied.   [10] Hart, p. 91.   [11] Hart, p. 231.
[12] Hart, p. 41.   [13] Hart, p. 95.

(c) whether the effect of non-compliance is a penalty or invalidity;

(d) whether the rule is mandatory or facultative;

(e) whether an internal attitude need be adopted towards the rule or not;

(f) whether the rule is intended for self-application or is to be applied by officials;

(g) whether or not the rule is one whose addition converts a set of rules into a system;

(h) whether or not the rule is supported by really serious social pressure.

It is clear that there is a good deal of overlapping between these categories. It is equally clear that they are not all identical. It remains to be seen for how many of these aspects Fuller's identification of Hart's distinction with that made by Hohfeld holds good.

(a) The contrast between duty imposing and power conferring rules

This is a most important aspect of the distinction between primary and secondary rules, and one to which Hart constantly reverts. It is equally important in any comparison with Hohfeld's work since the terminology is here at its closest. Thus Hart typically characterizes primary rules as imposing duties,[14] or obligations,[15] though he recognizes that this term is less commonly used among lawyers, or more rarely as conferring rights.[16] These are contrasted with secondary rules which are spoken of as conferring powers.[14] It is not made absolutely clear that the reference here is limited to secondary rules of change, since although the immediate context might suggest that the secondary rules of recognition are intended to be excluded, this is hardly consistent with the further reference to these rules in the next paragraph where they are said to be system-completing, which, it seems, must entail the inclusion of secondary rules of recognition. But Hart is not as rigorous in his terminology as Hohfeld. He himself concedes that the distinction is only 'very rough' and in places it does become somewhat blurred. This tendency is most marked in his discussion of the continuity of sovereignty[17] where the successor

---

[14] Hart, p. 79.   [15] Hart, p. 27.
[16] Hart, p. 48.   [17] Hart, pp. 53–58.

to a deceased sovereign is variously described as having the *right* to succeed, and the *right* to legislate. There is a danger of confusion here between Hohfeld's two groups. In his terminology the designated successor may well have both a right to be invested with sovereignty, and a power, when so invested, to legislate. The situation is obscured if the term 'right' is used for both. Nor is it improved by the equation which is made between 'right' and 'authority' in this context. Indeed the effect of this is to subvert Hohfeld's terminology completely since 'power' is itself here being contrasted with 'authority' to signify the mere physical ability of the ruler to enforce compliance with his rules. It is fair to note that parentheses[18] are used to emphasize that 'power' is being used in an unusual sense, but the total effect is not one of complete clarity. In general Hart's typical usage of the word 'power' does correspond to Hohfeld's in outline, and at one point[19] he even uses Hohfeld's opposite 'disability' to characterize a limitation upon a power. It still remains to be seen precisely what ambit Hart intends his primary and secondary rules to have. Are primary rules only to impose duties and create rights, or can they also confer powers? What is the range of effects which a rule can have to count as a secondary power conferring rule? It will be recalled that in Hohfeld's case it was suggested that the duty–privilege group referred only to the presence or absence of a rule constraining action. One would expect Hart's primary rules to be similarly limited. For the most part this is so, but in two places he allows room for doubt. In one[20] he refers directly to primary rules as conferring powers. And as already indicated the rule giving binding force to treaties is equated with primary rules in another. It seems certain that Hart does not intend to give this impression, but it may be at least psychologically significant that in both cases the secondary rule is a private rule of change, and, as will be seen, these seem to diverge from other secondary rules in a number of respects.

Turning now to the permitted range of effects of a power-conferring rule it will be remembered that it was argued that Hohfeld seemed to leave this important question open. Hart

---

[18] Hart, p. 62.   [19] Hart, p. 68.

[20] Hart, p. 134. It should be made clear that this passage occurs in the context of a different argument, and that Hart recognizes it as an inadvertent error.

similarly gives no unequivocal guidance. At some points he seems to limit the ambit of a power-conferring rule to the creation and extinction of duties. Thus he says, 'the powers which they [secondary rules] confer are powers to make general rules of the latter sort [primary rules] or to impose duties on particular persons who would not otherwise be subject to them',[21] and 'rules of the second type [secondary rules] provide for operations which lead not merely to physical movement or change, but to the creation or variation of duties or obligations.'[22]

But this doctrine is sometimes qualified, as in the passage immediately following the former of those passages, in which Hart says that it is only said 'at the cost of some inaccuracy' that 'whereas rules like those of the criminal law impose duties, power-conferring rules are recipes for creating duties.' It is not made clear what the inaccuracy is, nor whether it relates to the whole of the proposition or merely part, and if so, which. Sometimes an altogether more catholic view is expressed: 'There are other varieties of law, notably those conferring legal powers to adjudicate or legislate (public powers) or to create or vary *legal relations*[23] (private powers).'[24] Legal relations seem here, as they do for Hohfeld, to encompass more than just rights, duties, and privileges. Faced with these different formulations it is necessary to see whether any inference can be made from the uses to which the distinction is put. It then becomes at least tolerably clear that Hart does intend the variation of other secondary rules to lie within the ambit of secondary rules. Thus he refers to public rules which confer private powers as if they are secondary rules.[25] Similarly in his analysis of the structure of a legal system[26] he refers to the *relative* subordination of criteria for recognition, and to a *supreme* criterion. This implies that there must be at least one secondary rule about the criteria for recognition to establish such a hierarchy. Here public rules conferring powers on other public bodies to create further rules are regarded as a species of secondary rules. It seems then that secondary rules can be piled upon secondary rules indefinitely without altering their character as secondary rules. Position in the hierarchy is not signified by the adjectives

21 Hart, p. 33 22 Hart, p. 79. 23 Italics supplied.
24 Hart, p. 77. 25 Hart, p. 60. 26 Hart, ch. 6.

'primary' and 'secondary', but by a sub-division of the latter as either relatively 'superior' or 'inferior', culminating in a supreme rule. In this respect while neither Hohfeld nor Hart is completely unambiguous it is possible to regard their structures as identical.

(b) *The contrast between rules governing actions or rules*

This contrast is clearly closely connected with the preceding one. It will be demonstrated that it is not exactly the same. In this connection Hart asserts that,

> Under rules of . . . the primary type human beings are required to do or abstain from certain actions . . . .. Rules of the other type [secondary rules] are in a sense parasitic upon or secondary to the first.
>
> Rules of the first type [primary rules] concern actions involving physical movement or changes; rules of the second type [secondary rules] provide for operations which lead not merely to physical movement or change, but to the creation or variation of duties or obligations.[27]

He goes on to say that secondary rules are all *about* primary rules,

> while primary rules are concerned with the actions that individuals must or must not do, these secondary rules are all concerned with the primary rules themselves. They specify the ways in which the primary rules may be conclusively ascertained, introduced, eliminated, varied and the fact of their violation conclusively determined.[28]

In the light of the previous discussion it will be assumed, contrary to the tenor of these passages, that secondary rules may also be parasitic upon, or about, other secondary rules. It seems that one of the ways in which a rule can be 'about' another rule is by conclusively ascertaining its existence. Such a rule is a secondary rule of recognition. Its inclusion among the secondary rules throws doubt on the universal validity of the previous distinction between primary and secondary rules as being either duty-imposing or power-conferring. A rule of recognition need be neither. A rule asserting the validity of laws made by some long-deceased ruler cannot happily be regarded either as conferring a power upon him retrospectively

---

[27] Hart, pp. 78, 79.   [28] Hart, p. 92.

or imposing a duty upon those living today. It has accordingly been suggested that rules of recognition occupy a different place in Hart's system from that of any other secondary rules. It has been argued[29] that alone of all the secondary rules they are essential for any regime of rules, primary or secondary, since some measure of recognition must be accorded to any rule before it can be said to exist at all. A rule unrecognizable by anyone is inconceivable. Primary rules must be recognized by everyone, and secondary rules at least by officials. This is not true of any of the other types of secondary rule elaborated by Hart. Primary rules can exist without being varied, revoked, or adjudicated upon. Similarly these secondary rules themselves demand recognition before they can be said to exist, though they too can exist without being varied, revoked, or adjudicated upon. The flaw in this argument lies in its equation of recognition with recognition by reference to a rule of recognition in Hart's sense. Thus moral rules can be, and regularly are, recognized, but that does not mean that there is a rule of recognition in the moral sphere.[30] Indeed a most important feature of Hart's analysis is that in legal systems the recognition of primary rules is not casual, but governed by rules. Nevertheless it is still true that the rule of recognition differs from all other secondary rules in that its relation to them is of one-sided dependence. They cannot exist without it; it can exist perfectly well without them.

It may be accepted, then, that despite not conferring powers, rules of recognition are properly considered secondary rules as being at least 'about' other rules. Is it also the case that they are never 'about' actions, and conversely that primary rules are themselves always and only 'about' actions? It will be recalled that Hohfeld's analysis was seen to divide legal conceptions into two groups, both applying to any given situation so as to answer different questions which might be asked about it, namely whether it was permitted and whether it would effect a change in legal relations. Is this the same distinction? It may depend upon how one characterizes 'about'. In Hohfeld's system the concepts state the results of applying legal

---

[29] Summers, 'A Brief Rejoinder to Professor Mullock', [1965] Duke University Law Journal 76 at p. 78, n. 9.

[30] This point is made by Hart himself, *The Concept of Law*, p. 228.

rules to facts, just as Hart has explained.[31] It is not easy to understand Hart's distinction between primary rules which are about actions and secondary rules which are about rules in this way. In one sense both primary and secondary rules are 'about' actions in that they relate to events which take place in the world. But at the same time they are 'about' rules in that they categorize these events by reference to rules. For *A* to kill *B* and for *X* to hand a book to *Y* are both actions. Whether one amounts to murder and the other to a gift can be determined by applying rules. So in both cases rules are applied to actions. It may be the case that the consequences of this determination will be different, and that this difference will be intended to have a different effect upon conduct. This raises questions as to the *modus operandi* of the rules and their intentions. These are considered as the next two aspects of the main distinction between primary and secondary rules.

(c) The contrast between rules involving penalties and those involving invalidity in the event of non-compliance

Hart is here conscious of permitting a certain amount of distortion in his basic distinction as a result of conflating punishment and compensation as species of the genus penalty. He distinguishes primary and secondary rules by regarding the result of breach of the former as an 'offence' and breach of the latter as 'nullity', or potential nullity. He argues vigorously that it is confusing to equate the nullity which results from non-compliance with a secondary rule and the penalty which follows the commission of an offence prescribed by a primary rule; and that theories like that of Austin which seek to do so are misleading. He asserts that there is a fundamental difference between these two types of result. In the case of primary rules he says,[32]

It is logically possible ... that there should be such rules even though no punishment or other evil were threatened.

We can distinguish clearly the rule prohibiting certain behaviour from the provision for penalties to be exacted if the rule is broken, and suppose the first to exist without the latter.

We can ... subtract the sanction and still leave an intelligible standard of conduct which it was designed to maintain.

[31] 'Definition and Theory in Jurisprudence', 70 L.Q.R. 37.
[32] Hart, pp. 34–5.

Of secondary rules on the other hand he says,[32]

> We cannot logically make such a distinction. If failure to comply with this *essential*[33] condition [attestation of a will] did not entail nullity, the rule itself could not be intelligibly said to exist without sanctions.

And contrasting the two,[32] 'The provision for nullity is *part*[34] of this type of rule itself in a way which punishment attached to a rule imposing duties is not.'

This distinction is thus seen as a logical one, between secondary rules which cannot be understood to exist, even as rules prescribing behaviour, in the absence of nullity, and primary rules which can be so understood in the absence of penalties. This idea seems to be linked with the view of secondary rules of change as recipes for the creation of primary rules. Secondary rules are seen as essentially hypothetical. They simply prescribe the procedure appropriate for reaching a given result. They assume that the decision to use the procedure is motivated solely by desire for the result. Primary rules on the other hand are not recipes for creating sanctions. They assume that conduct is independently motivated, and the sanction is merely used to control it. This may well be true, but it is not clear that it is a logical truth. It may be, and indeed is, *socially implausible* to think of the rules of the criminal law as recipes for committing crimes and thereby attracting penalties, but it is not *logically impossible*. It is conceivable that the tramp's recipe for securing a night's shelter might be to knock off the policeman's helmet. The argument becomes still more plausible if rewards are considered. Payment of taxes may be taken as a hypothetical example. There could be a rule imposing a fixed penalty if payment is not made before a fixed date. The rule could equally well be cast in the form of a rule offering a fixed discount of equivalent amount if payment were made by the due date. It may be implausible to regard the first form as a recipe for paying the penalty. It is much less implausible to regard the latter as a recipe for securing the discount.

Conversely, secondary rules of change may sometimes be regarded as aimed primarily at the restraint of conduct other than that according to the specified procedure, rather than at

---

[32] Hart, pp. 34–5.   [33] Italics supplied.   [34] Italics in original.

providing for the realization of a legal result. It is possible to regard some stamping legislation in this way. The aim of the legislation may be seen as the use of unstamped paper rather than the provision of legal facilities. In other words the motivation to make use of the facility is equated with the motivation to avoid a legal penalty, as a means to secure the desired conduct, namely the use of nothing but stamped paper. This explains why nullity or penalties might be used quite indifferently in this context.

It is diffidently suggested that it is only when the procedure specified for realizing the result is itself devoid of value except as a means for securing that result, that the argument that the distinction is a logical one becomes convincing.

Hart uses the analogy of a game to support his argument.[35] He contrasts the foul rule which is regarded as analogous to a primary rule with the scoring rule which is analogous to a secondary rule. He argues that the scoring rules could not exist in the absence of nullity in the event of not scoring, whereas the foul rules could exist even if the players were not penalized. It is suggested that this confuses the physical phenomena with the characterization of those phenomena by the rules. It runs together the questions of what is to count as a score and whether scoring is to be counted. It is helpful to analyse the situation more closely. In the game of football rules provide that if the ball passes into the goal an alteration is made in the balance between the teams, and the game is restarted by giving the ball to the other side; other rules provide that in the event of a foul no adjustment is made to the balance between the teams and the game restarts with the ball given to the other side. The rule relating to the adjustment of the balance could as easily be attached to the one rule as to the other. In some games, as with the concept of the penalty try in rugby, it is indeed divided between them. Its incidence seems to make no difference to the meaningfulness of the conduct. It may be argued that this misses the point, and that it is not the physical conduct which becomes meaningless in the absence of the consequence of invalidity, but the concept of scoring itself. This seems plausible. It means that when the game provides for a score, however the rules say it is to be calculated,

[35] Hart, p. 238, n. to p. 28.

the notion becomes meaningless unless there is something else which counts as not scoring. This is true, but it proves too much for it is also true of all other concepts defined by the rules. Thus in the case of fouling, the rules which provide for fouling are meaningless unless there is some conduct which does not count as a foul. If this argument is accepted it may be seen that there is no distinction between primary and secondary rules in this respect. This has not passed unnoticed by other writers, even by those whose work in other respects Hart adopts. Thus Hume crisply and concisely observes,[36] 'It is impossible for men so much as to murder each other without statutes.' Rawls takes the same stand in classifying alike as rules of practices both the definition of an office and an offence, though in Hart's terms the former would be a secondary rule and the latter a primary. The object of both writers is to make clear the difference between the conduct regulated and the characterization of that conduct for the purpose of regulating it. And it is just as much the case that rules are necessary to transform killing into murder as that they are necessary to transform promising into contract.

The analogy of the game suggests a further defence of this aspect of the distinction. It might be argued that the game could survive without any concept of fouling, but not without any concept of scoring. It would then be the game itself which became meaningless without a scoring rule, but remained meaningful without a fouling rule. A more diluted form of the same argument would be that the character of the game would change more radically if the scoring rule were changed than if the fouling rule were changed. If the game is understood as the counterpart of a legal system Hart could perhaps be supposed to favour this argument since the addition of secondary rules is the decisive step in constituting a legal system. But if the maintenance of social life is understood as the counterpart of the game then he would have to be regarded as taking the opposite view since it is the presence of primary rules which determines whether men can live together at all. In any event this interpretation of the game analogy breaks down. To assert that the game became meaningless because there were no scoring rules would amount to denying that the game could

[36] *An Inquiry Concerning the Principles of Morals*, Sect. IV *in fine*.

be played without keeping the score. But as previously remarked it is perfectly possible to imagine a game in which the only consequence of scoring is to restart by giving the ball to the other side. To assert that the character of the game would be more radically changed by altering the scoring rule than the fouling rule, would in the case of football be to fly in the face of historical evidence. The transmogrification of football into rugby was accomplished by disregard of the foul rules, and changes in the scoring rules were simply consequential. It is worth pursuing the analogy of the game a little further. What is to be made of the rules defining the field of play? Are they primary or secondary? In football it is not a foul to kick the ball out of play, but the side doing so is penalized by giving the ball to the other side to kick or throw depending upon whether the ball has passed over the goal-line or touch line. Adjustments are not usually made to the score[37] so questions of nullity in that sense do not arise. And what about the rule defining the jurisdiction of the linesman which Hart briefly mentions in his note? His function is to advise the referee. His adjudication is neither necessary nor sufficient for either penalty or nullity.[38]

It is time to revert to Hart's legal example. It was the attestation of a will. He referred to this as an *essential* condition, noncompliance with which must entail nullity. His reference is to the situation in England under the Wills Act which does indeed make attestation essential. But it is only essential if the rules make it essential. Wills can be understood as a concept in the absence of attestation. In many countries it is not an essential condition to validity. It is characteristic of law that its main institutions like crime and contract, or even murder and sale, are composed of a myriad of sub-rules none of which is essential, in the sense that the institution would remain even if the sub-rules were different, though not perhaps if they were all different.[39] The structure of such institutions is extremely complex and has never been satisfactorily explained. The simplified

---

[37] Five-a-side football is exceptional in this respect.

[38] A possible legal parallel to such rules might be found in those provisions of the Marriage Acts relating to the formalities of marriage, breach of which does not affect the validity of the marriage nor attract a penalty.

[39] By analogy with the terminology coined by J. Raz in ' *The Concept of a Legal System* ' (1970) this is the difference between a momentary and a continuing institution.

analogy of a game is once again helpful. It may be asserted that in a broad sense both scoring and fouling are essential to make conduct into a competitive game. But these broad institutions require reference to a number of sub-rules. In the case of scoring for example, some of these refer to physical events like the passage of the ball in space and time, and others to further rules of the game. Thus rules define the dimensions of the goal, and other rules determine whether the passage of the ball into the goal shall be disqualified by reason of an immediately precedent breach of the foul rule. Any of these rules might be varied in any way, but the institution would remain as defined by the other rules. Thus there is at present a rule that balls passing over the crossbar do not count as goals, but this could be abandoned without making either the concept of scoring or of a ball passing over the crossbar meaningless. Similarly in law the rules relating to the length of the perpetuity period can be changed without making the concept of a perpetuity meaningless. Most legal rules are of such a character. Hart however is concerned with the broad institutions which lie behind the rules, although he puts it round the other way, ' *Behind*[40] the power to make wills or contracts are rules relating to *capacity*[41] or minimum personal qualification (such as being adult or sane) which those exercising the power must possess.'[42] 'Consider first those laws which lie *behind*[40] the operation of a law court.'[43] 'The rules which lie *behind*[40] the exercise of legislative powers are themselves even more various than those which lie *behind*[40] the jurisdiction of a court.'[44] Those rules which are referred to as lying behind powers are those which are in the very forefront of a lawyer's field of vision, and beyond which he is rarely inclined to look. He is not so concerned because it is these rules which define concepts and prescribe consequences. The main institutions might indeed become meaningless if there were no such rules, but this would be as true of those primarily dependent upon penalty imposing rules as of those primarily dependent upon nullity imposing rules. The real difference between these institutions lies in their functions. The difference is between that which is characterized· as an offence and that which is not, and whether it is so

---

[40] Italics supplied.   [41] Italics in original.   [42] Hart, p. 28.
[43] Hart, p. 29.   [44] Hart, p. 31.

characterized depends not upon the consequences which follow, but upon the function as conceived by the lawmaker and the subject. Before moving on to these questions in the next section, it is worth referring back to Hohfeld. He purported to describe *fundamental* legal conceptions. He could not have thought of further rules lying behind or in front of his concepts. For him they were the atomic components of a legal system. So in this respect there is a gulf between Hohfeld and Hart. Hart does recognize that there are further sub-divisions to be made, and his insight is surely clearer in this. It will be necessary to examine the delineation of such sub-rules in one area later. It is sufficient to remark that for Hohfeld, as for other scientific pioneers, what seemed to them to be atoms may turn out to have been molecules.

(d) *The contrast between mandatory and facultative rules*

This and the next two sections deal in different ways with the function of rules and mental attitudes towards them. Hart several times says[45] that it is characteristic of primary rules that they bind people whether they wish it or not, whereas secondary rules bestow facilities upon them for realizing their wishes. This is seen as a difference of social function. Primary rules are obligatory and mandatory, while secondary rules are facultative and optional. This requires further consideration. There may, in a given state, be a rule which requires all drivers to have licences and another which gives effect to written wills. These rules can certainly be regarded in the case of the former as prohibiting unlicensed driving, and in that of the latter as bestowing the facility of making a will. But can they not also be regarded as bestowing the facility of driving upon licensed drivers, and as requiring wills to be made in writing? And suppose that before these rules were introduced the old rules provided that no one should be allowed to drive in any circumstances, but that any form of will was effective. Could they then be best regarded in the first case as prohibiting conduct, and in the second as bestowing a facility?

The difficulty is that primary and secondary rules are both obligatory in some respects and optional in others. One can choose whether or not to drive or make a will. But once having

<hr />

[45] Hart, e.g. pp. 27, 78.

chosen, one must get a licence and put the will in writing. It may be said that there is a difference because the function of primary rules is to regulate conduct in drawing a line between freedom and constraint, while in the case of secondary rules the function is to prescribe legal consequences. This is however somewhat self-justifying since freedom is defined in terms of particular legal consequences. Thus penalties and compensation are regarded as symptomatic of the absence of freedom while nullity is not. If freedom of action were to be the acid test one might have expected the availability of injunction and specific performance to be more significant. But neither Hohfeld nor Hart is prepared to adopt such a test, and freedom acquires a special, limited, and legal meaning different from 'all that cannot be prohibited or compelled at law'.

In the case of secondary rules the interaction of privilege and potentiality is more complicated. It is, at least, necessary to distinguish freedom in respect of the power being conferred from freedom to exercise it once it has been conferred. It has already been remarked that to have a power is not necessarily to have a privilege to exercise it as in the example of the alienation of another's property. Nor equally does having a disability imply the absence of a privilege. Here Hohfeld's analysis can help to avert confusion. His two groups must be kept separate. Privilege or duty is one question, power or disability another. It may be the case that primary rules impose duties while secondary rules confer powers, but if so it is not then the case that primary rules impose duties while secondary rules confer privileges. These are separate distinctions, and if Hart is referring to the freedom to exercise the powers he is in danger of running them together. Thus on this view Hart and Hohfeld are poles apart. But Hart might be thinking of the power being conferred. If so it becomes necessary to distinguish a specific and generic sense. This may be illustrated by the power to marry. In a generic sense this is conferred by rules as to capacity. And this, it may be noted, is by no means wholly optional. In so far as it relates to age it is not optional at all. On acquiring the required age one has the power whether one wishes it or not. But there is also a more specific sense in which this power can be understood. The power to marry a particular person is not conferred by law, but does depend upon choice.

It is the choice of a private individual, but is still not that of the power holder. It is the choice of the liability holder, if one may so express it. Whether a girl has the power to marry a particular bachelor depends firstly upon the general rules relating to capacity which bind her whether she wishes it or not, and secondly upon the choice of the bachelor to propose to her. This too operates independently of her wishes. She can choose whether to accept or not, but she cannot choose not to make that choice. It thus appears that in neither of these senses either can it be said that secondary rules necessarily involve freedom of choice.

The difference between these latter two senses, or something close to it has however been made the focus of a general attack on Hart's distinction between primary and secondary rules. It has been asserted that he conflates the two quite different concepts of powers and capacities.[46] It is said that powers are conferred upon specific individuals or classes, and can be delegated, surrendered, or revoked, and their possessors can be impersonated, while none of this is true of capacities. It is said that capacities are concerned with the definition of those who can do certain things, while powers relate to what it is that they can do. It is argued that there is a fundamental difference between bringing oneself, or others, within the ambit of existing legal rules and changing the rules themselves. There are a number of different points here which should be distinguished. Some of them raise issues which have traditionally been discussed more within the context of Hohfeld's analysis. Legal linguistic usage does seem to support the distinction claimed between the generality of capacities and the specificity of powers. The most typical use of the word 'power' in private law is probably in the phrase 'power of appointment', and it is virtually unknown for lawyers to talk of powers to marry or to make contracts; these are capacities. This distinction has some affinity with that between a licence to walk across a neighbour's field, and the liberty to walk along a public highway. It has worried a number of commentators in their consideration of the concept of privilege in Hohfeld's analysis.[47] His term is redolent of specific exemption from a generally

[46] Cohen, Book Review (1962), 71 *Mind* 395.
[47] E.g. Williams 'The Concept of Legal Liberty' (1956) 56 Col. L.R. 1129.

binding duty, as he himself realized,[48] though he wished to apply it more widely to all cases where the actor was not constrained by a duty to do the opposite. Even in the limited case of a specific exemption from an otherwise general duty there is scope for further refinement. Thus one might wish to distinguish the situation where a private individual claims the protection of an exemption offered by the general law, say a privilege in the law of evidence, from that where one private individual is invested with the privilege by another, for example a licence to walk across the other's land. Hohfeld's failure to mark the distinction between specific privilege and general liberty is mirrored in the inadequacy of his distinction between rights *in rem* and rights *in personam*. His purely quantitative approach is much less convincing than the qualitative approach of Kocourek, at least in part for this reason. Kocourek is obviously alive to the problem of specificity which he brings into both aspects of his approach. Thus he employs on the privilege–liberty distinction the, admittedly unsatisfactory, categories of nexal, simple, and naked relations. On the *in rem–in personam* question he writes of polarized and unpolarized conceptions. Cohen's criticism of Hart runs along similar lines in that he is alleged to conflate general and specific abilities to change the legal situation, just as Kocourek and others accused Hohfeld of conflating general and specific freedom to act.

The major line of attack adopted by Cohen is the assertion of the importance of the distinction between changing rules and applying them. The argument is that it is wrong to regard, say, making a valid marriage in just the same way as legislation redefining the scope of matrimonial rights and duties. The former is to employ a capacity, the latter to exercise a power. This is however special pleading. The argument cannot be applied generally. There are some undoubtedly private powers, among them the most typical power of all—the power of appointment, which do not redefine rights and duties but merely alter their incidence. The position of an appointee is no different from that of the ordinary purchaser. Yet sale is clearly the exercise of a capacity on Cohen's view. The point is obscured

---

[48] *Fundamental Legal Conceptions* (1964), pp. 44–5.

by Cohen's concentration on public powers in his efforts to break down Hart's category of rules of change. This same preoccupation prevents him from seeing the very close analogy between some other private rules of change, say those conferred by the articles of association of a company, and the public powers conferred on, for example, a subordinate legislator. Nevertheless Cohen's criticism does indicate further distinctions which may be made beneath the broad umbrella of secondary rules of change. These will be considered in a little more detail later.

In what sense then are the functions of primary and secondary rules different? To revert to the simple examples at the beginning of this section it may be said that transcending the particular sub-rules there is a broad sense in which unlicensed driving is an offence and making a will a facility. It is necessary however to bear in mind that it is the institutions, not the individual rules, which are being considered. The difference in function may then be ascribed to the attitudes of the lawmakers, or the attitudes of those subject to the laws. To say that the institutions have different functions may mean that the law-makers intend to accomplish different aims by setting them up. Perhaps that in establishing offences they intend to prevent certain types of conduct, while in bestowing facilities they intend to help people achieve their own ends. But this is all very nebulous. It is never very clear to talk of the intentions of law-makers, at least not in sophisticated modern societies, and it is still less clear to talk of their aims or those of the population at large. The situation is further complicated by the range of techniques available to the law-makers. In the late eighteenth century for example it was not unknown for the legislature to make particular conduct an offence in one section of a statute, and in the next to offer a reward for its converse. Taxing rules are difficult to fit into this simple pattern. It is, however, clear that recourse to the complexities of such generalities cannot be avoided by a simple equation of primary rules with constraint and secondary rules with freedom. Indeed Hart himself resiles from this view in his account of the 'voluntarist' explanation of international law by admitting that secondary rules relating to the binding force of treaties 'are binding independently of the choice of the party bound by them'.

(e) Internal and external attitudes

A further key distinction made in 'The Concept of Law' is that between an internal and an external attitude to a rule. This is a difficult distinction and cannot be considered in any detail here. It is however used as a factor tending to differentiate primary and secondary rules in that Hart says,[49] 'The assertion that a legal system exists is a Janus-faced statement looking towards obedience by ordinary citizens and to the acceptance by officials of secondary rules as critical common standards of behaviour.' It is thus necessary for officials to take an internal attitude towards secondary rules. It is not made absolutely explicit how this applies to private secondary rules. Some passages certainly seem to suggest that in this case the internal attitude must inhere in those employing the secondary rule. Thus Hart asserts,[50] 'Rules conferring private powers must, if they are to be understood, be looked at from the point of view of those who exercise them.' There is also something similar in a further passage,[51] 'For the operations which these rules make possible are the making of wills, contracts, transfers of property, and many other *voluntarily*[52] created structures of rights and duties which typify life under law.' These extracts may imply a fully developed internal point of view. A weaker version is put forward in the discussion of international law and the binding effect of treaties,[53] 'The individual or state who *wittingly*[52] uses these procedures is bound thereby.' A further possible view is that only the officials of the system need take an internal view of private secondary rules, and that it is sufficient that they regard the procedures as capable of creating valid law. The difficulty with any stronger view is that of reconciling it with what actually occurs. We all make contracts of sale and carriage much as M. Jourdain talked prose. We do not have a point of view about the exercise of these powers just because we do not 'wittingly' use the procedures. And any other view would apparently require of ordinary private individuals a more profound acceptance of the rules determining when a contract was binding than of the obligations imposed by it, which would be absurd. It would seem to be the better view then that it is necessary only for the officials to take such

---

[49] Hart, p. 112.   [50] Hart, p. 40.   [51] Hart, p. 94.
[52] Italics supplied.   [53] Hart, p. 220.

an internal view of private secondary rules of change. This in turn seems to imply that there can be no such secondary rules outside the context of a legal system, since the existence of a legal system is so closely associated with the appointment of officials. But Hart is reluctant to accept this implication since he admits that promises can create obligations for individuals, and treaties for states, even outside the context of a legal system. The best escape route may lie in the view that if there are no officials, and no legal system, then those employing the rules must adopt an internal attitude towards them. Exactly who must hold exactly what attitude to which secondary rules is too complex to be considered here. It is probably enough to note that Hohfeld never addressed his mind to this very important question, and that Fuller's identification of his distinction with Hart's is seriously misleading in diverting attention from it.

(*f*) *Self or official application*

In the light of Hart's view that someone at least must take an internal attitude to secondary rules but that this is not necessary for primary rules, it might be thought strange that he should regard rules of the criminal law, which are typically primary rules, as principally intended for self-application by those whose conduct they bind. Thus he writes,[54] 'They [private individuals] are expected without the aid or intervention of officials to understand the rules and to see that the rules apply to them and to conform to them.' 'The members of society are left to discover the rules and conform their behaviour to them.' This squares well enough with his view that primary rules prescribe conduct, but perhaps less well with the idea that an internal attitude towards such rules is unnecessary. The explanation seems to be that while not necessary it is both desirable and desired by the legislators that such an internal attitude should be taken.[55] If it is true that an internal attitude towards secondary rules is required only of officials, then this difference between primary and secondary rules seems to be one merely of emphasis. That is to say that the desire that private individuals take an internal attitude towards secondary rules is less intense. It will normally be enough for the officials

---

[54] Hart, p. 38.   [55] Hart, p. 113.

to do so. This point of comparison again finds no counterpart in Hohfeld's work.

(*g*) *System completing*

It is fundamental to Hart's analysis that the addition of secondary rules to a set of primary rules[56] 'may fairly be considered as the step from the pre-legal into the legal world.' It is not made clear exactly which rules are necessary to accomplish this transition. As previously noted, it may only be public secondary rules which are essential. The quotation above is itself taken from a paragraph dealing with public rules. Whether private secondary rules can by their addition lead to this development is made especially dubious by Hart's criticism of 'voluntarist' theories of international law, which culminates in the inclusion of rules providing for the binding force of treaties among a *set* of rules of international law. The question of whether any of the other types of secondary rules may similarly be dispensed with will not be considered. Thus in this respect it seems that private secondary rules of change cannot be distinguished from primary rules.

(*h*) *Degree of social pressure*

In his discussion of the nature of rules imposing obligations Hart stresses the seriousness of the social pressure which is necessary to support the basic rules which make social life possible. Since these are rules imposing obligations they may be regarded as primary rules, though there are also references to rules requiring the keeping of promises or the fulfilment of a role as imposing duties. This might possibly be construed as a reference to some secondary rules as being duty-imposing were this not so strongly contrary to the main tenor of the argument. That leads one to construe these references as being to the result of applying the secondary rules. If these passages are disregarded there are then none which insist on a correspondingly serious social pressure. This is comprehensible when it is remembered that social life itself would be impossible without primary rules, while only the development of a legal system is dependent upon the introduction of secondary rules. It is natural that pressure for the former should be greater than for

[56] Hart, p. 41.

the latter. Here again Hohfeld paid no attention to such questions, a deficiency completely ignored by Fuller's equation.

A TAXONOMY OF POWERS

Hart has pointed out[57] that a taxonomy of legal rules remains to be accomplished. This is true, and what follows is merely a preliminary sketch of one small segment of the whole field. There are a number of ways of escaping from the criticisms that Cohen makes of Hart's position. The least defensible seems to be the one to which Cohen himself inclines, namely, to reduce secondary rules to conditional antecedents of primary rules. Hart's own defence is that the most illuminating results follow from presenting legal rules as falling into two broad categories. A further possibility is to break down the categories still further. This should lead, at least, to some further clarification of the nature of the broad categories. It may also help to bridge the gap between the analysis of Hohfeld and the theory of Hart.

As Hart points out there are many different types of secondary rules, and it is proposed to deal here only with rules of change. Nothing that is said should be taken as applying automatically to rules of recognition, adjudication, or enforcement. Hohfeld intended to show that adjectival relations were fundamentally similar to substantive relations, but died before attempting the task. Here too adjectival relations will be excluded, but for the different reason that they are not believed to be susceptible to precisely the same analysis.

In this sketch it is not proposed to coin new words, nor to express ideas by adopting limited special meanings of already familiar words. The spectre of the oblivion into which Kocourek's work has sunk haunts the first possibility. He indeed attempted a similar task to that undertaken here in chapters ten and eleven of his book 'Jural Relations' which deal with 'mesonomic' and 'prozygnomic' relations. He makes some of the distinctions proposed below, but in a way so obscured by the terminology in which it is expressed that very little has been derived from it. Hohfeld adopted the second approach, remarkably successfully, but not without controversy and the result has been a distracting succession of terminological quibbles

57 Hart, p. 32.

which has tended to inhibit more fruitful criticism of his work. It is also the case that as one continues to sub-divide so the stock of available words becomes diminished. To avoid this difficulty it is proposed here to take advantage of the facility provided by grammar of combining words in circumlocutions. It is appreciated that it gives a less elegant impression.

The previous discussion has indicated a number of points of distinction which may be made between different types of power, or rules of change if the former term appears to beg an important question. Here a number of such points of distinction will be suggested with a brief indication of the sort of questions to which they give rise. It is certainly not claimed that these are the only distinctions which can be drawn,[58] but it is hoped that their use might clarify discussion of particular rules on the one hand, and indicate the role that might be played by particular examples in the construction and criticism of broader theories.

(a) *Source of power*

This first distinction relates to the origin of the power, and in particular whether it comes from a public or a private source. The notion of a source here relates to the designation of the person or body bestowing the power upon the power-holder. Thus an agent generally receives his authority from a private source, while a local authority receives its from a public one. There are difficulties with this classification however. For example, a local authority may appoint an agent, and in that case the agent's authority would have a public source. More fundamentally, as Kelsen has argued,[59] all private and public sources may be traced back to a common source thus eliminating the possibility of distinguishing public and private in this sphere. Perhaps a more promising approach is to look not at the source from which the power emanates in terms of the status of the person or body conferring it but instead to the status of the rule by which it is conferred. This involves accepting the conventional view of the status of such sources somewhat unquestioningly. Thus the rules of agency are conventionally

---

[58] For a different set see A. Ross, *Directives and Norms* (1968), pp. 130–3.
[59] *General Theory of Law and State* (1961), pp. 87–90; *The Pure Theory of Law* (1967), p. 282.

regarded as a body of private law rules, and so the source of the authority of an agent appointed by a public body would on this view be said to be private. Two other possibilities may be considered. The first which can be quickly rejected is that one should have reference to the legal source of the power. This is just not appropriate as examples make clear. Thus the power to make a will which is universally accepted as private is plainly derived from a public general statute, while the power of the legislature to make laws which is archetypically public has no discernible source at all. A further attempt to distinguish between public and private in this general area of law has been made by Kelsen,[60] and, following him, by Ross.[61] They attempt it by distinguishing between the heteronomous or autonomous character of the rules made by the power holder. Thus public powers can be used to make rules binding others beside the power holder without their consent, while private powers cannot. There are a number of comments which may be made about this. The first is that it tends to run together a number of different points at which one might wish to distinguish these rules. Thus it applies to the source of the power, the status of the power-holder and the range of application of the power. In particular in the last respect it seems to imply a limitation upon the range of relations which are to be considered in determining whether a power is public or private. Its most plausible application is to duties, but it does not hold universally even there. Thus the acquisition of easements by prescription effects the imposition of duties upon a private individual by another, and so far from this being dependent upon the consent of the former, his consent would actually prevent the duty arising. Similarly in other situations the doctrine can only be preserved by adopting a very general view of consent. Thus, in the case of joining a trade union where under the rules the committee has power to create duties in the members, the view has to be taken that the general consent to joining under those conditions overrides the lack of consent to their exercise in a particular way. This is a view which did not appeal to the House of Lords in *Bonsor's* case. Finally in a number of other cases this view necessitates taking

[60] *General Theory*, pp. 204–5; *Pure Theory*, pp. 280–1.
[61] *Directives and Norms*, pp. 132–3.

a very legalistic view of consent, for example, in the case of insurance contracts where insurance is compulsory and all the companies insist upon the same terms. Once one moves away from the limited range of duties the view becomes even less acceptable. Thus powers to accept offers are continually being conferred upon people without their consent, and so too are a multitude of rights, privileges, liabilities, immunities, and disabilities. It is not disputed that distinctions turning upon the range of application of powers are valuable; it is suggested that this is a different distinction from that between public and private powers.

(b) Power-holder

If the status of the power-holder is distinguished from the status of the source of the power, the former becomes a further relevant focus for distinguishing between different rules in this area. Here again the most obvious, but by no means the only, distinction is between public and private power-holders. That the two questions of status are different may be illustrated by considering the case of the Public Trustee, undoubtedly a public body, being designated under the ordinary private rules to administer a trust fund, or conversely by the case of the private individual who is empowered under the rules of administrative law to insist upon an inquiry before a planning decision is given final approval. It is appreciated that not all cases will be so easy to classify. Argument could rage quite fiercely over the private or public status of, for example, the British Steel Corporation or British Petroleum. There are also many other questions relating to the status of the power-holder with implications for the nature of the powers conferred. They may relate to his capacity as an individual human being, whether he is an infant, lunatic, or married woman; or as a corporate body, whether a purported corporate body has been duly incorporated, or a trade union registered. It does not matter what principle of classification is to be employed, all that is asserted is that rules can usefully be distinguished according to the character of the user.

(c) Mode of investment

Here the question is related to the way in which the power

holder is designated. A power may be invested in someone specifically as in the case of the appointment of an agent or in the delegation of rule-making powers to a particular authority; or it may be done generically where the powers are given to a particular class and apply to each member of that class such as solicitors affected by the Solicitors' Act or local public health authorities by the Public Health Acts; or universally where a power is given to everyone without explicit exception, such as the power to make a will conferred by the Wills Act. There may, of course, be implicit exceptions even to apparently universal investments, perhaps inherent in the language used. Thus the Wills Act does not apply to corporate bodies, not because they are specifically excluded, but because it only relates to dispositions upon death, and corporate bodies are not usually regarded as capable of death. These forms of designation are by no means exclusive but may be combined in various ways. Thus a class may be defined generically but made subject to a specific exclusion, for example, a power might be given to all the sons of the testator except a named one. The questions discussed here are of course reminiscent of those dealt with by Kelsen[62] and Kocourek[63] in their analysis of rights *in rem* and rights *in personam* which is made to depend upon similar considerations. Here however the question is simply transferred from the analysis of the designation of the duty bearers in their schemes to the power-holders in this.

(d) *Freedom to exercise power*

Here the questions relate to the position of the power-holder in relation to the exercise of the power. They are clearly connected with further questions as to the procedures for its exercise, and the uses to which it may be put, but these questions are logically distinct since it is perfectly possible to imagine a power which the power-holder is bound not to exercise. Thus an auctioneer who is auctioning goods which unknown to him have been stolen, while he may have the power to alienate them is under a duty not to do so since this will amount to conversion, and if the true owner were to discover in time, he could prevent the auction from taking place. Conversely a power-holder may be under a duty to exercise his power,

---

[62] *General Theory*, pp. 85–6.   [63] *Jural Relations* (1928), pp. 201–2.

not all powers imply the freedom not to exercise them. This explains the learning devoted to distinguishing between powers coupled with duties and bare powers in cases like *I.R.C.* v. *Broadway Cottages Trust.*[64] It is also the explanation of what occurs in a collateral contract. The privilege to enter the main contract by exercising a power of acceptance is by the collateral contract transformed into a duty to exercise it. It may be argued that the extremes of absolute freedom and absolute obligation do not exhaust the possibilities, and that the exercise of the power may be made conditional upon some other factors. In this case the conditions will generally relate either to the procedure to be followed in exercising the power, or to the range of objects to which the power may be applied, and will be dealt with under those headings. Another possibility is that the conditions will operate as either precedent or subsequent to the power. In such a case the condition does not restrict the freedom of the power-holder to exercise the power, but instead operates as a factor determining whether the power exists at all.

(e) Form of exercise

This is an important factor in differentiating between different rules of change, and one which is highly productive of litigation, especially in the public sphere where it contributes much of the substance of administrative law. In private law the formalities are often less elaborate, and in some cases, such as discretionary trusts, are virtually non-existent where often all that is required is a genuine exercise of the discretion. However there other areas where the formalities may be simple but are nevertheless important, such as the law of succession where the provisions for the attestation of wills lead to a fairly constant stream of litigation.[65]

The requirements are however generally more elaborate in public law, and most elaborate of all in the formalities required for passing a public statute, though in that case compliance with the formalities can rarely be challenged. In the case of rules made by less august public bodies such as local councils or subordinate legislators there are often detailed requirements

---

[64] [1955] Ch. 20. For an illuminating application of jurisprudential analysis to these problems see J. W. Harris 'Trust, Power and Duty' (1971), 87 L.Q.R. 31.

[65] e.g. *In the Estate of Bravda* [1968] 2 All E.R. 217.

which must be followed minutely.[66] Nor is this formality limited to the strictly public sphere since a similar situation prevails in relation to other corporate bodies like trade unions and limited liability companies. Here too there is some litigation though it is somewhat confined by the rule in *Foss* v. *Harbottle*. The reason for this similarity is not far to seek. It is that both public bodies and private corporate bodies have to act through individual human beings and the formality serves to distinguish the capacity in which any given action is done. This is reinforced by the tendency for such bodies to act in a collegiate forum which itself entails the establishment of rules determining the procedure of the body, and particularly the way in which it should arrive at its decisions.

(f) Range of application

This factor relates to the range of persons, things, and relations which can be affected by the power. This is probably the most characteristic facet of powers since it is to this which the doctrine of *ultra vires* relates in its most typical form. It has already been remarked that Kelsen and Ross use this notion to distinguish between public and private powers. That argument was rejected, but it is clear that this is an important point at which different types of power can be distinguished from each other. Thus it is on this basis that special and general powers of appointment are distinguished. It is these considerations which determine the incidents of various contracts, and covenants binding land.

Very often the objects for which a power can be exercised are precisely set out, in a trust deed, in the articles of association of a company, or in the terms of an agency agreement. If they are exceeded, remedies can be sought. Exactly the same principles apply to public rule-making bodies whose powers are often defined in a formal constitution, as in the United States for example, in a statute, or in some other formal document.

Another form of restriction upon the range of application of a power is by the specification of certain standard incidents which must be fulfilled. Thus in some contexts a sale must involve a consideration in money or money's worth. The degree to which the standard incidents of transactions of a particular class may be altered varies a good deal. In some cases, like marriage, the standard incidents are invariable except, and then only to a very limited degree, by further transactions, such as settlements. In the law of contract considerations of public policy set a fairly broad outer limit to the range of permitted deviation, indeed there is really no standard case at all. Between these two extremes one might place the conveyance of land. The normal incidents of ownership can be altered by the reservation of casements or by the insertion of restrictive covenants, but again not in a completely unrestricted way.

Finally there is the consideration of the range of modalities which may be affected by the transaction. It sometimes seems as if writers assume that only changes in rights and duties are sufficiently important to characterize the ability to accomplish them as powers, or rules of change. But this seems an unduly limited approach. It is surely as important, at least, from the point of view of juristic analysis, that privileges, powers, and immunities are changed. One possible theoretical objection to such a view is that it might allow an infinite expansion of juristic relations. Thus if it is argued that one should distinguish between p^1 which is a power to alter rights and duties, and p^2 which is a power to alter powers, why should there not be a p^3 which is a power to alter powers to alter powers, and so on to p^n. In practice this would not give a moment's difficulty. The law is just not so refined as to conceptualize chains of powers in this way. All that is necessary is the basic distinction between powers to change powers, and powers to change other things. In this way the imaginary succession of powers can all be allocated to the first category.

(g) *Variety of changes*

This aspect relates to the sort of changes which it might be desired to bring about, and is perhaps most clearly illustrated by concentrating on the changes which might be made to a set of legal relations in respect of a piece of land. There are three basic possibilities, relations may be created, extinguished, and varied. It is also worth dealing separately with transfer even though it is really a special case of extinction and creation. Thus I can create a licence in my neighbour to walk across my land, and by revocation I can extinguish it. I can vary the terms of the licence by allowing him to walk across the land only at set times. There may, of course, occasionally be some difficulty in distinguishing variation from creation and extinction. Finally by selling the land I can transfer most of my rights and duties in respect of it to the purchaser. There may be restrictions upon my freedom in any of these respects. I may have covenanted not to re-sell some property I have bought, for example. There are many cases when I cannot transfer legal relations which I possess. This is especially true of powers, which have been conferred upon me by specific designation, where the restriction is so well established as to be entombed in the maxim 'delegatus delegare non potest'. The whole area is a fruitful one for litigation both in the public field, and in the private where it gives rise to much of the law of assignment.

(h) Effect

A final point at which one can usefully distinguish between different rules of change is that of the effect which a purported exercise of the rule can have. There must obviously be at least two possibilities, that the change has been effective, and that it has not. Thus a will may be valid or invalid. In most legal systems there is also the further possibility that a transaction is conditionally valid. Thus in the law of marriage the doctrine of nullity distinguishes between those defects which make the marriage void, and those which make it merely voidable. A similar distinction is made in the public sphere, for example in respect of subordinate legislation. The converse situation of a transaction being conditionally void also occurs, for example in the case of some contracts with infants which become valid only if they are ratified when the infant attains full age.

These eight factors are all points at which powers or rules of change can diverge from each other. Some are more important than others. In some there are only two alternative possibilities, in others there are an infinite number shading into each other. By reference to these factors powers and rules of change could be sub-grouped in hundreds of different ways. It is suggested that the range of this variety of types of rule of change should be borne constantly in mind in considering the general theories advanced to explain legal systems. Thus it can be seen that Cohen's criticism of Hart is really too facile. He has used one or two of these distinctions as a warrant for saying that Hart was wrong to regard rules of change as being one unified group. But once the range of possibilities is appreciated, the structure of the rules can be seen and rival schemes of abstraction more fruitfully evaluated.

XI

On the Functions of Law

J. RAZ

I

The concept of the functions of law is, quite obviously, of major importance to any theory of law which attempts a general explanation of the nature of law. Like so many other jurisprudential concepts, it is also relevant to a number of other disciplines concerned with the law. It is pertinent to the considerations of lawyers, judges, and officials faced with problems of the correct interpretation and application of the law. It is relevant to sociologists and political scientists wishing to explain the interaction of the law with other social norms and institutions. It is indispensable to moral and political theorists elaborating general principles to which the law should conform and for deviation from which it should be criticized. In a more indirect way the concept of the functions of law is also of interest to normative philosophy, for it bears on a more general explanation of the functions of norms, which is part of the elucidation of the nature of normative systems whether legal, moral, social, or other.

Bearing in mind the importance of the concept there is little wonder that statements relating to legal functions are often encountered in many discussions concerning the law. It is, however, surprising that legal theorists have paid so little attention to the elucidation of such an important notion. Not that legal theorists did not pronounce on the functions of law. Indeed such pronouncements were often made. They were, however, too often made in an attempt to emphasize a particular way of viewing the law, which the philosopher concerned thought, quite often correctly, had been neglected. They were not meant to be comprehensive classifications of the functions of law.

Consider for example, the following quotations:

For the purpose of understanding the law of today I am content with a picture of satisfying as much of the whole body of human wants as we may with the least sacrifice.[1]

Law is the enterprise of subjecting human conduct to the governance of rules.[2]

The norms of a legal order regulate human behaviour.[3]

What, then, is this law business about? It is about the fact that our society is honeycombed with disputes. Disputes actual and potential; disputes to be settled and disputes to be prevented.[4]

All these statements are correct and important, they all draw attention to important aspects of the law or illuminating ways of considering it. Yet it is curiously difficult to evaluate them, even to judge whether they are compatible or not. It would seem that this difficulty is not overcome by filling in more about the context in which these statements were made, for what all these philosophers fail to provide us with is a comprehensive reasoned scheme of classification of the functions of laws. It is the purpose of this article to contribute to the elaboration of such a general classification.[5]

Before undertaking this task, however, two further clarifications are in place.

Philosophers have occasion to refer to the functions of law in at least three different contexts. Some are concerned with the functions that all legal systems necessarily fulfil, thus regarding certain functions as part of the definition of a legal system, or as entailed by this definition and certain universal facts of human nature. (As the definition of a legal system should not be arbitrary but has to be justified, the contention that all legal systems necessarily fulfil certain functions is, if true, extremely important.) Similarly, the performance of certain functions might be a defining characteristic of certain branches of the law (e.g. the law of contracts or the criminal law etc.). On the other hand, theorists are often interested not in functions fulfilled by all legal systems but in those fulfilled by some or most;

---

[1] R. Pound, *Introduction to the Philosophy of Law* (1922, 1961), p. 47.
[2] Lon L. Fuller, *The Morality of Law* (revised ed. 1969), p. 106.
[3] H. Kelsen, *The Pure Theory of Law* (1967), p. 31.
[4] K. N. Llewellyn: *The Bramble Bush* (1930, 1960), p. 12.
[5] It is not my purpose to discuss the concept of function itself.

their enterprise may lie in comparing the degree to which these functions are carried out and the techniques by which they are promoted in various legal systems. Finally, theorists are interested in claims that legal systems in general or under certain circumstances ought to fulfil certain functions in certain ways. Rather than putting forward any such claim, it is the aim of this essay to help in formulating a general classificatory scheme, by the use of which such claims can be made and evaluated.

Such a classificatory task can be carried out in great detail. Only the most general classifications will be proposed here, as only they are likely to prove of general interest. More detailed classification is bound to be made within the framework of the general categories. The exact way in which it is to be carried out depends, however, on the purpose at hand, which varies from one context to another.

II. NORMATIVE FUNCTIONS

It is important to distinguish between normative and social functions of the law. The distinction is not meant as a classification of functions. It is rather a distinction between types of classifications, between different principles of classification of functions. Every legal norm has necessarily a normative and usually also a social function. When discussing the law it is essential to keep the two separate by being clear at every moment which principle of classification is being used. Normative functions are ascribed to laws by virtue of their normative nature, their mode of normativity. Social functions are attributed to laws because of the social effects they have or are intended to have. (The distinction between intended and actual social functions of laws is of great importance in assessing the performance of laws. It figures in many discussions of law reforms. It will not, however, be dealt with here.) Laws fulfil their social functions because of their particular normative character. The normative function of laws is part of the means by which they perform their social functions.

The normative function of laws is determined by their normative nature. Legal systems are normative systems. Every law is either a norm or has some logical relation to a legal norm by means of which it affects the existence, application, or interpretation of such a norm, thus indirectly contributing to the meaning of the norm. Only laws which are norms have a normative function and their functions are uniquely determined by the type of norm they are. It is common to all norms, legal or otherwise, that they guide human behaviour; they are reasons for performing or abstaining from a certain action. Because they guide human behaviour they fulfil also a second corollary normative function. They provide a standard for evaluating human behaviour. On the basis of norms acts and omissions can be judged as wise or foolish, effective or ineffective, right or wrong, etc. This subsidiary normative function becomes the major one in the case of retroactive laws. Purely retroactive laws do not guide behaviour for they are enacted after the behaviour in question has occurred. They only serve to evaluate it. This is, of course, part of the reason for their generally obnoxious character.

All legal norms, as norms, have these general normative functions in common: they guide behaviour and thereby also serve as a standard for evaluating it. Saying this, however, is not saying much. It does not clarify how this guiding function is performed, nor does it distinguish between the various modes in which the law can and does guide behaviour.

In looking for the ways in which the law provides reasons for action (and in action omission is included), we should of course disregard any reasons for the behaviour which exist independently of the law and would have existed even were there no law bearing on it. We should, furthermore, disregard the fact that the mere existence of a law is for many people a reason for complying with it. Though this is a very common phenomenon it is not essential to the existence of a legal system. Legal systems can exist, and some undoubtedly have existed, even though the vast majority of the population abhorred them and even though many people were only too glad to violate the law whenever it was safe to do so.[6]

The aim should be to look for reasons provided by the law itself. Not because these are the best or most important reasons for action, but simply because it is of the nature of law as a normative system to guide behaviour by providing legal reasons

---

[6] See on the problem of the attitude of the population and its relevance to the existence of a legal system: Hart, *The Concept of Law* (1961), pp. 109-14.

for action and the means by which this is achieved are being investigated here. The only assumption to be made is that the legal system in question is generally efficacious, i.e. that its duty-imposing rules are generally followed and enforced. This is a necessary, though not a sufficient, condition for its existence precisely because were it largely ineffective it would fail to provide reasons for actions and would not guide human behaviour. The degree to which the system as a whole is efficacious and various particular rules are enforced will determine the strength of the reasons provided by these laws. It will be convenient, however, to disregard this factor in the following discussion.

The only way in which laws can provide reasons for action is by determining that certain legal consequences follow on the performance of certain actions. Reasons for actions can be expressed in terms of the intrinsic desirability of the actions and their consequences both in themselves and as part of a general pattern of events. Laws guide behaviour by adding to their natural, non-legal, consequences additional consequences, thus affecting the reasons for or against the performance of these actions. When this happens the relevant law itself can be said to be a reason for the action or for avoiding it.[7]

The legal consequences attached to actions by law are immensely varied. They include liability to sanction upon the violation of a duty, the duty to perform a contract resulting from having concluded it, the granting or deprivation of rights by making a new law, the duty to maintain a person incurred by marrying her, etc. The various legal consequences of action can, nevertheless, be divided into two groups. Some are consequences which are generally regarded as undesirable by human beings, for example, deprivation of life, liberty, property, or other rights or the infliction of physical suffering. To this category should be added the consequence of being compelled to perform an action as a result of not performing it on a previous specified occasion. Other legal consequences of actions are not generally undesirable. They may be regarded as generally beneficial, or they may be desired by some men

---

[7] In this sense, the law is said to be a reason for action because of its content. The possibility that the mere existence of a law regardless of its content may constitute a reason for action was mentioned above.

in certain circumstances while others will prefer to avoid them. Examples of consequences of this second type are the rights and obligations incurred for oneself and others by acquiring property, accepting an appointment in the civil service, concluding a contract, and the rights and duties imposed by making a new law.[8]

By stipulating that such consequences follow upon the performance of certain actions the law guides behaviour. It makes the consideration of the legal consequences relevant to the desirability of the actions bringing them about. It does so in two quite distinct ways. The law provides what can be termed *determinate guidance*, when stipulating consequences of the first, generally undesirable, type. It provides *indeterminate guidance* when stipulating consequences of the second type.

In determinately guiding behaviour a law, by making the performance of a certain action the condition for an unpleasant consequence, provides a reason for avoiding this action. When guiding behaviour indeterminately a law makes the performance of an action sometimes more desirable and sometimes less desirable than it would otherwise be. It depends on the wishes and needs of the persons concerned, given the particular circumstances they are faced with in particular situations. By definition it is generally desirable to avoid a generally undesirable consequence. On the other hand, in certain situations a person will want to acquire a certain property, to marry a certain lady, to undertake certain obligations in exchange for certain rights etc., while in other circumstances he will wish to avoid all these results. This is what makes the first type of guidance determinate and the second indeterminate.

It should be clear that nothing is here implied as to the psychological ways in which legal consequences affect people's behaviour. They may be taken into account when people deliberate and plan what course of action to take. They may

---

[8] It is of interest to note that all the consequences of the second type are changes in legal situations, i.e. changes of the rights and duties of certain persons. Some of the consequences of the first, rather unpleasant, type are not of this nature. For example: deprivation of life and the causing of suffering. The law of course does not make this happen, it merely directs people to bring it about. This gives logical primacy to laws stipulating the first type of result. As to the reasons for this as well as an explanation of the relations between the different types of laws see J. Raz, *The Concept of a Legal System* (1970), pp. 156–66.

affect people in other, indirect ways, or they may fail to affect them at all. By stating that a reason for action exists a normative remark is made, not a psychological one. Similarly, stating that there is a reason for a certain course of behaviour does not mean that it is a conclusive or overriding reason. Other reasons may be there, some working for the same conclusion and others opposing it. Nothing can be said in general about the rational outcome of such deliberations, let alone their actual conclusion.

Another point which the previous discussion makes clear is that much of the difference between determinate and indeterminate guidance by a law depends on the fact that determinate guidance is achieved by stipulating a legal consequence which is in itself an independent reason for action because of universal features of human nature. In cases of indeterminate guidance the legal consequences are partial and incomplete reasons variously completed by other factors in various circumstances. Whether the legal consequences are reasons for performing or refraining from the action depends on these changing factors, which explains the indeterminate nature of the legal guidance.

The analysis I have presented of the general normative guiding function of the law into two normative functions of determinate and indeterminate guidance leaves one major factor unmentioned, and it is time to supply the omission. The notion of guiding behaviour implies purposive action. That the law guides human action implies not only that it creates reasons for action, but also that these are provided with the intention of affecting human behaviour in certain ways. It is tempting to ascribe the intention to the law-maker. This solution has many attractions but, though the law-maker's intentions when they exist should not be ignored in this context, the solution is bedevilled with many well-known difficulties. It is often impossible to ascertain the intentions of law-makers. This is always the case where customary laws are concerned, and frequently also in the case of judge-made and enacted laws. Furthermore, many laws persist even when circumstances have changed. They are maintained, applied, and justified on grounds very different from those which prompted their creators. It would seem, therefore, unreasonable to have regard only to the law-maker's original intentions. Professor Hart suggested that what the population in general and the law-enforcing officials in particular take the intention of the law to be should be taken into account. This view will be adopted here.[9] It is convenient to refer to the 'intention of the law', regarding it as a theoretical construct logically connected to the attitudes of the population and particularly of the law-making and law-applying organs as expressed in the legislature and its committees, court opinions, etc.

In conclusion, two normative functions can be ascribed to the law: it guides action determinately by expressing the intention that it shall be performed and stipulating a generally undesirable consequence to follow when it is not performed. It guides behaviour indeterminately by stipulating certain legal consequences to follow upon the performance of the act, which are not generally obnoxious, with the intention that these legal consequences will affect people's decisions to perform the action.

This analysis of the normative functions of law attempts to clarify the techniques used in law to guide human behaviour. Such an analysis should precede and partly determine the shape of a taxonomy of laws. In determining the fundamental types of laws the normative functions of laws are a major consideration, but not the only consideration, to be borne in mind. Some laws are not norms, they do not guide behaviour. Such laws relate to norms in various ways. They may determine the interpretation of norms, or their scope of application. Or they may set conditions for their applicability or even for the existence of legal norms or of other laws. Laws which are norms fulfil one or the other of the normative functions.[10] Thus, duty-imposing laws guide behaviour determinately, whereas power-conferring laws guide behaviour indeterminately. Other types of legal norms, such as legal principles, also fulfil one or the other of the normative functions.[11] It is possible to offer various subdivisions of the two normative functions discussed. This is

[9] See Hart, *The Concept of Law*, p. 39; 'Kelsen Visited' 10 *U.C.L.A. Law Review* 709. Whether the population or the officials approve of the law is immaterial.

[10] See on laws which are not norms *The Concept of a Legal System*, ch. 7. On the problem of the taxonomy of laws cf. ibid., pp. 140–7.

[11] See on legal principles, R. M. Dworkin, 'Is Law a System of Rules?' (1967) 35 U.Chi. L. Rev. 14 also published in R. S. Summers (ed.), *Essays in Legal Philosophy*.

of great importance for any attempt to present a complete taxonomy of laws. This matter will not be pursued here.

These remarks do not amount to a complete analysis of any type of legal norms for two distinct reasons. First, they concern only the normative functions of laws and disregard all the other factors which should be taken into account in a taxonomy of laws (for this reason, e.g., the relations between duty-imposing and sanction-stipulating laws were not discussed). Secondly, although every type of legal norm has a characteristic normative function, some of the norms of that type may not function in the way described here. For example, it is characteristic of duty-imposing laws that they are backed by legal sanctions. But some laws are rightly regarded as duty-imposing even though they are backed only by social, and not by legal sanctions. A complete analysis of duty-imposing laws should account also for the ways in which the notion was extended and applied to laws not backed by legal sanctions. Similar explanations are a necessary part of any explanation of any type of legal norms.

Before turning to the examination of the social functions of law, I wish to point out an important asymmetry between the two normative functions of the law. When determinately guiding behaviour the law intends a certain action not to take place. Stipulating generally undesirable consequences in the event the action is performed is a means to that end, the end being preventing the action. The law is primarily interested in the guided action, yet when behaviour is guided indeterminately the intention of the law is that the action be performed if the legal consequences are wanted by the individual or official concerned.[12] The guided action is merely the means. The law's attention is, as it were, focused on its legal consequences. The law provides a way in which certain ends can be achieved by those who want them. This explains why actions determinately guided are usually of some importance, at least when repeated by many, whereas actions indeterminately guided are usually of no consequence apart from those stipulated by law. Obligations and rights are incurred by word of

---

[12] Occasionally the law does superimpose determinate guidance on indeterminate guidance, making it obligatory or prohibited to use certain powers on certain occasions.

mouth, by signing a piece of paper or performing an innocuous ceremony. These are the acts indeterminately guided by the law. It is because the law's intention is to provide easy means for achieving certain legal results that such actions are particularly appropriate for its purpose.

III. SOCIAL FUNCTIONS OF THE LAW

The normative functions of the law are the ways in which the law guides human behaviour. They are determined by the reasons provided by the law for human behaviour. In considering the variety of these reasons the actual behaviour of people is immaterial. The social functions of laws, on the other hand, depend on the degree to which laws are obeyed and applied and on the effects of the existence of laws on human behaviour, attitudes, etc.

Distinguishing between the various normative functions of the law is a relatively easy task. They are closely connected with the basic types of legal norms, and, therefore, the classification of legal norms provides a guide to the analysis of normative functions. Indeed, the two tasks are intimately interconnected. Inasmuch as every legal system necessarily contains both power-conferring and duty-imposing laws it can be safely asserted that every legal system performs the two normative functions. Turning to the analysis of the social functions of the law as determined by its social effects one is treading on much more slippery ground. No firm guide to the classification, comparable to the analysis of types of norms, is available. It is much more difficult to provide a classification with any claim to exhaust all the social functions that legal systems ever perform. It is even more risky to maintain that all legal systems necessarily perform some or all of these social functions to any extent. It is difficult to propose even a very general classification which would be more than an *ad hoc* device useful for very limited purposes, a classification which would serve as a firm basis for the further analysis of law by lawyers, philosophers, sociologists, and political scientists alike.

A special danger awaiting any analysis of the social functions of law is that it may be so closely tied with particular moral and political principles as to be of no use to anyone who does not completely and exclusively endorse them. Bentham's plan for the natural arrangement of the law is a good illustration of this danger. Bentham had the brilliant idea of arranging and expounding the law in a way which would not only facilitate the memory and make for easy retrieval of any relevant legal material by lawyers and laymen alike, but which would also enable everyone to see what the social effects of the law were, and would make the criticisms and reform of the law an easy matter. He thought he had discovered a single method of arranging the law which would achieve all these diverse purposes. Laws should be arranged on the basis of the actions they command or prohibit:

With respect then to such actions in particular as are among the objects of the law, to point out to a man the *utility* of them or the mischievousness, is the only way to make him see *clearly* that property of them which every man is in search of. . . . From *utility* then we may denominate a *principle*, that may serve to preside over and govern, as it were, such arrangement as shall be made of the several institutions or combination of institutions that compose the matter of this science. . . . Governed in this matter by a principle that is recognized by all men, the same arrangement that would serve for the jurisprudence of any one country, would serve with little variation for that of any other. Yet more. The mischievousness of a bad Law would be detected, at least the utility of it would be rendered suspicious, by the difficulty of finding a place for it in such an arrangement. [13]

In proposing his scheme for natural arrangement Bentham does not confuse the roles of the expositor and critic of the law. He does not confuse the law as it is with the law as it ought to be. But his method of expounding the law as it is is designed to serve the critic as well. This in itself is an admirable purpose, which should be served by every analysis. The trouble, however, is that the way Bentham conceived of the function of the law was so closely tied to one particular way of evaluating it, namely his own, that his scheme for a natural arrangement is likely to be of little use for anybody but a utilitarian of the Benthamite brand. The aim of the analyst should be to propose

[13] *A Fragment on Government* (Blackwell, 1960), p. 24 f. See also on the same subject: *Introduction to the Principles of Morals and Legislation*, pp. 398–403, and *The Works of Jeremy Bentham*, ed. J. Bowring (1863), iii. 172, and elsewhere.

a classification of the social functions of the law which is of use to the reformer, but is not too closely tied to any particular viewpoint.

It is my hope that the classification proposed below avoids all these pitfalls and successfully meets all the requirements mentioned. It seems to me that all legal systems necessarily perform, at least to a minimal degree, which I am unable to specify, social functions of all the types to be mentioned, and that these are all the main types of social functions they perform. These claims will not, however, be argued for here. Instead the classification will be simply put forward and explained in general outline. It should be further clear that the price of making such claims is that only the most general and broad categories of social functions can be indicated. Apart from the need for justification the analysis proposed demands further elaboration and refinement.

It is possible to ascribe to every legal norm one normative function which explains its normative character. It is not possible to ascribe one distinct social function to every law or legal norm. Social functions are characteristically performed by legal institutions established and regulated by numerous laws. It is most common to inquire about the social functions of the banking system, ownership, the limited company, marriage, etc., rather than the function of any particular law involved in regulating these institutions, though occasionally it is useful to investigate the function of particular laws as well. Furthermore, one and the same legal institution, sometimes one law, often performs several social functions, though at the high level of generalization at which the present analysis is conducted it is easier to point out one type of function performed by each institution.

The social functions of the law can profitably be divided into direct and indirect functions. Direct functions are those the fulfilment of which is secured by the law being obeyed and applied. Indirect functions are those the fulfilment of which consists in attitudes, feelings, opinions and modes of behaviour which are not obedience to laws or the application of laws, but which result from the knowledge of the existence of the laws or from compliance with and application of laws. The indirect functions which laws actually fulfil are the results of their existence or of following and applying them. It must be remembered, however, that the acts of following or applying the laws are themselves part of the direct, rather than the indirect, functions of the law. The intended indirect functions of laws are those results which it is the laws' intention to achieve, whether or not they are actually secured. The indirect functions are most commonly fulfilled not only as results of the laws' existence and application but also of their interaction with other factors such as people's attitudes to the law and the existence in the society concerned of other social norms and institutions. The direct functions of the law often depend for their fulfilment on similar factors, but this is not always the case. A person may conform to laws imposing obligations without knowing that they exist. He may exercise legal powers without realizing that his actions have any legal effects. Though such cases are relatively rare, it is quite common for people to perform their duties and exercise powers for reasons which have nothing to do with the law. When doing so they contribute to the fulfilment of the direct social functions of the law. For example, curtailing the use of violence is a direct function of the law for it is secured if the relevant provisions of the criminal law are obeyed. Inculcating certain moral values in the population is an indirect function, for its success consists in something more than mere conformity with the law.

Direct functions will be dealt with first. They can usefully be divided into primary and secondary functions. The primary functions are outward-looking, they affect the general population and in them is to be found the reason and justification for the existence of the law. The secondary functions are the functions of the maintenance of the legal system. They make its existence and operation possible. They are to be judged by their success in facilitating the fulfilment of the primary functions by the law. Thus providing a national health service is a primary function. Regulating the operation of law-making organs is a secondary function.

IV. PRIMARY FUNCTIONS

There are four primary functions:

(a) *Preventing undesirable behaviour and securing desirable behaviour*

This function is mainly performed by parts of the criminal

law and the law of torts. It is served by prohibitions on murder, assault, unlawful imprisonment, libel, certain forms of sexual behaviour, revealing official secrets, etc., as well as duties of care while engaging in dangerous activities, duties of parents and guardians, etc. It may be claimed that this function is the most basic and elementary the law performs. It has attracted much attention and there is no need to discuss it in any detail here. It should be obvious that by talking about undesirable behaviour it is not implied that the behaviour is really undesirable or that the majority of the population considers it undesirable. It is regarded so by the law. Such views are attributed to the law in a way similar to that by which intentions were attributed to it above. It may be regarded undesirable for any reason. But, and it is important to remember this, in so far as a mode of behaviour is prohibited because it is regarded as likely to affect adversely some other direct social function of the law it does not fall into this category. Though this function is mainly performed by duty-imposing laws, it sometimes involves power-conferring laws as well. Thus the law may confer certain powers and make it compulsory to use or refrain from using them under certain circumstances, because their use is deemed desirable or undesirable.

(*b*) *Providing facilities for private arrangements between individuals*

The main bulk of the private law as well as large parts of the criminal law and the law of torts are concerned with this function. Most of the institutions of private law serve primarily this purpose. Contracts, negotiable instruments, private property, marriage, companies, co-operatives, banks, trade unions, and other forms of incorporation are all created to serve this function. They all form patterns of legal relations into which individuals enter of their own free will if and when they consider it will serve their ends or be to the good of somebody with whose well-being they are concerned.

In establishing and regulating such institutions both duty-imposing and power-conferring rules giving rise to rights under private law are involved. It is a mistake to think that only rights and powers have to do with this function. Rights and powers to conclude contracts, acquire and dispose of property, establish corporations, marry, etc., would be pointless and without effect but for the duties to perform contracts, respect property rights, etc. Duties imposed by the law of torts and the criminal law in respect of institutions designed for the performance of this function should, therefore, be regarded as contributing to its performance. Such duties include the provisions against trespass, theft, etc. The duty to avoid negligent harm is an instance of a duty serving both the first and the second functions. It serves the first function by protecting, e.g. against causing bodily harm, and it serves the second function, by protecting, e.g. property against negligent damage.

When fulfilling this second function the law sometimes provides ways of securing legal protection for arrangements that could be achieved by non-legal means. Often, however, it makes possible the achievement of ends that could not have been otherwise achieved in human societies. People can and often do reach agreements which are not legally binding. Men and women can and sometimes do establish lasting relations without marrying. The limited company, however, makes possible recruitment of capital from the general public to an extent that would not have been possible without some legal arrangements.

By prohibiting undesirable behaviour the law directs human activities in ways it finds appropriate. The law itself decides on ends which are desirable or undesirable and it limits individual choice to guarantee the achievement of the proper ends. By providing facilities for private arrangements between individuals the law helps individuals in pursuing ends of their choice. It does not impose its will on individuals but serves them in realizing their own will. The individual's freedom of choice is restricted only in consequence of his previous free decisions and actions.

While doing so the law makes the use of the facilities provided depend on observing various conditions. It does not allow individuals to invoke the protection of the law for any arrangement they may like. It creates frameworks within which individuals must make their arrangements and pursue their objectives if they are to enjoy legal protection. These restrictions are necessary to protect one party to an arrangement from being exploited by the other party, and to protect third parties from unfair consequences affecting them resulting from arrangements in which they did not participate. Hence the various restrictions on the freedom of contract, the limitations on the ways in which companies can be established and operate, etc. The more far-reaching the legal protection provided, the more it is likely to affect third parties and consequently the more severe will be the legal restrictions on the freedom of individuals to agree on the terms of their own arrangements. Thus, under the law of contract individuals have a wide freedom to decide the terms of their agreement, for they create rights *in personam* affecting only the parties to the agreement. But individuals have a very limited choice to decide the content of any rights *in rem* they may acquire. Basically it is a package deal. The law determines the consequences of the right and the individuals have to choose whether to take it or not and decide the price. Similarly, the less equal are the parties to an agreement likely to be the more will the law tend to restrict their freedom. These last remarks concern, of course, principles which should guide the law-makers. They do not pretend to reflect the way the law always operates.

(c) The provision of services and the redistribution of goods

This function has become of great importance in recent times, but as the following examples show it has always been performed by legal systems. The law performs it by making arrangements for defence against outside enemies (keeping internal order mainly belongs to the secondary functions discussed below), by providing for education, health service, road construction and maintenance, sewage and rubbish clearing, subsidizing industries or the arts, the payment of social security benefits, etc.

It is not generally possible to distinguish between redistribution of goods and the provision of services. When a law of agrarian reform is made, or when it is made compulsory to divide some of an industry's profits among its workers, or when a law stipulates a compulsory form of distributing the estate of deceased persons, it clearly provides for the redistribution of goods. Likewise, when a service is provided under the law against payment based on cost incurred as, for example, might be the case with a state-run railway service, this is a clear case of services rendered with no element of redistribution of goods. But many of the services stipulated by the law are paid completely or partly from the general budget. This means that they are largely paid out of taxes, and there is no guarantee that the amount of taxes paid by a man is proportionate to the benefit he derives from services provided by the law or to the cost of these services. Therefore, it is not possible to separate in general the provision of services from the redistribution of goods.

The previous remarks make also the well-known point that tax laws serve this social function. They also, of course, serve the secondary functions discussed below. Only the provision of services and the redistribution of goods by public bodies exercising public powers belong to this category. It does not include e.g. private gifts or voluntary labour contracts. Hence it is mainly the public law which is involved in the performance of this social function. Both laws conferring powers on officials and laws prescribing how these powers are to be exercised are involved as well as other duties. Quite often the law grants rights to these services to individuals enabling them to enforce the correlative duties on officials to provide the services.

(d) Settling unregulated disputes

It will be submitted here that laws regulating the operation of courts, tribunals, arbitrators, etc. fulfil both primary and secondary social functions. They fulfil a primary function inasmuch as they stipulate procedures for settling unregulated disputes, the so-called cases of first impression. They fulfil a secondary function inasmuch as they stipulate procedures for settling regulated disputes, that is, cases where the law is clear and cannot be changed by the judicial organ. They fulfil both these functions when they apply to partly regulated disputes, that is, disputes governed by existing law which is either unclear or can be changed by the judicial organ.

Both the distinction between regulated and unregulated disputes, and the corresponding distinction between the social functions of the law are likely to raise many objections. The distinctions will, therefore, be explained at some length with the aid of three simplified models of different types of normative systems.

Type A. Let us imagine a normative system fulfilling all or some of the three first functions. It may or may not have norm-governed procedures for changing its norms. But it does not have any norms stipulating procedures by which disputes can be authoritatively settled. Such a normative system will guide behaviour, and in doing so will prevent many potential disputes. When a dispute does arise reference to the norms will often help in reaching an agreed solution. Two important features characterize such a system. (1) There will be no authoritative way of deciding what is the correct solution to disputes governed by the norms of the system, that is, regulated disputes. (2) There will always be disputes which cannot be solved simply by reference to the norms either because the case is not dealt with by the norms as they exist at the time it occurs or because the norms existing at that time are vague concerning the issue in dispute. These are disputes which are not completely regulated and the system does not help in settling them.

Type B. The second type of normative system is similar to the first except for the fact that its norms include some establishing authorities for settling disputes and regulating their operation. These authorities, however, have only power to settle questions of fact and pronounce about the correct application of existing norms to the case. Faced with cases not governed by existing norms, or cases with regard to which the existing norms are vague, the authorities will simply decline to make any decision. A system of this type has three distinctive features: Firstly, such a system fulfils at least some of the first three social functions. Secondly, it provides for settling regulated disputes, but, thirdly, it does not provide any way for settling disputes which are not fully regulated.

Type C.[14] Normative systems of the third type are very different. They do not include any norms guiding the behaviour of ordinary people and performing any of the three first social functions. All their norms are concerned only with instituting organs for settling disputes, regulating their operation and,

---

[14] This type is discussed by Hart: *The Concept of Law*, p. 139. See also R. M. Dworkin 'Judicial Discretion', in (1963) 60 *Journal of Philosophy* 624.

sometimes, they include norms making it a duty to bring disputes before the relevant organs.

When faced with a dispute the organ may decide it in any way it likes. It does not state its reasons and is not bound to reach similar decisions in similar cases.

This type of system can also be characterized by reference to three features: Firstly, it does not fulfil any of the first three social functions, and does nothing to guide human behaviour in daily life. It does not help prevent potential disputes. Secondly there are under it no regulated disputes,[15] thirdly it provides procedures for settling all unregulated disputes.

Systems of type B differ from those of type A in having special organs improving the efficiency of the system. Their norms may be identical in content, affecting the same potential or actual disputes and performing the same primary functions. But in addition systems of type B provide recognized ways for official and authoritative settlement of disputes, which can be dealt with only informally under systems of type A. They fulfil an additional secondary function—they provide norm-applying organs, thus improving the efficient functioning of the system. Systems of type C, on the other hand, are not more efficient than those of type A. They differ not in their secondary but in their primary functions. They do not prevent undesirable behaviour, they provide neither facilities for private arrangement nor services to individuals. But they provide procedures for settling disputes whenever these occur. They perform only the fourth of the primary functions.

Legal systems are a combination of types B and C. They provide both for the settlement of regulated and unregulated disputes. (Though usually there are certain types of unregulated disputes with which legal systems will refuse to interfere.) Many legal systems by establishing some principle of *stare decisis* transform automatically every unregulated dispute once it is brought before the courts into a regulated or at least a partially regulated one. Therefore, legal systems perform both the primary function of providing ways for settling unregulated

---

[15] I disregard disputes concerning the operation of the dispute settling organs themselves.

disputes and the secondary function of instituting law-applying organs for settling regulated disputes.

The distinction between the two functions is obscured by the fact that usually the same organs perform both. Furthermore, it is obscured by the fact that many disputes are partly regulated. To some extent this is inevitable and is due to the inherent vagueness of laws (both rules and principles). But to a large extent it is official policy of law-making organs to use very vague terms (e.g. reasonable care) so as to leave much to the discretion of the courts. When dealing with a partly regulated dispute the courts, and therefore the laws regulating their operation, perform both primary and secondary functions.

V. SECONDARY AND INDIRECT FUNCTIONS

Secondary Functions

The law's secondary social functions have to do with the operation of the legal system itself. They provide for its adaptability, its efficacy, and its smooth and uninterrupted operation. There are two secondary functions: firstly, the determination of procedures for changing the law, and secondly, the regulation of the operation of law-applying organs. To adapt Kelsen's formulation: the law regulates its own creation and its own application.

The law regulates its own creation by instituting organs and procedures for changing the law. These include constitution-making bodies, parliaments, local authorities, administrative legislation, custom, judicial law-making, regulations made by independent public bodies, etc. The law regulates its own application by creating and regulating the operation of courts and tribunals, the police and the prison system, various executive and administrative bodies etc. In the performance of these functions are involved laws securing the financial resources necessary for the maintenance of these organs, and laws arranging for the recruitment of the appropriate personnel. This is mainly the domain of the public law, though an important role is played by the criminal law in the performance of these functions. Both duty-imposing and power-conferring laws are involved.

The discussion makes clear the key position of the court system in all legal systems. They perform the primary function

A Table of the Functions of Law

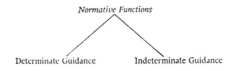

Normative Functions

Determinate Guidance   Indeterminate Guidance

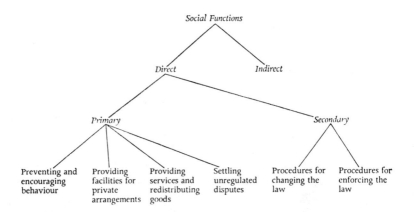

Social Functions

Direct   Indirect

Primary   Secondary

| Preventing and encouraging behaviour | Providing facilities for private arrangements | Providing services and redistributing goods | Settling unregulated disputes | Procedures for changing the law | Procedures for enforcing the law |

of settling unregulated disputes. They perform the two secondary functions of law-applying and law-making. They also perform important indirect functions. In many societies the courts are the most respected of legal institutions. They are often most directly connected in the public mind with the idea of the law and the rule of law. Consequently they play a vital role in promoting respect for the law and the values sustained by it.

Throughout the preceding discussion it has repeatedly been pointed out that the types of normative functions of the law are not co-extensive with types of social functions. Laws of all the normative types are involved in the performance of every social function. It was further emphasized that duty-imposing laws contribute to the performance of all legal functions. Duty-imposing laws, though not the only type of laws, are the ultimate basis of the law. Only because the other types of law have various logical relations to the duty-imposing laws, can they perform all the functions, normative as well as social, which they do perform.

Indirect social functions

The social effects of the law which come under this heading almost always depend for their achievement on non-legal factors, especially the general attitude to the law and its inter-action with social norms and institutions. Some of these func-tions are performed by particular legal institutions, others by the existence of the legal system itself. The indirect social effects of the law are numerous and vary enormously in nature, extent, and importance. They may include such things as strengthening or weakening the respect given to certain moral values, for example, the sanctity of life, strengthening or weakening respect for authority in general, affecting the sense of national unity, etc. The law helps in creating and main-taining social stratification, it sometimes helps in creating a sense of participation in running the country, sometimes it contributes to a feeling of alienation. Some laws are created with the intention of securing indirect effects. For example, conferment of certain privileges on certain classes of people may be done with the intention of enhancing their status. Therefore, the distinction between intended and actual func-tions applies to the indirect functions as well. The previous example shows also that sometimes securing the indirect func-tion is the main reason for enacting a law. Consider, for ex-ample, an exemption of university students from the draft as a measure of encouraging enrolment in the universities, or an employment-tax law as a means to increase efficiency in industry and commerce. These examples should make clear that the indirect effects of the law as conceived here are far from being relatively unimportant by-products of the law. They are part of its essential function in any society. Lawyers and legal theorists have paid little attention to the law's indirect functions. Sociologists and political scientists have great interest in them but found them a very elusive factor difficult to pinpoint and quantify. There can be little doubt that our understanding of law will remain partial and deficient until the social sciences succeed in tackling more fully the problems involved in assessing the indirect functions of the law.

VI. ON SOME COMPETING CLASSIFICATIONS

The classification of legal functions outlined above has not revealed any unknown functions of the law. It was not meant to do so. People have been thinking about the law long enough to have discovered all its main functions. But in discussing them they have often disregarded some and confused others. It was my aim in this essay to attempt a comprehensive classification of the main legal functions, trying to distinguish between those functions which have often been confused and to separate various levels of analysis. Doing this is not solving the problems of the functions of laws, it is merely presenting them. In assessing the merits and failures of the proposed classification it may be useful to compare it with the ideas of other writers. I will conclude this essay with some remarks (no complete analysis is intended) on the classifications suggested or implied by one political and one legal theorist.

Political theory was for a long time held captive by theories of the separation of powers with their concomitant doctrine of the three functions of government.[16] Modern political analysts have, however, fought loose from the constraints of this doctrine and paid more careful attention to the analysis of the various functions of the political system. One notable example is the analysis proposed by G. A. Almond and G. B. Powell Jr. in *Comparative Politics: a developmental approach*.[17] An important part of their analysis of the political system consists of the analysis of the conversion processes by which the system converts its input in the form of various types of demands and supports into its output. The conversion processes are briefly explained in the following passage:

We need to look into the ways in which (1) demands are formulated (interest articulation); (2) demands are combined in the forms of alternative courses of action (interest aggregation); (3) authoritative rules are formulated (rule making); (4) these rules are applied and enforced (rule application); (5) these applications of the rules are adjudicated in individual cases (rule adjudication); and (6) these various activities are communicated both within the political system,

[16] See on the development of these: Vile, *Constitutionalism and the separation of powers doctrine* (1967).
[17] 1966.

and between the political system and its environment (communication) (p. 29).

The output of the system resulting from these various conversion processes are four:

These are: (1) extractions, which may take the form of tribute, booty, taxes, or personal services; (2) regulations of behaviour, which may take a variety of forms and affect the whole gamut of human behaviour and relations; (3) allocations or distributions of goods and services, opportunities, honours, statuses, and the like; (4) symbolic outputs, including affirmations of values, displays of political symbols, statements of policies and intents (p. 27).

Apart from the conversion processes the system performs also system maintenance and adaptation functions which include recruitment and socialization (e.g. pp. 29–30). All these together make possible the assessment of the system's capabilities 'that is, the way it performs as a unit in its environment.' Almond and Powell distinguish between regulative, extractive, distributive, and responsive capabilities, the last indicating the system's responsiveness to demands.

No direct comparison of the classification proposed above with that of Almond and Powell is possible. They analyse the functions of the political system, not those of the law. But as the law partakes in the political system a partial and careful comparison can be profitable. Almond and Powell do not distinguish between the political functions performed by the law and those to which the law does not contribute, nor do they discuss the various ways in which the law contributes to the performance of various functions. Classical political theorists were always careful to analyse the place of the law in the political system. The neglect of this problem by modern theorists is to be regretted. It may also lead to confusion. It is quite clear that the law has but little to do with some functions of the political system, for example, handling foreign affairs, socialization, etc. Almond and Powell discuss some such functions and yet their analysis of the conversion processes with the crucial role ascribed to rule-making and rule-application, concepts which they discuss in legal terms,[18] suggest that the law is the only means through which the political system functions.

[18] Cf. *Comparative Politics*, ch. 6.

One may suspect that they did not free themselves from the spell of the separation of power doctrines and their concomitant analysis of the functions of government.

Further traces of the doctrines of the three functions of government are to be found in their distinction between rule-applying and rule-adjudication functions. No one can deny the importance of the courts in political as well as in legal systems, some remarks concerning this subject were made above. Almond and Powell's classification, however, breeds confusion for it obscures the fact that adjudication is not all of one nature. It is sometimes a part of the law-applying function and sometimes the performance of a distinct primary function of settling unregulated disputes. By considering rule-adjudication as a separate function they obscure the first fact and disregard the second.

The most obvious counterpart of the primary functions in their analysis is their classification of the output of the political system. There are three points to be made here. First, Almond and Powell fail to distinguish between the direct and indirect functions of the law. This is in keeping with their general neglect of paying attention to the role the law has in the political system. The distinction is however crucial to the understanding of both law and politics. Its neglect obscures the nature of the extractive, regulative, and distributive functions because all these are sometimes direct and sometimes indirect functions. It also obscures the fact that the symbolic output is different in kind from the others being the only one secured only by non-legal means and by the indirect functions of the law.

Secondly, the regulative function conflates two distinct functions, those of preventing undesirable behaviour and providing facilities for private arrangements. For their regulative function includes 'provisions for public safety, controls over markets, and rules pertaining to marriage, health and sanitation' (p. 26), which is a mixed bag of provisions performing both primary functions mentioned.

Thirdly, Almond and Powell mention one important category not included in the classification proposed above, that of extraction.[19] By extraction they do not mean all the demands

---

[19] This, like the other categories, applies also to the relations between one state and another. This aspect is here disregarded.

of the systems from individuals and groups, for that would include restrictions imposed on individuals' freedom of action. Extraction includes only the extraction of property rights and personal services. It might be tempting to have a special category for demands the system makes on individuals, though the temptation should be resisted. But once one narrows the category by excluding certain types of demands, it seems reasonable to go further and subdivide the narrowed category of extraction according to the purpose served by the demand. Therefore, in the classification proposed above extraction was divided and absorbed by the primary function of providing services and the secondary functions of system maintenance. The demand for service in the army or in a jury, but not the demand to refrain from assault or to provide for one's family, would be considered by them as extractions. What can justify this difference but the reasons for the various demands, and if reasons for demands play a part in the classification why not distinguish between demands imposed in order to provide services and demands made in order to maintain the system.

Legal theorists of the positivist school, by concentrating on the criminal law, tended to emphasize the first primary function of prohibiting undesirable behaviour and to overlook the other functions. Bentham, e.g., thought that in arranging the law:

... the penal code ought to precede the civil code and the constitutional code. In the first, the legislator exhibits himself to every individual, he permits, he commands, he prohibits, he traces for everyone the rules of his conduct. ... In the other codes he has less to do with commandments than with regulations and explanations, which do not so clearly address themselves to everybody, and which are not generally interesting to those concerned ... [20]

In his general theory of law H. L. A. Hart[21] has paid special attention to the second primary function, that of providing facilities for private arrangements, as well as to the secondary legal functions. The analysis proposed here is largely an elaboration of his ideas. Hart, however, did not distinguish between normative and social functions. Consequently, his theory suggests a simple relation between types of rules and social functions, according to which duty-imposing rules

[20] Bowring iii. 161.   [21] In *The Concept of Law.*

perform the first primary function whereas power-conferring rules perform the second primary function. In fact both rules have to do with each of these functions. Furthermore, this simplified picture of a one to one correlation between types of rules and types of functions obscures the fact that legal systems perform two more primary functions, those of providing services and settling unregulated disputes.

The confusion engendered by conflating normative and social functions, is increased when Hart turns to the examination of the secondary functions of the law. At this stage he again identifies types of rule with types of social function, but now with the distinction between primary and secondary functions. By doing this he obscures the distinction between the primary function of facilitating private arrangements and the secondary function of law-making. He also obscures the important role of duty-imposing laws in performing the secondary functions. Finally, the careless reader, who came to identify the distinction between primary and secondary rules with that between duty-imposing and power-conferring rules, may be misled into regarding the rule of recognition as power-conferring, whereas in fact it is a duty-imposing rule. All these confusions are caused by the fact that the classification of rules into primary and secondary is meant to serve two incompatible purposes. It is sometimes regarded as a distinction between normative functions, sometimes as a distinction between social functions.

Index of Authors